CW01188327

WENMAN JOSEPH BASSETT-LOWKE

The artwork on the front jacket is entitled *Travel* and was executed by
Philip Green, May 1928, specially for W J Bassett-Lowke

WENMAN JOSEPH BASSETT-LOWKE

by

Janet Bassett-Lowke

Editorial assistance by John Milner

A memoir of his life and achievements

1877 - 1953

A Special Edition to mark the Centenary of the founding of the business of Bassett-Lowke in Northampton

1899 - 1999

PO Box 85, Chester. CH4 9ZH
UK

© **Janet Bassett-Lowke and John Milner**

All rights reserved. No part of this book may be reproduced in any form or by any means, electronic or mechanical, photocopying, recording, or by any information storage or retrieval system including the Internet, without permission in writing from the Publisher.

ISBN 1-900622-01-7 (Hardback)

British Library Cataloguing in Publication Data
A catalogue record for this book is available from the British Library
Bassett-Lowke, Janet
Wenman Joseph Bassett-Lowke : a memoir of his life and achievements, 1877-1953
Special Edition to mark the centenary of Bassett-Lowke Ltd
1. Bassett-Lowke, Wenman Joseph, 1877-1953
2. Bassett-Lowke (Firm)
3. Modelmakers - England - Northampton - Biography
I. Title
745.5'928'092

Typesetting and Design by:
*RailRomances, PO Box 85,
Chester. CH4 9ZH (UK)*

Image Setting by:
*Lazertype, Laurel Bank,
Gresford, Wrexham LL12 8NT*

Printed and Bound in Great Britain by:
*The Amadeus Press Ltd., 517 Leeds Road,
Huddersfield. HD2 1YJ*

Published by:
*RailRomances, PO Box 85,
Chester. CH4 9ZH (UK)*

Cover Design by:
*Jazz Design, The Old School,
Higher Kinnerton, Chester. CH4 9AJ*

Every reasonable attempt has been made to identify, where not known, the owners of copyright illustrations and material appearing in this book and in some cases this has proved to be impossible. The author and the publisher extend their apologies to anyone who may feel aggrieved by lack of acknowledgment, and would welcome notification in order to provide such credits in the future. All photographs not credited to a particular source are from the Bassett-Lowke family records.

'Bassett-Lowke' and 'Lowko' are registered trade marks of Corgi Classics
Limited and are used within the context of this book with their permission.

Dedication

To my revered and only uncle
'Uncle Whynne'
1877 - 1953

W.J.Bassett-Lowke, on 5th May 1925, with his two nieces Vivian on the left and Janet, author of this book.

Opening Comment

NORTHAMPTON BOROUGH COUNCIL

R.J.B. Morris MA LLM (Cantab) Solicitor **Chief Executive and Town Clerk**

This personal memoir of W.J.Bassett-Lowke by his niece provides for the first time a vivid portrait of one of Northampton's famous sons. He was a name which, to echo Macaulay's phrase, every schoolboy would have known and which is still, at his company's centenary, synonymous with the finest model-building and miniature engineering.

Janet Bassett-Lowke both knew and worked for "W.J.", as she still calls him, during the early years of her life and at the height of his success and confidence. There is no-one else now who can record as she has done the personality behind the lectures, the exhibitions and the catalogues. Moreover that personality went beyond his engineering skills : he was adept at still and cine photography, a senior member of Northampton County Borough Council for many years, and of course through his wide-ranging interest in design, a patron of Charles Rennie Mackintosh and the modern movement in architecture.

Accordingly this book will appeal not only to students of railways and model building but also to the burgeoning number now recognising the value of the legacy which, through transforming 78 Derngate and building "New Ways", never saw it, and that "W.J." was colour blind!

The author mentions Frank Hornby – he who invented Meccano and produced Hornby trains. She regrets that when young she did not ask her uncle the questions she now wishes she had asked about his career and his achievements. I can echo that : as a boy I knew my grandfather's cousin Fred Mason who in Liverpool helped Frank Hornby cut (in wood) the original templates which became Meccano. I wish I too had asked him more!

Nevertheless she has provided a colourful narrative which adds significantly to our knowledge of this important figure and his company. His legacy will continue in his matchless models which will continue to give pleasure and profit.

Roger Morris

Foreword

Wenman J Bassett-Lowke was a remarkable industrialist, patron and citizen. His business, which started in a corner of his father's engineering company, grew into an international concern. Its products entranced generations of children of all ages; provided valuable precision equipment during both wars; and delighted Indian maharajahs and owners of stately homes alike. His two homes in Northampton, commissioned from Charles Rennie Mackintosh and Peter Behrens, introduced modernism to Britain. He once declared : *Have nothing in your home which predates your birth*. His involvement as a founding member of the Northampton Repertory Theatre and the Councillor Chair of Northampton Baths Committee provided his home town with two major resources. In addition he was a Fabian, member of the Design and Industries Association, keen photographer, traveller and author. All of these achievements were carried out with impressive energy, perfectionism and single-mindedness. *I do what I have to, come what may* was the motto in his first Northampton house. His biography is long overdue.

Janet Bassett-Lowke worked for her uncle as assistant and secretary for almost 15 years, from 1932 to 1946, and has been gathering together material for this biography over the past 20 years. Her account interweaves valuable personal recollections with the history of the company, descriptions of his commissions and other achievements. Previously Bassett-Lowke has tended to occupy subordinate roles in accounts of Mackintosh's career, the history of the Design and Industries Association or model making in Britain. This text provides a necessary and revealing fuller picture. It is clear, for example, that Bassett-Lowke's progressive tastes in interior design were well formed several years before the important remodelling of 78 Derngate. He was a complex man: a pacifist who made substantial profits during the Great War; a sophisticated cosmopolitan who remained loyal to Northampton; an open-minded, and probably ruthless, entrepreneur whose energy and charm appear at times more American than English.

The publication of his biography is timely, coinciding with the centenary of the founding of Bassett-Lowke, and the campaign by the 78 Derngate Trust to secure the long term future of this remarkable house for public enjoyment. The text and the centenary exhibition at Northampton Museum and Art Gallery will hopefully encourage further research into this rich subject and rightly draw attention to Northampton as the home of some of Britain's most important early 20th century architecture.

Given his expressed views, one can only speculate on Bassett-Lowke's reaction to the proposed restoration of 78 Derngate, some 80 years after its completion. Without question, however, he would have been proud to think that the writing skills he had encouraged in his young niece had been used to such good effect and with such determination.

Pamela Robertson
Senior Curator
Hunterian Museum and Art Gallery,
University of Glasgow

Contents

Opening Comment 6

Foreword 7

Introduction 9

Chapter One - *Early Glimpses of WJ* 11

Chapter Two - *The Bassett-Lowke Ancestors* 15

Chapter Three - *WJ's Youth and Scattered Incidents* 23

Chapter Four - *The Beginning of the Business* 31

Chapter Five - *Personal Headway in his Twenties* 55

Chapter Six - *Pursuits and Interests* 67

Chapter Seven - *Mackintosh and 78 Derngate* 81

Chapter Eight - *Candida Cottage* 103

Chapter Nine - *Post War rebuilding* 111

Colour Supplement 121

Chapter Ten - *Wonderful Models* 137

Chapter Eleven - *A Whirlwind Life* 161

Chapter Twelve - *'New Ways'* 169

Chapter Thirteen - *Life in the 1930s* 189

Chapter Fourteen - *The Model World of Ships* 199

Chapter Fifteen - *Later Years and The War* 213

Chapter Sixteen - *The End of an Era* 223

Postscript 237

Acknowledgements 239

Bibliography 240

78 Derngate Trust 241

Appendix 1 - *Prof. Dr. Peter Behrens - Letter 1926* 242

Appendix 2 - *Chronological events 1899-1953* 245

Index 250

Introduction

The thought that I might one day write my memoirs of my uncle, Wenman Joseph Bassett-Lowke, lay dormant in my mind for several years after his death. I knew he had been considering his autobiography in the late 1940s but there were other activities filling his life; several committees, business planning for the future of his company Bassett-Lowke Ltd, the question of when he would retire, and his entertaining of friends with his wife, my Aunt Jane. Time was taken up too with the writing, in company with his friend George Holland, of his first full length book about the ships he loved and the men who built and sailed in them. During World War II, he enjoyed his holiday visits to the Lake District and after it was over experienced the new exhilaration of travelling by air to Switzerland, seeing the various railways there and meeting old friends. So the weeks and months passed and his life story was shelved until it was too late.

After my uncle's death in 1953 I saw my Aunt Jane regularly. She was happy to see me and welcomed my young family to her home *New Ways* and, from time to time would add to my store of memorabilia about WJ. Old photographs, newspapers and letters from the past, diaries, old medals, all faithfully handed on to me neatly packaged with *Janet* written clearly on the outside. Later, as she decided to leave her modern home for a smaller house, I received some of the Mackintosh furniture.

We talked often about her life with uncle and I began considering the work of the Borough Council eventually, in 1970, being elected as a councillor for St. George's; the self-same ward that WJ represented in the 1930s and 40s. I spent a very busy and worthwhile 13 years on the Council before giving this up to have more time with my seven grandchildren. During my years in office, Mr. William Nicholson the Borough Architect spoke to me about Charles Rennie Mackintosh. He and his wife were both interested to know about 78 Derngate, WJ's first home when he married, which was then in the possession of the High School and its connection with the famous Scottish architect. I decided to learn more about Mackintosh and the intensely developing interest in his work. I visited Glasgow and was taken around some of his work by the then Keeper of the Mackintosh archive at the Hunterian Art Gallery, Roger Billcliffe.

It was time to start on my adventure in finding out all I could about my uncle and this book about him is the result.

It is the story of a boy born in the days of Queen Victoria; a serious lad. His mother had little difficulty in packing him off to school. He was, for those days, a scholar of sorts and, leaving at the age of 13, he carried on with the studies which interested him; Machine Drawing, Perspective, Sound Light and Heat, and geometry. He was also well grounded in his love of books realising, I think, they had uses for the future. His father was an understanding man and agreed to him starting off working in an architect's office, but must have considered this a strange request, as the natural thing he would have hoped was that his son would follow in his footsteps into the family engineering business. However, his patience was rewarded about 18 months later when the young man returned to the fold to tackle his apprenticeship in engineering.

I traced the years as the business progressed. How, with unerring instinct, he seemed to find the craftsmen for his demanding standards and trained them. How he developed his own life and became knowledgeable about most in the world which held his interest.

55 years on, when WJ was 70 years old, Percival Marshall who in 1898 started *The Model Engineer and Amateur Electrician* magazine said : *I knew him when he was just emerging from the chrysalis stage when he was an apprentice at his father's works and he had ideas. I have watched him hundred of times since then and I have seen him trying to grow up, but he has never grown up. He is just as much a boy as ever, and I am sure we all hope he will still preserve that delightful outlook on life. In the same way W J Bassett-Lowke has extended his personality right through the staff of the great company he started*. In sixteen chapters I have endeavoured to follow his career and the life he lived, crowding into it thrice the achievement most of us have time for. He linked fittingly in tandem his joint maxims *Fitness for Purpose* and *Perfection in Miniature*. He travelled millions of miles over the world by various means – bicycle, train, taxi, ship, aeroplane and car (but never owned one). Nevertheless, most Sundays he found time to quietly attend church as he had done since a young boy. He got the maximum out of life and I salute him.

Janet Bassett-Lowke
February 1999

1877 - 1953

BASSETT-LOWKE
LIMITED

Chapter One

Early Glimpses of WJ

As a child I cannot recall my first meeting with my Uncle, but have the faint and blurred vision of a man of speed. Speed in every way - swiftness of speech, nimbleness of foot, activity of mind! Throughout life he seemed to have us all on the run.

In those early days Wenman Joseph Bassett-Lowke was just an uncle whom we were advised to treat with deference. In 1953, reading Sir Gordon Russell's obituary of him in *The Times*, I regretted my lack of foresight in only then realising the breadth of his remarkable talents. It was in October of that year that his valediction read :

> *Occasionally the founders of colleges, schools and businesses become legends in their lifetimes. W.J. Bassett-Lowke certainly became a legend to me. As a boy I waited more impatiently for his catalogue of model locomotives than for almost anything the postman brought. His standard of accuracy was so high that I remember being impelled to measure a railway bridge with exemplary care and making a model of it in which even rivets were not forgotten, in order to live up to his scale model permanent way! But when, just after the 1914-1918 War, I came to know him as one of the Founders of the Design and Industries Association, I realised that his interests were far wider than railway engineering, on which his knowledge was encyclopaedic.*
>
> *He was passionately keen on improving standards of design in every day things. In order to encourage architects who were thinking along new lines he built a house which appeared revolutionary to his neighbours in the 20s, but has since come into its own. He used to boast that there was nothing in it older than himself! On the other hand he took a great interest in the Museum and Art Gallery at Northampton, which like many other good causes in the city, owes much to his help and encouragement, always practical and quietly given. He retained his zest for new ideas into old age, and his death will sadden many of all ages and conditions and many walks of life.*

The only significant item not mentioned by Sir Gordon was my uncle's meeting with the well-known architect Charles Rennie Mackintosh. In the year before uncle married, Mackintosh transformed his small Georgian house at 78 Derngate, Northampton, into a very modern, before its time, dwelling. On March 21st 1917, it became the first home for Wenman Joseph and his bride Florence Jane Jones, daughter of Charles Jones founder of the Northampton shoe firm, Crockett & Jones, a business which is still today well in being. After a spring honeymoon which, due to the 1914-1918 war, was just a few days in Bournemouth, Mr and Mrs W J Bassett-Lowke returned to live in their unusual house.

As it happened, my father and mother lived nearby and in our childhood years there were often brief sightings of uncle. He would be at the door with a query to my mother *Where's Harold?* or *Where's the kid?* My sister and I would be playing in the front room and would look up as his head popped round the door. There were lots of laughter lines on his puckish face as he took off his glasses and crinkled his eyes with the usual 'password' to us : *Hello kids - and what do monkeys eat?* We always came back with the required reply in a shrill chorus *Nuts*! In a few minutes, sometimes merely seconds, he would be off to my father's workroom, talking away in his brisk manner, then in next to no time, he would be back again in the hall, the front door shutting, his footsteps hurrying down the garden path and away.

From my very first recollections, I considered him a smart *grown up*. He always wore a homburg hat. His clothes were well cut, his shoes gleaming. What puzzled me at first were the things in cloth which covered these. Eventually mother informed me that they were gentlemen's gaiters, commonly known as 'spats'! Also, I always looked at the carefully chosen shirts and distinctive ties he wore. At our tender ages we did not realise we were looking at a successful businessman, and that my aunt made sure everything matched as he was colour blind.

An invitation to 78 Derngate meant that we put on our Sunday outfits and were drilled by mother on the *children should be seen and not heard* dictum of her Edwardian upbringing. From these visits I was able to gaze at Auntie Floss. She was a pleasant and elegant small lady who always wore pretty dresses, I thought. Tea was set out on a trolley or small table and our Aunt was a first-class cook, who made mouth-watering cakes. Her tiny sandwiches were of the 'cucumber' variety and we soon made them disappear. As a great treat afterwards, we were allowed to watch the working of some of uncle's mechanical toys. We knew where they were to be found and, when permission was given, demurely fetched them from a special drawer and took them out gingerly from their neat boxes. Uncle, of course, always wound them up and repackaged them. We were allowed to put the boxes away - a very careful mission.

I do not remember much about the Derngate house, but I know I realised it was quite a different sort of home from ours. I used to feast my eyes on the fascinating design on one wall of the lounge/hall facing as you came through the front door, and which I now know was the Mackintosh Screen. This screen hid the stairs going up to the next floor. It was a lattice work screen composed of squares of various kinds. Some squares were leaded lights with ornamental patterns in gold and orange colours. In the centre there was a semi-circular niche the height of 3 squares, where a vase of flowers could be placed. The other squares, the background of the design, were in the same pale cream colour. There were also a number of square apertures in the screen - fascinating. If, by chance, I went upstairs it was fun on the way down to peep through, at this different view of the room, and without being seen. Another object, which drew my attention, was the immense circular candelabra attached to a decorative ceiling piece, which again, was full of intricate squares; the whole fitting unerringly drew the eye of the beholder. It was an exciting room with dark walls that had bright touches, such as the settee covered in dark moiré silk and with enormous cushions of shot purple and yellow silk, edged with emerald green ribbon. How was I to know that this kind of design was a Charles Rennie Mackintosh trademark?

Occasionally at weekends, uncle would come along to us and ask my father to take some photographs. The brothers were both keen on photography, but my father, Harold Austin, chose to stay with still photography, whereas Wenman Joseph eventually became keenly interested in cine photography. Father had a dark room and, at quite a tender age, we girls were initiated into its mysteries and given useful little jobs to do with developing, printing and enlarging. These were not favourite chores but we knew we all had to take turns. When my two sisters Vivian and June and I were aged between three and eight years old, uncle became interested in a magazine called *Wonderful Playthings*. All of us, in particular June the youngest, were photographed with many kinds of superb toys to decorate the pages of this trade magazine. Photographs taken by my father for this magazine survive but, alas, copies which uncle helped with in the 1920s, seem to have disappeared without trace. I fear that we three girls were a disappointment both to uncle and my father, who must have wished for a male Bassett-Lowke for the next generation. Father threw off his regret by being a taskmaster to his daughters, making us work hard both at school and at sport. A talented sportsman himself, tennis being his favourite game, he was soon urging us on competitively. We were allowed to go gently through kindergarten, but not long after that, in the light mornings of the year, we were early risers and practising on the tennis courts in the nearby park, before we set off to school.

Our parents took us through some unusual projects! There was the *back to health in 40 days* routine when we all took a course of sultanas soaked overnight in lemon juice, but worst of all, we decided, was the Aberdonian Bath! This was an ice-cold bath every morning, summer and winter, when each member of the family took turns to get into the freezing water and immerse up to the neck. The jumping out afterwards and brisk rub down with a warm towel usually brought us back to life again, but I shiver to think of those days. Again on holiday we were introduced to expensive tastes. We learnt to love to eat prawns, shrimps, lobsters, crayfish, crabs, oysters and Dublin prawns. Evidently the Lowke family, headed by Grandpa and Grandma, way back in the 1890s, had discovered the Channel Islands where these shellfish abounded and were not looked upon as luxuries. The whole family clan spent holidays there when uncle and father were young. Uncle, years later, handed over to me from his store of old photos, pictures of himself and father as boys, including those showing poor Grandpa and Grandma Lowke looking like over-clothed *souls of the sand*, who had missed their way on a promenade walk. We were lucky to have visited the islands and Guernsey in particular, in the days when they were quite beautiful, peaceful and unspoilt.

Grandma Porteous, my mother's mother, owned a bungalow at Jerbourg, on Guernsey, overlooking the little known Pea Stacks, a set of rocks jutting out from the coast into the sea. Most days of our holidays were spent clad in sun bonnets, cotton dresses and sandals. Carrying buckets and spades, we used to proceed, walking along lanes with hedges laden with blackberries and verges bright with many kinds of wild flowers - to Petit Port, the lovely sandy bay approached down a cliff with 197 steps. One never to be forgotten day father and mother took their prawning nets round the rocky pools and that evening, on our Primus stove, we cooked the $26^{1}/_{2}$ dozen prawns they caught. Those were the days!

Uncle was not really keen on sport, but took an interest in his nieces when they began to show promise. Sister Vivian, very close to me in age, and I continued working at our tennis and, eventually, we did achieve the status of first couple in inter school matches. But another sport intervened. One Guernsey holiday we met, as a family, the Channel Islands swimming champion and her coach from London. Before we returned home, our parents had arranged for us to go to London during school holidays and train for speed swimming, learning strokes like the crawl and back crawl, as well as the orthodox breaststroke. We linked up with other promising pupils for training. It was my sister Vivian who was to prove the star, showing great ability in speed swimming.

Uncle became proud of us, taking a positive interest in the exploits of Vivian and, as a reward for her successes, said he would take her on his summer week's cruise in the fjords of Norway. He added he would include me in this largesse provided I wrote him an essay account of the trip. On our return I battled away and produced *Impressions of My First Cruise* presenting it to him typed, more or less neatly, by myself. This cruise was, to us, a new and exciting experience and uncle appeared chuffed to be in the centre of interest, as a relative in control of the two young lasses who swam round the ship in the glacial waters of the Eid Fjord! For the first time in my life I was really able to talk to my uncle. In fact, both Vivian and I were not afraid to speak when spoken to, and we really had a happy time. Auntie and uncle were with a party of friends, who all appeared to be kindly disposed towards us.

This Norwegian cruise came towards the end of my schooldays. I had matriculated and was staying on for another year. The headmistress had written to my parents, indicating that I should stay on at school without further fees, to work on a preparation course and, hopefully, sit for entrance to university, perhaps even Oxford! Just at this time, my father had business problems and my mother told me that no way could they afford to accept this chance for me at present. In those days, parents had to pay for everything in further education, there were none of the grants students have today. This was a bitter blow. Crushed, I felt in a kind of limbo, playing out time studying German, shorthand, typing, bookkeeping and working on a project on the Italian painters.

Uncle spoke to me about what I was going to do when I left school and I truly said I did not know. Towards the end of that week when we were cruising in the fjords; in another world, Uncle brought me down to earth when he said, *Why not come and work for me?*

Chapter Two

The Bassett-Lowke Ancestors

My great grandmother Tryphena, daughter of Thomas White, a shoemaker who lived in Mill Lane, Northampton, was born in 1826 and was married on Christmas Day 1849 to Joseph Lowke, a tobacconist and son of John Lowke, a maltster. These sparse details are given on their marriage certificate; also that both parties were *of full age* and resident at that time in the district of St. Peter's in Northampton. They were married in the lovely old sandstone Parish Church of St. Peter's, according to the rites and ceremonies of the Church of England.

On St. Valentine's Day 1850 the funeral service of Joseph Lowke took place but I have not been able to trace any registration of his death. This may be accounted for by the fact that in the winter of 1849/50 there had been a smallpox outbreak in East Haddon, which was the village where Joseph's family lived. Sadly it appears that he gave help in the village during the outbreak and succumbed to the disease.

The local Register for 1850 records on the 19th September 1850 the birth of a boy, Joseph Tom, to Tryphena Lowke, formerly White. She was at that time living in Horseshoe Street, not far from Kingswell Street; the street which was to feature very much in her later life.

Sometime after her first husband's death, Tryphena went as housekeeper to Absalom Bassett, taking her very young son Joseph Tom with her. On the 15th October 1854, Tryphena eventually married Absalom, who came originally from Gloucestershire. The marriage certificate describes him *of full age*, a bachelor, and whose trade was boiler making. His father Thomas was a gardener. In June 1855 they had their first son, Harry, and a second boy, Thomas, in 1857. Their address at that time was 7 Gas Street and Absalom was described as *boilermaker journeyman*. Nearly a decade later, in April 1866, a third Bassett son was born, Frederick George, and by then the family had moved to No.18 Kingswell Street, where Absalom had started an engineering business in 1859.

I have just one picture of my great grandmother Tryphena as she stands outside the works in Kingswell Street next to her burly second husband, he wearing a top hat. This seemed to me somehow incongruous, as he is in shirt sleeves rolled up to the elbows, as if he had just come up from the yard. But it must have been quite an occasion, as Tryphena is wearing a becoming bonnet and smart afternoon apron. All other members of the family pictured in the photograph are wearing hats, including a very small boy, Wenman Joseph, who wears a most striking style of *halo* headgear and certainly appears to have a good mop of hair. The others are my grandmother Eliza, my grandfather Joseph Tom, and the eldest Bassett son Harry who evidently had an interest in cycling. Very clearly visible along the shop and works front are the words *Central Works Bassett and Sons - Iron and Brass Founders - Gas Engine and Shoe Machinery erected and repaired*.

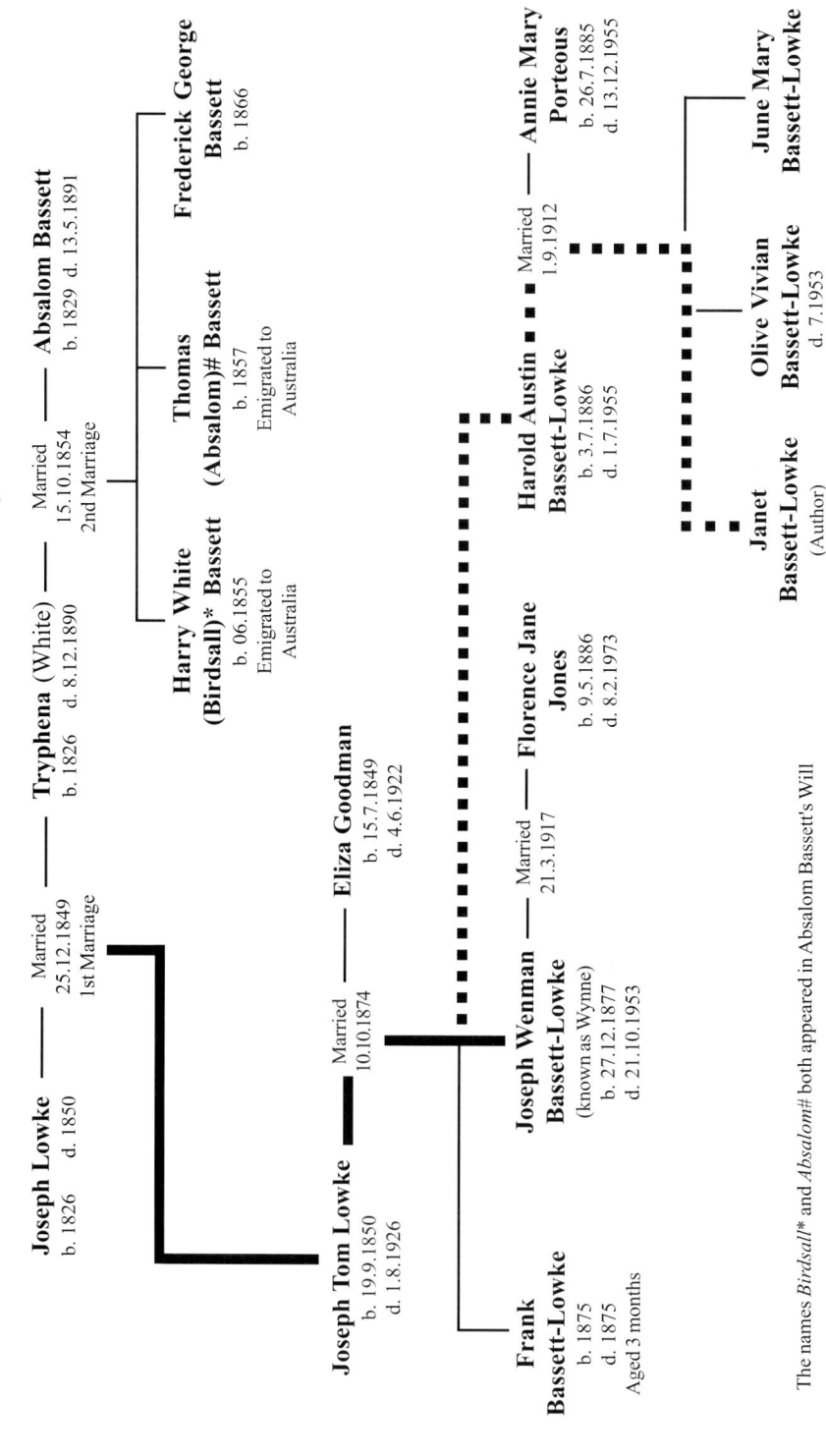

The Bassett-Lowke Family Tree

Joseph Lowke — Married 25.12.1849 1st Marriage — **Tryphena (White)** — Married 15.10.1854 2nd Marriage — **Absalom Bassett**
b. 1826 d. 1850 — b. 1826 d. 8.12.1890 — b. 1829 d. 13.5.1891

Children of Tryphena & Absalom Bassett:
- **Harry White (Birdsall)* Bassett** b. 06.1855 Emigrated to Australia
- **Thomas (Absalom)# Bassett** b. 1857 Emigrated to Australia
- **Frederick George Bassett** b. 1866

Joseph Tom Lowke — Married 10.10.1874 — **Eliza Goodman**
b. 19.9.1850 d. 1.8.1926 — b. 15.7.1849 d. 4.6.1922

Children:
- **Frank Bassett-Lowke** b. 1875 d. 1875 Aged 3 months
- **Joseph Wenman Bassett-Lowke** (known as Wynne) b. 27.12.1877 d. 21.10.1953 — Married 21.3.1917 — **Florence Jane Jones** b. 9.5.1886 d. 8.2.1973

Harold Austin Bassett-Lowke b. 3.7.1886 d. 1.7.1955 — Married 1.9.1912 — **Annie Mary Porteous** b. 26.7.1885 d. 13.12.1955

Children:
- **Olive Vivian Bassett-Lowke** d. 7.1953
- **June Mary Bassett-Lowke**
- **Janet Bassett-Lowke** (Author)

The names *Birdsall** and *Absalom*# both appeared in Absalom Bassett's Will

The Bassett-Lowke ancestors outside the works of Bassett & Sons in Kingswell Street in the early 1880s. From left to right Absalom Bassett, Tryphena Bassett, Wenman Joseph, aged about 4 – 5 years old with his mother Eliza Lowke, Joseph Tom Lowke and, with the tricycle, Harry White Bassett.

J Bassett-Lowke Collection

WJ, known to us as Uncle Whynne, could not be more than 4 to 5 years old, which places the date of the picture around 1882/3. From this only view I have of my great grandmother, I consider she was a pleasant looking woman with a serene face. Sadly I do not know how my own great grandfather looked; I just imagine him as a fine young man carried away in the flower of youth. Nevertheless his genes have been transmitted down the years, my eldest grandson having inherited engineering from both sides of the family. His father is descended from a line of Wellingborough engineers, whose business was first established in 1870.

According to *Kelly's Directory*, Absalom actually set up business in Kingswell Street in 1859 where his engineering yard was situated. The previous places where my forbears had lived - Mill Lane, Gas Street, Horseshoe Street and St. Augustine Street - disappeared years ago when new bigger roads were constructed, but Kingswell Street is still in being. Absalom and Tryphena stayed in Kingswell Street and, according to records in 1891, they lived at No.18. Eventually Joseph Tom, Tryphena's firstborn, went to live at No.13 when he married Eliza Goodman on the 10th October 1874. She was the daughter of John Goodman, baker of Augustine Street, whose wife's maiden name was Campion and first name was also Eliza. No.13 is a house I remember vaguely. Usually, when we children called with mother to visit, our grandma used to meet us at the door with her finger to her lips and say *Hush my dears - your granddad is having his nap*. We used to tiptoe into the back kitchen and sit there quietly munching one of her home-made biscuits. The little hall had a fascinating glass cabinet that contained all sorts of treasures. We were told grandpa had brought these back from the Holy Land.

Just one thing I do vividly recall about this small home . There was no garden, but upstairs was a verandah, which was reached by climbing out of a bedroom window, and in the summer there was a shrub growing up the wall and stretching along the verandah balustrade. This plant had very pretty leaves and little star-shaped white flowers, which gave out a delicious scent. It was the white jassamine which contrived to make the little balcony - although it overlooked an uninteresting yard - a place I loved to visit. I think the room I passed through was at one time the boys' bedroom.

Eliza Lowke, the author's paternal grandmother. She was born in July 1849 and died in June 1922, and was a seasoned traveller with WJ in the early years of the 20th century. She was a kind lady who did good voluntary work among the needed of Northampton.

J Bassett-Lowke Collection

Our grandma Eliza had been a private governess before she married. We children knew little about her as she died when we were quite young. In 1922 Mr Flinton-Harris JP, a close friend of uncle's, wrote for the local weekly magazine :

A loveable little lady has died this week. Very few, if any Northampton ladies have visited more parts of the Continent so much as she, and I have had personal opportunities of knowing how she would make these holidays an additional opportunity of unselfishly striving to study the comfort of those around her. Her last visit to the Continent before the war was with her elder son, Mr W J Bassett-Lowke, Sir Leo Chiozza Money and myself. She mothered us throughout a long tour through Germany, Denmark, Sweden and through the Norwegian Fjords. It will remain a cherished memory to us all.

A. BASSETT,
ENGINEER, AND PRACTICAL BOILER MANUFACTURER,
KINGSWELL STREET, NORTHAMPTON,

Every description of Boilers, Cornish, Portable, and Upright; Kitchen Ranges; and maker of improved Tubular Boilers for Greenhouses, Tanks, Girders, and Cisterns. Fire Boxes fitted to Portable Engines with the best Material and Workmanship. Every description of Repairs to Portable or Stationary Engines executed with the best attention, and at the lowest prices.

An early advertisement in Kelly's Directory for Absalom Bassett's business. He was W J Bassett-Lowke's step-grandfather.

Courtesy Northampton County Records Office

The local newspaper itself also spoke of her as *a lady much mourned*, she went about doing good in an unobtrusive way. She was a helper for the Christmas Dinner Fund, The Fresh Air Fund, Special Schools for the mentally deficient, and was associated all her life with the Doddridge Church in Northampton. Also, being a member of the committee of the University Extension Movement, she was a reader and thinker above the average.

What a pity I did not know all this to appreciate her before she died. We children were not afraid to speak to her, but did not dare to say much to grandpa because he appeared to be either hard at work or taking a snooze!

My grandfather died on the 1st August 1926 at the age of 76. Members of the Fire Brigade in their full uniform with helmets carried his coffin and amongst the floral tributes was one from *Whynne and Floss* (WJ and Mrs B-L). The Press reported that *his eldest son W J Bassett-Lowke was unable to attend because he was in Norway on business* but he was represented by his brother Harold. The *Northampton Independent* spoke of my grandfather as an expert engineer and a well-known inhabitant of Northampton. At an early age, he began to work with his stepfather and he evidently soon showed an aptitude for engineering. He was a willing worker learning quickly and helping to build up the business of A Bassett & Sons, which grew and prospered and, at the time of Absalom's

---

| 58 | COUNTY ADVERTISEMENTS. | [1877. |

A. BASSETT AND SONS,
ENGINEERS & PRACTICAL BOILER MANUFACTURERS,
KINGSWELL STREET, NORTHAMPTON.

Every description of Boilers, Cornish, Portable and Upright; Kitchen Ranges; and makers of improved Tubular Boilers for Greenhouses, Tanks, Girders and Cisterns. Fire Boxes fitted to Portable Engines with the best Material and Workmanship. Every description of Repairs to Portable or Stationary Engines executed with the best attention, and at the lowest prices.

An advertisement appearing in Kelly's Directory, eighteen years after the business was started by Absalom Bassett.

Courtesy Northampton County Records Office

The Long Service medal presented to WJ's father, Joseph Tom Lowke, in recognition of 45 years voluntary service to the National Fire Brigades Union. He served the local fire brigade as a voluntary engineer.

J Bassett-Lowke Collection

death, was firmly established. Two of the three Bassett sons, Harry and Thomas, became interested in the cycling trade and went abroad to Australia, but trace has been lost of them. In his Will, Absalom bequeathed : *to each of my sons Harry White Birdsall Bassett and Tom Absalom Bassett, now residing at Melbourne Australia, the sum of 50 pounds.* An old lady living in New Zealand sent me details of a Thomas and William Bassett in Christchurch, New Zealand who, in 1905, were agricultural implement importers. A friend of my sister's in Tasmania relates that she had seen a Bassett cycle years ago in her family's garden shed. Whether or not these two items were in fact anything to do with my grandfather's half brothers has not been established.

My grandfather's greatest interest outside his business was the Volunteer Fire Brigade, for which he acted as chief engineer over many years and was awarded a treasured long service medal. He made this fire brigade work his chief hobby and put all his capabilities into striving for efficiency. He was popular for his honesty, good workmanship, and all round interest in the town.

After the voluntary fire brigade was disbanded he maintained a keen interest in the Northampton Fire Brigade and members showed their respect for him at his funeral when they acted as bearers at Doddridge Church and at the General Cemetery. He was the last survivor of the old Volunteers.

He and grandma Lowke were a devoted couple. Both had a keen affinity in their love of travel and study and were regular worshippers at Doddridge Congregational Church.

Grandma and grandpa Lowke had three sons. Their first child, Frank, was born in 1875 but died in December of that year aged 3 months. Joseph Wenman (Uncle Whynne) came next, born on 27th December 1877, followed 9 years later by Harold Austin on the 3rd July 1886. Up until the time grandpa married he was usually spoken of as *Joe Bassett* working in the Bassett engineering business. When it came to his banns of marriage being called, he had to consider and put down his true name, Joseph Tom Lowke. I would think grandma Lowke would have been the person to organise this and on her boys' birth certificates she made sure that compromise was effected. On my Uncle's Birth Certificate his Christian Names appear as *Joseph Wenman Bassett* and his Surname as *Lowke* and,

ADDRESS FOR TELEGRAMS
BASSETT, KINGSLEY PARK TERRACE, NORTHAMPTON.

New Haven
Kingsley Park Terrace,
Northampton,
June, 1896.

Dear Sir or Madam,

I beg to inform you (as already locally announced) that my association with J. T. Lowke, usually known as J. Bassett, has now ceased and that it is my intention to re-open premises in this town for the purpose of carrying on business as consulting and general Engineer, Boiler Maker, and Machinery Agent. Pending further notice I shall be pleased to hear from you at the above address, when any enquiries will receive the same careful attention as heretofore.

Trusting for a continuance of your esteemed favors

I remain

Yours faithfully,

(OWN SON OF THE LATE ABSALOM BASSETT) FRED. G. BASSETT.

P.S.—I have a competent and efficient staff of workmen under my own personal supervision for repairs to Engines, Boilers, and Machinery, in town or country.

Distance no object.

Notice in respect, in 1896, of the business separation of Fred G Bassett from his stepbrother Joseph Tom Lowke, both of whom were offering the same service.

J Bassett-Lowke Collection

likewise, my Father's name as *Harold Austin Bassett* and *Lowke* respectively. At the date of birth the address is given as 13 Kingswell Street.

Joseph Tom Lowke followed in his stepfather's way and became an accomplished engineer. Tryphena died on the 8th December 1890 and Absalom on the 13th May 1891 both at the early ages of 64 and 62 years respectively. Absalom's death was from bronchitis and the information on his death certificate was that Joseph Tom was present at his death. I feel that there must have been good comradeship between these two. Absalom's Will left the business between Joseph Tom and the youngest Bassett, Frederick George, and it was carried on for a time by them both. When the Duke of Clarence died in 1892 a memorial service was held at All Saints Church and the Freemasons marched to the service ………*at Messrs Bassett & Sons Works in Kingswell Street 21 mortars were discharged.*

In June 1896, Frederick decided to start his own business. With grandfather now as sole owner, the name was changed to J T Lowke and Sons, the firm with which Wenman Joseph Bassett-Lowke was to serve his engineering apprenticeship, and which helped him well in the early days of his model enterprise. In the *Northampton Mercury* on the 1st January 1897 he announced the change :

> **Established 1859**
> *J.T.Lowke (Generally known as Joseph Bassett)*
> *Begs to inform his customers that he is carrying*
> *on the Old-Established Business of the late*
>
> **BASSETT & SONS**
> *Engineers, Boiler makers & Iron Founders*
>
> *Central Works 18,19,20 Kingswell Street.*
> **Experienced workmen sent to all parts of the country**
> **For repairs to engines, boilers and machinery**

Chapter Three
WJ's Youth and Scattered Incidents.

I hold, amongst the few relics from my uncle's very young days, a fragile scrap of fine paper, bearing a few treasured words which must have been written early in the 1880s by my great grandmother.

My dear Grandson Wenman Bassett,

You are getting quite a little man to write to your Grannie Bassett and I am pleased with your letter. I went to Chapel this morning the preacher talked about Timothy's Grandmother Lois. She was such a good Grannie don't you wish I was as good. The second epistle of Paul to Timothy, ask Mammie to read a bit of it to you. Are you good to your Mammie, give my love to her, it is so long since I see you both ..... will you ask my dear Eliza to get $5^1/_2$ yards of that shirting for Gramp. I know he will like it ..... Bless you both I will pray for your safe return.

Your loving,

Grannie Bassett

Pleased with your drawing. I believe you will be clever.

I wonder, would his grandmother's letter and its Biblical reference have been beyond a small boy's understanding? I think so, but these same writings do give me, her great-granddaughter, a singular insight into her thoughts and feelings. I salute her, a good Christian, interested in her son's son and kindly disposed as the mother-in-law of her son's wife, Grandmother Eliza. Also the main channel of my being born a Bassett-Lowke.

From time to time I gleaned facts about Uncle from himself. He left school at 13. A teacher whom he really liked made WJ realise, as a young schoolboy, the value of knowledge from books. In later years he encouraged me the same way and would, from time to time, pass on a book that he thought I should read.

I found among his treasured possessions two small textbooks. The first, which had a Preface dated Jan 1st 1881, is entitled *Gill's Academic Series - The Academic English Grammar and Analysis* from Gill and Sons, Warwick Lane, Paternoster Row, London. It is ornamented with a few choice decorations from the pencil of a mischievous schoolboy, and we are left in no doubt that the book belonged to a certain Wenman Joseph Bassett of 13 Kingswell Street, Northampton, from these words stamped on the cover and on several pages inside. On the front flyleaf is a pale pencilling of an ostrich resplendent running! At the back of the book is a most lifelike lobster, filling the back inside flyleaf, while the inside back cover sports six small pictures of matchstick figures rowing boats in some sort of race and, below the sea level, a few fishes swimming beneath the waves! He had made

An early school photograph with Wenman Joseph Bassett-Lowke in the centre (with sailor collar) of the third row. The slate says 'All Saints', Northampton, and this is thought to be All Saints Church School, Horseshoe Street.

J Bassett-Lowke Collection

certain to have full claim on this book. You could take your pick of several other pages, with his name plastered there. It is printed 5 times on the inside front cover alone! Then, three times in colour on a different page, stamped smartly with a rubber stamp. The boys of those days certainly had ways of making sure they retained their property!

This little book is fascinating to me in other ways. The unfamiliar words used in those days: Part I *Orthography*, Part II *Etymology* (the study of the sources and developments of words and morphemes), Part III *Sub-division of the Parts of Speech Inflections of the Adjective*. Would the average school child today be familiar with such a word as a morpheme? The second textbook, *The Scholars Handbook of English Etymology*, was issued by George Philip & Son, 32 Fleet Street, London, and inside is inscribed in copperplate *Wenman Joseph Bassett A.S.C.S.*, which I take to mean All Saints' Church School[*]. This small book had no pictorial ornamentations, just the rubber stamp with his name and address. The preface is not dated but says: *The present little work has been carefully drawn up for the use of the UPPER STANDARDS of our elementary schools*. Slipped between the pages of this *Scholars Handbook* was a Northampton Grammar School Scholarship Exam paper, which WJ sat at the time; an example of the standard of work set in those days.

---

[*] No reference to All Saints' Church School has so far been found. It is recorded that in 1889 there was All Saints' National School in Adelaide Place, off Horseshoe Street which was next to Kingswell Street, and the Middle Class Boys School in Kingswell Street run under John E. Mawbey - Editor

These school books, particularly the second, gave more advanced knowledge than I remember at school and I therefore surmise that teachers were certainly masters of their subject and that Wenman Joseph had a brain and aptitude above the ordinary. After he left school, he continued his education and attended evening classes studying Advanced Machine Drawing, Perspective, Sound, Light and Heat and finally Geometry.

My father was 9 years younger than Uncle Whynne, so I learnt very little from him about his brother's early childhood. However I do possess just one letter which he wrote to *Win* (Uncle Whynne) in the year 1899 in which, schoolboy like, he discusses the course of the Boer War in South Africa. Most young people these days may not have heard of this war 100 years ago, but it was fought in South Africa between the British Empire and two Dutch Boer republics, the Transvaal, and the Orange Free State.

The discovery of gold on the Rand led to the arrival in the Transvaal of a large foreign (Uitlander) element to whom the Boers had denied the franchise and other civil rights. Cecil Rhodes, then Prime Minister of the Cape, had one aim in life to unite all South Africa under the British Flag. South African statesman Stephanus Johannes Paulus Kruger on the other hand, hoped for a purely Dutch Afrikaans country and had other ideas and began to prepare, while Britain, hoping for peace, was taken by surprise. The stage of the resulting campaign, up to the time of my father's letter to Win in the autumn of 1899, and at the time of the Boer ultimatum, was that there were 27,000 British troops over the whole of South Africa, whereas the Boers could muster 45,000 men plus 110 guns and could call on reserves at will.

Combined forces of the Boers launched two offensives. The first from the west towards Mafeking and the diamond mining centre of Kimberley, and the second from the east converging on the British forces under White at Ladysmith, where they were put under siege at the end of October 1899. This success by the enemy caused General Bullen, British Commander in Chief, to alter his plan to relieve Kimberley and Ladysmith.

My father's letter enters at this point, when we are told that Lord Methuen was entrusted with the plan to relieve Kimberley. He had 10,000 men on the Orange River, south of the town, and this force fought three successful actions at Belmont, Graspan and Modder River.

Mrs. Eliza Lowke, on the right, with her niece Alice Lovejoy, W J Bassett-Lowke's cousin. Alice Lovejoy's maiden name was Alice Maud Eyden. She looked after Joseph Tom Lowke after his wife Eliza died in 1922.

Henry Greenly Collection

NORTHAMPTON GRAMMAR SCHOOL.

DECEMBER, 1888.

ENGLISH HISTORY.

1. What was the origin of Queen's Cross, on the Hardingstone Road?
2. Write a short account of Thomas à Becket.
3. Give some account of the Crusades, naming the English Princes who took part in them.
4. What do you know about Magna Charta? Mention, if you can, its chief provisions.
5. Give an account of the wars with France in the reign of Edward III.
6. Write a brief biography of John Hampden.
7. " " " Sir William Wallace.
8. " " " Wickliffe.
9. " " " Simon de Montfort.
10. " " " Oliver Cromwell.
11. " " " The Black Prince.
12. When, and between whom, were the following battles fought:—Naseby, Neville's Cross, Flodden, Northampton, Bosworth.
13. What do you know of the introduction of printing?
14. Give a brief account of the Reformation in England.
15. Explain the terms: Witan, Feudal System, Indulgences, Cavaliers, Constitutions of Clarendon.
16. Name the sovereigns, with their dates, from Edward I. to Henry VII., inclusive.

[Ten questions only may be attempted. They may be selected from any part of the paper.]

W.M.

The exam which W J Bassett-Lowke sat for entrance to Northampton Grammar School when he was 11 years old, and interesting to compare with examinations set today. There is no record of whether or not he passed.

J Bassett-Lowke Collection

This last action is described in my father's schoolboy letter written to my uncle, who was then 22 years old. Obviously a fanatical follower of the war news, my father writes:

Dear Win,

I am writing in answer to your statement about my letter..... as for my letter I sent you it was so right that you could not answer it - you had to say it was a 'Baby's letter'. That baby's letter struck you up though. I gave some sense and I do see where this great victory came in, you don't allow me to explain. Methuen had only 8,500 before the battle....the Boers had nearly 10,000 before the battle - 8,000 according to you. I also fail to see that. They had built a fort of moulds and earth works at the top of a steep hill on the banks of the Modder, very nice, was it not, the British, after tedious days and weeks march are ordered to storm it. Now I want you to picture our poor soldiers, do use your sense, poor chaps needed one bidding to do it and they did it, not one hesitating, you cannot contradict it. They went up the hill in the heat of the day while the Boers were peacefully sitting under cover. They had to drag their great heavy guns up after them, if you have ever read of the heat in S. Africa you would know what it is, after lugging and pulling for an hour or so they at last got in range. Then Lord Methuen addressed his brave men saying "Come follow me" and stepping aside t(ey rushed up up up, in the face of a storm of lead - picture it boy do, they reached the top and bravely stood at bay with the Boers beating them back and after several charges, drove them out, is that a victory? "yes it is". If the English were driven out of Ladysmith you would soon say they were defeated, is it not right - and this victory was of great importance - we were able to cross the river after the bridge was repaired that is the importance. He wanted to cross the river and he did. I hope you will answer this letter in a fair manner. I am reading the war news greatly now.

I am yours ever,   Harold.

My father always addressed his brother as *Win*.

Lord Methuen was repulsed in a bloody battle in a mighty attack on Magersfontein, the last Boer position covering the siege of Kimberley. That news must have saddened my father's young heart in the black week in December 1899 when the English also suffered defeat near Stormberg in northern Cape Colony and at Colense in Natal.

Reading this schoolboy letter, I remembered mother telling me that young Lowke, experimenting in the science lab at school, produced an explosion with the result that he was rushed off to hospital. The rumour circulating at the girls' school she attended had the result that there were tears. It was thought he would lose his sight. When I mentioned this one day to uncle I had the impression that he was vexed that *the kid*, as he so often named him, had worried their mother. Reflecting on the slightly disputatious theme of the South African letter, I came to note that this reaction often surfaced throughout their lives, as I grew up working for my uncle and was closely in touch with both of them. The age difference may have caused this to a certain extent and their different temperaments, but they both enjoyed photography and took an interest in each other's achievements in this respect.

A holiday group of the Lowke family and relatives in Guernsey at the turn of the 20th century. In the back row Alice Lovejoy and her brother, Wenman Joseph behind his father Joseph Tom Lowke on the left, and the author's father (WJ's brother) next to his mother Eliza in the front.

J Bassett-Lowke Collection

Yet many years on, when uncle was in hospital and coming to the end of his life, my father was upset and kept visiting him. They had, maybe, come to terms with each other and decided that blood was thicker than water. I hope so.

Amongst my father's belongings is a small Collins Pocket Diary for 1899, written when he was 13 years of age. The Sunday entries were routine: *went to Chapple [Chapel] in the morning, went to Chapple with Win*, [his spelling throughout was *Chapple*], *Went to Chapple with Win and Mother and went to Granny Goodman to take her a pork pie* or *Went to Chapple with Win in morning and photographed a cannon with a pocket Kodac* [Kodak]. On February 27th there was the entry: *Went to school as usual. Went to Win's exhibition of models* and, later on that week, another entry: *again went to Win's Exhibition of models*. On March 12th, his first entry was: *Win went away to Leeds on Saturday,* and then the constant note about *Chapple*. In May, he went to Wolverton with his father to see the carriage works. Thought it a fine sight. Went in the Royal Train and took some snapshots and a day or two later *wrote to Win* (probably relating his carriage works visit). Then: *went to school and also bought a big cannon off Win, paid 4s -6d for it,* and another day: *saw Win work a 30 shillings loco model.*

This year would be the time when WJ was working on his student apprenticeship with Crompton Parkinson at Leeds and York. The fact that several times my father mentions photographic work he did strengthens my belief that the brothers started early in their interests in this hobby. WJ was fond of cycling and used to go all over the place in search of interesting subjects and he was on the look out for some way to earn money toward advertising the early small items he was making. Luckily one week, when he happened to be in Northampton, he heard that there was an accident at Wellingborough Station 8 miles away and, as we shall see later, WJ sped away on his bicycle to the scene and quickly photographed and produced pictures of the accident scene. One of the rooms on the premises of 18 Kingswell Street was fitted up as a dark room for WJ's use and my father also became very keen. In August of 1899 the family went to the Channel Islands, the first mention being for August - *Started from house on our journey for Guernsey via Waterloo.........Got on very well and reached Southampton at 1.30. At night started for Guernsey.........Arrived at Guernsey at 6.30 - good passage. I was not sick. Went to Mrs Snell* [possibly their landlady] *and walked round Clarence Battery in morning.* The various places mentioned during the month, when family and friends were there, showed they knew the islands well, visiting Sark, Herm, Alderney and Cherbourg besides practically every bay of Guernsey. This year of diary entries has given a good picture of my father's school days and his relationship with his elder brother WJ. With a gap of 9 years between them it gives the feeling that he looked up to WJ and obviously kept in touch with what he was doing. There is a hint of brotherly friendship and interest between them.

Captain H L Rokeby of Arthingworth Manor, near Market Harborough, engaged J T Lowke & Sons to construct a Hyler-White steam car for him, which was then being described in the English Mechanic magazine as a DIY series. It is seen here at the J T Lowke Works c. June 1902 and not yet fitted with its bodywork.

Alan Burman Collection

Chapter Four

The Beginning of the Business

It is obvious to me that WJ had an excellent start to his working life with the help and encouragement of both his parents. He had a discerning and intelligent mother who, unusually for her time, was not afraid of foreign travel. Probably her example was the spur that prodded her energetic son into taking up the selfsame interest. She several times accompanied him on his trips to the continent, meeting the families of his business acquaintances, and in so doing saw many lovely parts of Europe.

He was a diligent pupil at school and was on good terms with his father. At some period, soon after he left school at the age of 13, which would have been around 1890-91, he persuaded his father to let him go into an architect's office, where he worked for a period of 18 months, to test his wish to become an architect. At that time there were half a dozen main architectural practices in Northampton. It is not known which practice he joined but there are three possible candidates, all with family connections at the time. One of these was Matthew Holding, who was well known for being the local architect selected to design the second stage of Northampton's Guildhall, following E W Godwin, who, under the nom de plume *Non Nobis Domine* was chosen in 1864 to be the initiator of this grand Victorian building. The Holdings were a local family who were well known to the Lowkes. Edith and Edward de Wilde Holding, the children of Matthew Holding, and my parents were members of the Kingsthorpe Tennis Club (long since disbanded and built upon). The other possibilities are Keightly Cobb, who was a friend of both WJ and my father, and my grandfather's business architect Alexander Ellis Anderson. Of all three, Cobb is perhaps the most likely. The early basic knowledge that WJ gained of architecture was to prove exceedingly useful in his later life.

My uncle realised that architecture was not his future, although he had as yet no decisive idea as to what he really wanted. His father persuaded him to take up an apprenticeship within his own business, and so he started work in the blacksmith's shop of the boiler-making department of the business. Here he was put to work operating the bellows for the hearth and generally helping the blacksmith. He openly admitted that he was not really built for heavy manual work.

J T Lowke & Son were described as engineers, boilermakers, and iron and brass founders. Around their yard in Kingswell Street was a conglomeration of buildings housing the foundry, blacksmith's shop, and fitting cum machine shop. The business was also the Northampton agent for Tangye Gas Engines. With Northampton being the centre of the shoe making industry, it is not surprising to find that the firm made Collier sandal moulders and heel builders for the Northampton Machinery Co.

About 1902 the English Mechanic magazine ran instalments on a do-it-yourself project for the construction of a Hyler-White steam car, designed by Thomas Hyler-White, son of a London silversmith, who had worked for the Daimler Motor Company. D J Smith & Co., engineers in the East End of

London, supplied the castings and parts. A local reader, Captain H L Rokeby of Arthingworth Manor near Market Harborough, engaged J T Lowke & Sons to construct one for him. It was a very large car for that period. A Serpollet-type flash boiler mounted behind the rear axle supplied the steam for a vertical twin cylinder marine engine, located under the front seat. In June of 1902 David Smith, of D J Smith & Co., visited Northampton and conducted trials on the running chassis. After a run of two or three miles, visiting Mulliners coach works in Bridge Street, and probably the other well known Northampton coachbuilder Joseph Grose, David Smith commented that the workmanship was excellent, in fact the work was really too good in parts.

Although there were two coachbuilders in close proximity, the bodywork for the steam car was made in Newport Pagnell by Messrs Saloman & Sons. The car ran briefly during the summer and in October Captain Rokeby said that he was pleased with the result as *an experimental car and a good strong knockabout toy .... and we may be able to improve it into something better this winter*. This was not the only steam car to visit Northampton, as we shall see later in our story.

Eventually WJ was transferred into the fitting shop to learn fitting and machining work, under the watchful eye of William Vaughan who was to become a very close friend. *Here I was happy* he related, *I could manage the work and what was more I found that I liked it, and at last I really began making progress in a job that I found congenial and interesting*. Whilst serving his apprenticeship with his father, WJ attended the Kingswell Street College where he took evening classes in Advanced Machine Drawing, Perspective, Sound, Light and Heat, together with Geometry. He was very much thinking to the future.

WJ began to take an interest in model engineering and, as his skills increased, he started to make small stationary engines from castings and parts, supplied by various firms in the business at that time. Miniature boilers were made in the firm's boiler shop, and thus a new occupation was found, in which he had profound interest. Model engineering by this time was already a well established and developing hobby, and many people were building model steam locomotives and engineering models in their spare time. Model locomotives are almost as old as their full size prototypes, examples having been recorded as far back as 1829.

Gradually, WJ became aware that there were a lot of people who were also interested in the hobby of model engineering. The amateur's workshop at this time was very basic and the ability to make precision parts such as whistles, safety valves, water gauges, pumps, etc. was lacking. *Here was an idea!* To quote WJ: *Why not start selling small fittings and parts that I made in my spare time to other enthusiasts who needed them for their model making?* This was the birth of Bassett-Lowke & Co. - model makers to the world! WJ persuaded his father to allow him to show the fittings and parts produced in his spare time, and other models and fittings which he bought in for resale, in the display window next to the office in Kingswell Street. WJ was fortunate in that he found support for his new venture from Harry F R Franklin, who was his father's bookkeeper, and who also had an interest in model engineering. Having decided to make this a commercial venture, the two became close friends as well as business partners; a combination that does not always succeed.

Harry Foldar Robert Franklin was born in 1875 at Chesterfield. The family moved to Bedford when he was quite young and then, some years later, to Northampton where Franklin senior came to the firm of accountants, A C Palmer and Co. His son Harry joined him in this employment when he left school. Palmers were called into J T Lowke and Sons to set up an accounting system, after which young Harry was retained to act as bookkeeper. It was then that he met WJ and shared his interest in making models, cycling and photography, thus starting a lifelong friendship and business association.

In contrast to WJ, Harry was of a retiring, almost shy, personality quite happy to be concerned with the day to day activities of the business and leave his partner to travel, build up the business connections and deal with all publicity matters. Again, in contrast, WJ had little time to continue practical model making or to be interested in using models, while Harry maintained his interest in steam power. At his home in Leicester Parade, Northampton, he installed a 2" gauge model railway and, in later years, had a $10\frac{1}{4}$" gauge track laid in the grounds of his intended retirement home at Radwell in Bedfordshire.

For a number of years he also owned an American built *White* steam car, ceasing to run it only when replacement parts were unobtainable. The car, registration number NH1878, was a model O-O of 20 horsepower and is now in the car collection at Beaulieu. At one stage, it was registered in the name of E W Twining who also had a long association with WJ. A third contrasting feature in Harry's make up was that he was prepared to undertake direct responsibility for manufacturing and thus persuaded WJ to go along with him in setting up Ships Models Ltd. in 1921.

Harry senior had another interest, a steam launch named *Iolanthe* that he bought at Brentford and navigated along the Grand Union Canal to Blisworth and then the branch to Beckett's Park, Northampton. It was kept in a boathouse at Midsummer Meadow and, in the First World War, was used on many occasions to take parties of wounded soldiers on trips along the river Nene. Harry junior did quite a number of things in this way; he also took wounded soldiers in his steam car to various entertainments and concerts.

In the General Strike of 1926, Harry Franklin Snr. demonstrated his loyalty to the Government by driving for the L M S railway on the Northampton to London Euston run, with his son, also named Harry, acting as fireman. He married a second time and retired in 1938 to his house in the Bedfordshire village of Radwell.

W J Bassett-Lowke, the young photographer, complete with his transport, always ready to look for interesting subjects to capture on film - circa 18 to 19 years old.
J Bassett-Lowke Collection

At this time, there were only a few suppliers of fittings for steam engines, with probably Steven's Model Dockyard in London, Clyde Model Dockyard in Glasgow, John Claret of Tottenham (of which more later), and Bertrand Garside of Warrington being the principal players. With some of these fittings, especially pressure gauges, requiring precision equipment to manufacture them, and with J T Lowke not being equipped for this class of work, WJ bought these in for resale from suppliers like John Claret who did much work especially for him. He also started building complete models, steam engines, dynamos and so forth from castings and parts purchased from various firms, advertising them in the local paper.

Finance is a crucial issue when starting any business but help was on hand through a local disaster at Wellingborough station, about ten miles from Northampton. Just before the 7.15 p.m. express train from St. Pancras to Manchester was due to pass through Wellingborough station, on the 2nd September 1898, a platform trolley, which had been parked at right angles to the platform, rolled off onto the

Local disaster struck at Wellingborough station, on the 2nd September 1898, when a platform trolley, parked at right angles to the track, rolled off the platform and derailed the 7.15 pm express train from London. WJ was quickly on the scene and sold a quantity of prints some, it is believed, to the national Press, giving him the capital he required for his new business.

Courtesy Northampton Borough Council

Harry Franklin Jnr. (centre) joined WJ as a partner in the business and is seen here with Harry Franklin Snr. (left) when they volunteered for service on the LMS Railway during the strike of 1926, under the Local Voluntary Service Committee scheme. In all, 1,847 people, including 57 horse drivers and 68 women car drivers, were enrolled to run essential services.

Henry Greenly Collection

track. Despite efforts to retrieve it, the train hit it at full speed and ended up as a tangled mess at the north end of the station, killing the engine crew and five passengers. WJ relates that :

> *Harry and I visited the scene soon afterwards and we took a number of photographs of the smashed locomotive and broken, splintered coaches. We found that prints were much in demand and we sold a large number, including some to the National press and so we pooled the proceeds towards buying materials for our modelmaking venture.*

Photographs were even taken by WJ in stereograph (3D).

In 1899 a new magazine, which had only been started the year before, came to his notice - *The Model Engineer & Amateur Electrician*, described as a journal for amateur modellers. He lost no time in visiting the offices of this publication in Farringdon Avenue, London EC. It was from here that a club was formed on the 2nd November 1898, the Society of Model Engineers, with the new magazine's Editor, Percival Marshall A.I.Mech.E., as the mainspring in both convening and chairing the inaugural meeting. It was here, through Marshall, that WJ met Henry Greenly, a keen and talented man in the realm of model railways, an offshoot of his work with the Metropolitan Railway.

Both *The Model Engineer & Amateur Electrician* magazine and the Society of Model Engineers were in their infancy. This gave WJ, who was really relatively unknown at this time in the field of model engineering, a platform from which to develop his new business. He started to advertise his products in the new magazine and during 1899 produced his first catalogue. No ordinary catalogue, I should say, but reputed to be carefully compiled with actual photographs pasted in; no doubt taken by WJ himself. *A pointer to the spirit of these young merchant adventurers in an unexplored field of commerce, a pointer to their pride in their products and to their determination to compel attention* to quote George Holland on the occasion of the 50th Anniversary of Bassett-Lowke. A mail order business was thus established, but little did WJ and his partner Franklin realise the impact they would eventually have on the market.

A pastime today : a business tomorrow

The first review of WJ's products appeared in *The Model Engineer & Amateur Electrician* for February 1899 when his range of small pressure gauges was described; ranging from 4s. 6d. (20$^1/_2$ p) to 5s. 6d. (25$^1/_2$p) each. Most enterprising was the fact that he also offered 'dummy pressure gauges suitable for watch chain ornaments' at 2s. 6d. (12$^1/_2$p) each. Interestingly, one of WJ's competitors, Bertrand Garside of Warrington, also offered in 1898 a dummy pressure gauge but this was only priced at 10d (4p)!

The Conversazione, the first gathering of the Society of Model Engineers, also provided WJ with the opportunity to display his products at the Memorial Hall, Farringdon Street, London on the 11th November 1899. One important factor, which was to help WJ later on to develop his business, was that the Society recognised at an early stage the need to lay down standards where hitherto there had been none at all.

WJ, with the help of his marketing activities and the active help of his partner Franklin, was increasing his business. Elsewhere Henry Greenly became more and more interested in the *Model Engineer* magazine and eventually, in 1901, joined the editorial staff leaving his Metropolitan Railway post. His work progressed with the *Model Engineer* and, thrown together, Greenly and WJ formed an instant liking for one another. It was not surprising that they embarked upon a business association which developed into Greenly becoming WJ's consulting engineer in the same year; a relationship which lasted many years.

Either late 1901 or early 1902, Greenly drove a Lifu steam car up to Northampton where its wagonette body was rebuilt by the Joseph Grose firm of coachbuilders to provide a covered-in cab. The car belonged to Sir David Salomans, who was ex mayor of Tunbridge Wells and organiser of the first horseless carriage exhibition in 1895. The car was built in the Isle of Wight by The Liquid Fuel Engineering Company in East Cowes. Having a tiller which when moved to the left turned the car to the right which resulted in a disastrous maiden trip in London. No doubt the reason for selecting a firm of coachbuilders in Northampton was probably due to Greenly's connection with WJ.

As the time of WJ's learning period was coming to an end he discussed with his father his great interest in models, and the fact that he was not inclined to work in heavy engineering. His father listened and knew only too well that electricity was indeed the development for the future. He was extremely keen that WJ should gain some experience in this field of industry. WJ was thus sent to Crompton Parkinson of Chelmsford, a well-known firm of electrical engineers, for a period of about twelve months as a student apprentice. Whilst employed there he worked on installations at the Hunslet Goods Yard, Leeds, and at York Corporation.

With WJ being away from Northampton for this period of time, it meant that Harry Franklin had to carry on with the business very much on his own. There was regular, almost daily, correspondence between the two partners, each using a duplicating book so that they would have copies of their handwritten notes. The one surviving copy of these books, which was unfortunately destroyed in 1968, made interesting reading because they were very demanding of each other and sometimes abusive, but the day to day details were all dealt with; often spiced with footnotes concerned with the latest experience with the ladies!

If asked to pinpoint the most momentous decision in WJ's life, I consider this was his resolve to visit the Paris Fair in 1900; an event that had a far reaching influence on Europe in many ways, both culturally and commercially. WJ read in the local newspapers that the Fair contained a good collection of mechanical toys and continental scale models, all of which aroused his curiosity and interest. Throughout his life, he was noted for organising parties to visit various places of interest. On this Paris trip he took with him two friends; one was Frank Jones, of a Northampton shoe company and brother of the girl WJ eventually married, who wanted to see the leather section of the exhibition, and the other, Flinton Harris who was to eventually be the best man at his wedding.

WJ found the exhibition a wonderful place, with exhibitors from far and wide, and he was delighted with the excellence of German-based companies in their model work. To use his own words :

> *I was amazed at all I saw but especially I wondered at the high class toy productions. Many of them were miniatures of Continental railways with locomotives, coaches, wagons and other accessories, and these had a distinctive superiority over other toys; they were accurately built to scale, as far as was possible, for small working models. The only things to compare with them in England were stubby green engines with brass wheels, tall chimneys, crude driving arrangements, and fantastic names like 'Zulu' or 'Ajax', with little or no resemblance to the real thing.*

He was truly impressed by the quality of the design and craftsmanship displayed by these continental manufacturers, who were streets ahead and who were to dominate the toy market for years to come. What must surely have gone through his mind was the question as to why no British manufacturer had attempted to challenge the German domination of the market.

Two companies impressed WJ. The first was Bing Bros. run by Stefan Bing who was Governing Director and the second was Georges Carette, both based in Nuremberg and generally known as *The Toymakers of Nuremberg*. He looked very carefully at the sample models displayed and identified the possibility of having similar scale models built of British design and to the same quality standard. He made tentative arrangements with Stefan Bing to have a new range of model engines and accessories manufactured to his own design for the British market; but this was not to be until 1901.

He was obviously impressed by the German manufacturer's ability and willingness to produce scale locomotives of quality specifically for the British market. His enthusiasm was further endorsed by much correspondence in the *Model Engineer* at the time requesting manufacturers to produce a reasonable scale model locomotive at a reasonable price. For the time being he had to rely upon the manufacturing expertise and capabilities of his German counterparts. Model locomotives built by

WJ with, in 1902, his first comprehensivve catalogue which was the first one in which he used printed photographs. Only 25 years old, his catalogue design was very much ahead of its time in comparison to his competitors.

J Bassett-Lowke Collection

British manufacturers such as Stevens Model Dockyard made no attempt to resemble the locomotives of the day; they were basically regarded as toys - more commonly known as *dribblers* as they used to drip oil and water all over the floor. However, during this early period, WJ did include these models in at least one of his early catalogues which survives.

The first model produced by Bing for Bassett-Lowke in 1901 was a gauge 3 model of an L.N.W.R. locomotive *Black Prince*. It was described by Percival Marshall as *deserving great praise as a genuine step in the direction of more realistic model locomotives than have often been supplied by professional model makers*. WJ's decision to select *Black Prince* as his first project may well have been influenced by the fact that on the London & North Western Railway's stand, at the Paris Fair, was a very fine scale model of their 4-4-0 *Diamond Jubilee* of which *Black Prince* was also a representative example. This was the start of an era of supremacy for my uncle who, one must remember, was still only 24 years of age at the time.

Over the years WJ expanded his range of products, mostly imported from Germany, and supplemented by those of British manufacture including items that he was able to manufacture himself with his limited facilities.

At about the same time that WJ met Percival Marshall and Henry Greenly, he came into contact with another interesting man, John Claret, who had trained in the production of precision machining. The Claret family were based outside London in Tottenham, and Mr. Claret's first work in the model connection was in the building of model locomotives for private customers, and the manufacture of miniature steam fittings. His principal outlet in the model fittings line was with Bertrand Garside of

Warrington, but when in 1898 he met WJ and H F R Franklin, who were then on the brink of trading as W J Bassett-Lowke & Co., WJ soon found a larger market for Claret's products. As these friendly business relationships continued, the Claret family decided to move en masse to more healthy countryside and found a house at the village of Moulton, near Northampton. A partnership was formed between WJ, Franklin, Claret and one of his sons. Business progressed with workshop plant and machinery being installed at the house in Moulton. In 1912, John Claret's son sadly died; like his father, he was an excellent craftsman. John Claret carried on on his own, but as the war came much of the plant and machinery was transferred to Bassett-Lowke in Northampton and was used on war work such as gauge making.

During those early years of the 20th century, WJ was often at Moulton discussing business, and he valued John Claret as a first class metal worker. Claret was a Calvinist Baptist, a Sabbatarian and a strict Pacifist. He would have nothing to do with war work and so was not allowed to keep those who

John Claret had an established business in Tottenham, London, making model steam fittings. Through Bassett-Lowke he found a larger market for his products and the Claret family eventually moved up to Moulton, near Northampton. Circa 1914, his equipment was transferred to the Bassett-Lowke works for use on war work.

J Bassett-Lowke Collection

worked for him; hence the transfer of the business to Bassett-Lowke & Co. He just carried on working day in day out, working a full week alone, on his excellent model fittings and continued to be active until the last week of his life. He died in 1929 reaching the advanced age of 89. Among his family of three sons and two daughters, all knowledgeable on metal work, he had one son in the Navy and another, W.E. Claret, A.M.I.E.E., A.M.I. Mech.E., M.Inst.Fuel, was a well known power engineer. WJ was pleased to be an esteemed friend of the family. His youngest son, also John Claret, accompanied WJ on business trips to Germany acting as an interpreter.

William Barber, who attended the nearby Bluecoat School, recorded that his schoolmates and he were fascinated by the B-L works. They used to open the door to have a quiet look inside :

> *rows of little copper 'tubes', marvellous little engines, flywheels, bogie wheels, and to us youngsters it was such a wonderful sight ………we were such a nuisance opening the door for a peep that we were 'deterred' and eventually transferred our attention elsewhere!*

Another comrade whom WJ met around the turn of the century through Marshall and Greenly was Stuart Turner of Shiplake, near Henley on Thames, Oxfordshire, a young man well known at the time in the marine engineering world. In 1902, he became interested in the growing enterprise of model engineering, and had seriously discussed the design and construction of marine engine models with Henry Greenly. Greenly designed for him small vertical marine engines and went further with a larger high-speed engine suitable for driving an electric generator. This was essential for a workshop in the early days of this century in many places before a town electric supply became available.

Stuart Turner, also with a good eye for business and conscious of the fact that model engineering was an expensive hobby, was the first in the business to offer 'easy terms' to his customers. WJ later included many Stuart Turner manufactured items in the B-L catalogues; pumps, steam engines, and castings. The business of Stuart Turner was incorporated on April 6th 1906 and WJ purchased shares that month, paying £50 to acquire shares at 5/- (25p) each in four payments from April 21st 1906 to February 7th 1907. WJ maintained his interest in this firm throughout, with the result that his nieces inherited the shares in the company, which they hold to this day. Evidently 257 shares were issued, with Stuart Turner having one and for some reason his wife having 5.

Sidney Marmaduke Stuart Turner was born in 1868. He did many jobs; working in a bank, then a customs office, working for a millwright mending lawn mowers and suchlike, then moving on to work on the Clyde in a shipyard, and thence to join the Clan Line where he spent 2 years at sea. Later Stuart Turner ran an electrical business in Jersey which did not succeed but his next job, looking after a steam generating plant at Shiplake Court near Henley-on-Thames, was the crux of his future life. Here, working at Shiplake, he designed his first famous engine, the No. 1 Model Steam Engine. He made the patterns, had them cast, machined and assembled them, and showed the finished engine at a local exhibition. From publicity in the *Model Engineer*, orders came in by leaps and bounds and from then on Stuart Turner did not look back. He left the business in 1919 for South Africa and died in 1933. He was an interesting and highly successful friend of WJ's for many years and Henry Greenly, who first met him in 1902, also acted as consultant to him with perhaps, at times, a conflict of interest.

Greenly had joined WJ as his consulting engineer and in the following year, 1903, WJ asked him to have a look at current developments in France and Germany on behalf of Bassett-Lowke. WJ himself was tied up with work at Northampton but would try and join him later. Seeing the publicity value of such a visit, Percival Marshall had approved of this idea as the results would be reported eventually in the *Model Engineer* pages. WJ did later join Greenly, together with his mother Mrs. J T Lowke, in Munich. On that trip they went to several places on the continent, including tours to German manufacturers like Maerklins of Munich and Bings of Nuremberg. To Erfurt and to Jena - these

An early visiting card designed by E W Twining for W J Bassett-Lowke
J Bassett-Lowke Collection

THE BEGINNING OF THE BUSINESS   41

It was the 2 ½" gauge live steam model of the LNWR 'BLACK PRINCE' 4-4-0 locomotive, produced in 1902 with slide valve cylinders as opposed to oscillating ones, that provided Bassett-Lowke with the breakthrough to improve the standard of model railway equipment at that time. W J Bassett-Lowke is seen above demonstrating the locomotive to some young, and perhaps envious, admirers.
RailRomances Collection

Above, the 1¾" gauge model of the LNWR 'LADY OF THE LAKE' introduced in 1901. It was the first quantity produced model of scale proportions. Left, an LNWR 'GEORGE V', introduced in 1912 at a price of 12/6d (62½p), made from lithographed tinplate which revolutionised both production and quality.
RailRomances Collection

In 1909 a gauge 2 model was produced of a Great Western Railway 4-4-0 appropriately named 'COUNTY OF NORTHAMPTON'.
Courtesy Bob Burgess

young model railway enthusiasts covered many miles in search of new developments. My grandmother was not the only lady visiting foreign parts with WJ, but Greenly's wife, Lilley, also went and was able to enjoy a trip down the Rhine by steamer and from Mainz onwards by train, to Nuremberg.

The first alliance of the business of Bassett-Lowke was between WJ and his colleague Harry Franklin. Then came a third member to join them, William Rowe. He was a young man who soon volunteered to go with WJ on many of his speaking engagements, carrying the equipment needed and running the slides that illustrated the talks. The luggage would not be light for these talks as they were with lantern slides and all the paraphernalia concerned. I believe neither of them was daunted by wind or weather and the many rough journeys encountered on such occasions; WJ would not use a car so the journey would be by train or taxi. William (Bill) Rowe was known to me when I joined the firm in the 1930s. He started work at the age of 14 and was the son of Northampton's Chief Fire Officer, intending after this first temporary job to follow in his father's footsteps into the Fire Service. But, he was caught up under the spell of models and became the first storekeeper of the company. Bassett-Lowke Ltd. kept his interest and filled all his working life and he finally retired in the early 1970s at the age of 68, always a hard working servant of B-L Ltd.

The longest partnership, with the exception of founders WJ and Franklin, was that with Henry Greenly, famous in his own right for pioneer work in the world of railway modelling. This latter partnership came to an untimely and unfortunate end in 1938. In another sphere of railways WJ had evidently watched with growing interest the passenger carrying miniature railways which had come into existence as he grew up. These were generally owned by wealthy landowners - pioneers like Sir Arthur Heywood, who developed a complete 15" gauge system on his estate as early as 1874 with a commercial objective in mind, before WJ was born. Also, Sir Arthur built a similar system in 1895 for the Duke of Westminster, to service his estate at Eaton Hall, near Chester and this particular railway was to eventually play a key role in WJ's adventures into the field of miniature railways.

WJ became interested in the idea of miniature railways, as opposed to model railways, the difference being that miniature railways were of a larger gauge with the track laid on the ground and with trains capable of pulling adult passengers. He may well have been influenced by seeing a local miniature railway at Blakesley Hall, Towcester, in Northamptonshire, built by the owner Mr. C W Bartholomew, who had built the line to connect the house and the estate to the nearby station. He imported two American style locomotives to operate the line. These little 4-4-0 steam locomotives were built by a firm named Cagney in America, and were based on the New York Central Railways No. 999, which is claimed to have set a new world speed record of 112 mph on the Empire State Express in 1893. I can well imagine WJ being excited by the prospect of miniature passenger carrying railways, but I cannot imagine him being enthused by American locomotives which, whilst being very practical, were hardly very attractive in appearance. In fact it seems that he discussed the idea maturing in his mind that he, with the help and expertise of his father's facilities at J T Lowke & Son, might seriously consider building passenger-carrying railways for the public. One of the first projects that WJ ventured upon, where he had the aid of Henry Greenly, was the formation of a Company whose objective was :

The object of acquiring by purchase or otherwise, sell or otherwise dispose of, establish, develop and carry on the business of Model Engineers, Manufacturers of Miniature and Model Railway

Engines, Carriages and Trains, and other articles and things used in connection with the business of Exhibitors of Miniature Railways, Trains and other things either by payment or by way of advertisement or both.

In short, Miniature Railways of Great Britain Ltd., which came into being in December 1904.

Turning to the second page of the Memorandum and Articles of Association, I read several names on the list of shareholders whom I knew well. WJ (of course then living with his parents at 13 Kingswell Street), 50 shares; H F R Franklin, his partner, 50 shares; Ernest Arthur Trenery (timber importer, who was to play an important role in the new company and who also supplied B-L with timber), 50 shares; Alexander Ellis Anderson, the architect employed by the Lowke family for both business and private work, 60 shares; Joseph Tom Lowke, my grandfather, 50 shares; Thomas Keightly Cobb, architect friend of the family, 20 shares; Charles Henry Battle, a clerk and known to WJ as a member of his Doddridge Young Men's Class, later well known in connection with the Northampton General Hospital, and appointed in this instance as Company Secretary, 20 shares; and last but by no means least Henry Greenly, 50 shares.

As a start, and probably to gain experience, a complete miniature railway of $10\frac{1}{4}$" gauge was purchased in 1904 and installed adjacent to Abington Park, Northampton, opening on the Easter Saturday 1905, the fare being 2d (just under 1p). WJ wanted to lay the railway in the Park but the Council

With the formation of Miniature Railways of Great Britain Ltd in 1904, the first miniature railway was built on the edge of Abington Park, Northampton. It was of $10\frac{1}{4}$" gauge and opened on Easter Saturday 1905. The locomotive 'NIPPER' and equipment was purchased from the Bricket Wood Railway, St. Albans, which was owned by George Flooks and Fred Smithies. It was a great success and started Bassett-Lowke on the road to bigger ventures.

RailRomances Collection

refused and arrangements were made to put it on adjoining land. The locomotive was a little 0-4-4 Tank named *Nipper*. This had been designed by Henry Greenly for George Flooks of Watford, based upon the Class E locomotives of the Metropolitan Railway who, in association with Fred Smithies (inventor of the Smithies type boiler), had built a miniature railway at Bricket Wood, St Albans. Bassett-Lowke purchased the locomotive in 1904 after the Bricket Wood line closed. Fred Smithies became a very close friend of WJ's and was to have a long association with his miniature railway activities. It was in 1904 that WJ became a member of the Junior Institute of Engineers, which later became the Institute of General Technician Engineers.

Steam was to be the success of the new venture which resulted in W J commissioning Henry Greenly, who had already prepared drawings of small model locomotives for him, to design a 15" gauge locomotive for commercial use on a proposed line at Blackpool - the result in 1905 was a 4-4-2 Atlantic called *Little Giant*. When constructed, it was taken to the Duke of Westminster's Eaton Railway at Eaton Hall, Chester, for a day of intensive trials before being transferred to the foreshore at Blackpool.

The success of this first line prompted further railways, largely at national exhibitions, which were very much in fashion during this period in Great Britain and on the Continent. The $10^{1}/_{4}$" gauge line at Northampton was transferred to the Sutton Coldfield Pleasure Show on the outskirts of Birmingham in 1907, where *Nipper* was renamed *Kovek*. The line at Blackpool was moved to a new site at Halifax in 1909. The same year a line was laid at the Franco-British Exhibition at the White City in London which followed the 1908 Olympics, the stadium being named White City Stadium after the Chicago-influenced exhibition architecture. MRGB Ltd. was under contract to Sideshow Railways Ltd. to build the railway. All these lines were operated by further examples of the original *Little Giant*, the 15" gauge locomotive built for Blackpool. Also in 1909 another line was opened at Nancy in France.

Large exhibitions were all the rage on the Continent in the early years of the century before the 1914-1918 War and B-L locomotives and rolling stock were supplied to The Centenary Exhibition in Breslau, Germany; being the first English built miniature locomotive in Germany. WJ's dream of matching his German counterparts had come true and he had a foothold in Europe. Others followed. In 1909, the Exposition Universelle et Internationale in Brussels which, in 1910, had an attendance of 13 million people, was open for 7 months, but had a catastrophic fire which destroyed some of the B-L exhibits, and the exhibition lost £10,000. Then there was Roubaix in 1911, and Anglo Park at Budapest in 1912.

One of the most attractive was the Luna Park railway, built in 1912 at La Parc des Eaux Vives alongside Lake Geneva, in Switzerland. The design and construction was undertaken by Henry Greenly and the operation was supervised by John Wills, who originally worked in the Bassett-Lowke London shop. This leisure park lasted a very short while and overnight went into liquidation. Quick thinking John Wills loaded the locomotive and rolling stock on to a wagon and headed for home, at least saving some of WJ's losses on the venture!

Also in 1912 B-L built and supplied a complete 15" gauge railway for the King of Siam, whose name ranks amongst many of WJ's distinguished customers.

In the meantime, lines had been opened up at Halifax Zoo in 1910, Rhyl in North Wales in 1911, which was designed by Henry Greenly, the Llewellyn Miniature Railway at Southport in 1911 and, just

THE BEGINNING OF THE BUSINESS 45

Above, a further view of the railway at Abington Park, Northampton, and below, the 15 inch gauge 'Little Giant' Class locomotive 'GREEN DRAGON' (No.16), built by Bassett-Lowke in 1909 for the Franco/British Exhibition at White City. In the same year it won a gold medal at the Model Engineer Exhibition in London. It is seen here in the work's yard in Kingswell Street.

RailRomances Collection

With the success of the Abington Park railway, Bassett-Lowke commissioned Henry Greenly to design a 15 inch gauge 'Atlantic' 4-4-2 locomotive for the second venture at Blackpool. The result was 'LITTLE GIANT', seen here on test at the Duke of Westminster's railway at Eaton Hall, Chester, in 1905.

RailRomances Collection

Bassett-Lowke built the above 15 inch gauge locomotive in 1909 for Squire Charles W Bartholomew (front right), for his railway at Blakesley Hall, Northamptonshire. This 4-4-4 tank locomotive named 'BLACOLVESLEY', whilst of steam outline in appearance, it was fitted with a 14 HP internal combustion engine. Sitting on the left is W J Bassett-Lowke, with F Green with the bowler hat, Henry Greenly (the designer) with the 'boater', and on the right C W Bartholomew.

Courtesy Northamptonshire County Records

THE BEGINNING OF THE BUSINESS   47

Proctor Mitchell, W J Bassett-Lowke and John Wills visited the Lake District in 1916 and took out a three year lease on the derelict Eskdale Railway. It was rebuilt to 15 inch gauge and became the Ravenglass & Eskdale Railway. Here we see Bassett-Lowke built 'COLOSSUS' with a full load of holidaymakers.

RailRomances Collection

In 1916, Narrow Gauge Railways Ltd (associate company of Bassett-Lowke) built the Fairbourne Miniature Railway at Fairbourne, in Mid Wales. 'PRINCE EDWARD OF WALES' takes a photographic break in 1916 at Bathing Beach Halt with, on the left in a straw hat, W J Bassett-Lowke and John Wills on the locomotive.

Henry Greenly Collection

Trials of the Bassett-Lowke built Pacific JOHN ANTHONY (later COLOSSUS) took place in July 1914 on the Duke of Westminster's railway at Eaton Hall, Chester. Built for Capt. J E P Howey, the locomotive is here seen with journalist Cecil J Allen driving a test train with a load of coal. The locomotive remained at Eaton Hall until 1916 when it was purchased by the Ravenglass & Eskdale Railway.

RailRomances Collection

A site meeting, in April 1911, on the 15 inch gauge Rhyl Miniature Railway, in North Wales, with from left to right, Butler, Proctor-Mitchell, Roberts (foreman), Albert Barnes (Marine Lake manager), Grimshaw, W J Bassett-Lowke and Adrian Brough (seated). Below, is the station at the Marine Lake, Rhyl, with 'Little Giant' Class locomotive 'PRINCE EDWARD OF WALES', c. May 1911.

RailRomances Collection

Bassett-Lowke became a limited liability company in 1909 and in 1910 they acquired larger premises, at the top of Kingswell Street, to cater for greatly expanded sales and to enlarge the manufacturing facility.

RailRomances Collection

before the Great War (1914-18) started, lines were built at The Norwegian Exhibition, Christiania, near Oslo, in Norway, and The League of Work Exhibition in Cologne, the latter being brought to an untimely end by a disastrous fire, spelling the end of the Bassett-Lowke domination of the continental exhibition railways.

On the 8th December 1911 Miniature Railways of Great Britain Ltd was placed into liquidation and finally wound up on the 28th November 1912 , to be superseded by a new company Narrow Gauge Railways Ltd.

This failure was by no means a slur on WJ's abilities; both he and Franklin honourably repaid B-L for the original investment in MRGB Ltd. The general consensus is that building these miniature railways on the Continent was an expensive exercise and that their profitability was not sufficient to make it truly viable.

Undeterred by the outbreak of war, WJ was still on the outlook for more ambitious lines on the home front. In 1915 his attention was drawn to a derelict 3ft 6ins gauge mineral line in the Lake District running from the small seaside village of Ravenglass some 7 miles into the hills, advertised for sale in the *Model Engineer* magazine.

The line was taken over and re-laid to the 15" gauge and a collection of locomotives and rolling stock acquired from other lines was assembled to run it. These included the locomotive and coaches from the Christiania exhibition in Norway and a B-L locomotive built for Captain Howey. This was a much larger version of the *Little Giant* being a 4-6-2 Pacific and named *John Anthony*, later renamed *Colossus* at Ravenglass, and was for his private line at Staughton Manor. Another line laid in 1915 was at Fairbourne on the Mawddach Estuary in Mid Wales, and was operated by John Wills who also became Postmaster and spent the rest of his life at Fairbourne. In due course many of these lines were passed to local operators and were no longer worked or operated by the B-L management.

Henry Greenly and WJ continued to co-operate for many years on smaller gauge models and a number of miniature railways of smaller gauges, that is $7^{1/4}$", $9^{1/2}$", and $10^{1/4}$", were built with B-L locomotives and rolling stock between the Wars. Notable smaller Exhibition lines were built, such as the Children's

Welfare Exhibition at Olympia in 1914, on which Mrs. Winston Churchill and Mr. Cadbury, of chocolate fame, travelled, and the Empire Exhibition at Wembley when, on the 14th May 1925, King George V and Queen Mary were passengers on the Treasure Island Railway. The carriages at the Wembley exhibition seated two people facing each other and the principal engine was named *Peter Pan*, a Bassett-Lowke *Atlantic* painted for the occasion in Canadian Pacific railway colours and which belonged to Terence Holder, one of WJ's valuable customers. The King invited a small boy to accompany him, but he was so shy that his place was taken by a very bold young girl - an event which delighted the Press and which gave B-L front-page publicity in the *Daily Mirror*!

One of the *Little Giant* class locomotives named *Green Dragon* was awarded a Gold medal and Diploma of Merit at the Model Engineer Exhibition in London, 1909. A similar model named *Entente Cordiale* was also awarded a Gold medal at the International Exhibition, Nancy, in the same year.

Most of the lines mentioned have now gone except for the lines at Rhyl, Southport, Ravenglass and Fairbourne which are there today, albeit with different motive power but as a stark reminder of WJ's foresight. Several of the *Little Giant* class locomotives exist today, including the original built for the Blackpool Miniature Railway in 1905, which has been superbly restored. The last *Little Giant* was built in 1923 for the well-known racing driver of the day, Count Louis Zborowski. Shortly after delivery, he was killed at Monza in a racing accident and the engine was purchased for the Fairbourne Railway in 1924 and appropriately named *Count Louis*, where it stayed until 1986. The majority of miniature railways today are of the $7^1/_4$" and $10^1/_4$" gauges, and several still operate Bassett-Lowke locomotives.

During this period Henry Greenly was an essential factor in the development of the miniature railway side of the business; there was simply nobody else who could have fulfilled this role. This is acknowledged by WJ in his 4th edition of the *Model Railway Handbook*, which is jointly signed by WJ and Greenly. Greenly did all the drawings for the *Model Railway Handbook* as well. Here was the ideal combination of a person with excellent business acumen supported by one with outstanding technical expertise. WJ considered that Henry Greenly had a mind like quicksilver when it came to grasping a problem.

An imposing photograph of the young managing director, WJ, imaculately dressed and driving a $9^1/_2$" gauge Great Northern Railway 'Atlantic' at speed.

Courtesy Simon Townsend

THE BEGINNING OF THE BUSINESS 51

The Treasure Island Railway at Wembley on the 14th May 1925, when King George V and Queen Mary were passengers. Above, a little boy is helped from the train having refused the priviledge of sitting with the King and, right, his place is taken by a young lady who has no fear at all.
John Hall-Craggs Collection

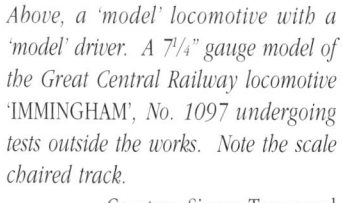

Above, a 'model' locomotive with a 'model' driver. A 7¼" gauge model of the Great Central Railway locomotive 'IMMINGHAM', No. 1097 undergoing tests outside the works. Note the scale chaired track.

Courtesy Simon Townsend

The Bassett-Lowke stand at the seventh MODEL ENGINEER EXHIBITION, *held at the Royal Horticultural Hall, Westminster, London, in 1924. In the showcase in the centre is a ⅛ inch to the foot model of the Royal Mail Steam Packet Co.'s* ALMANZORA, *which was one of eight models ordered by the company for exhibition at Wembley that year.*

J Bassett-Lowke Collection

THE BEGINNING OF THE BUSINESS 53

Elenora Howard Greenly, Henry Greenly's daughter, keeping a watchful eye on a Great Northern Railway 'Atlantic' undergoing steam test, and photographed by W J Bassett-Lowke. 1907.

Henry Greenly Collection

Vivian Sharpe and fellow employees in the model locomotive department at St. Andrews Street, late 1920s.

RailRomances Collection

This 9½" gauge model, designed for Bassett-Lowke by Henry Greenly, of a Great Northern Railway 'Atlantic' No. 1442 became a standard production model. It is seen here on test outside the works with a full load of passengers!

Courtesy Simon Townsend

W J Bassett-Lowke in his office, circa 1910, which is decorated with a Vienna Secession style stencil; an early indication of his modernistic approach to design, and interestingly some time before his involvement with Charles Rennie Mackintosh.

J Bassett-Lowke Collection

Chapter Five
Early Progress

What else was developing in WJ's busy life during the early years of this 20th century? He had a partner. He had chosen a clever and brilliant consulting engineer. He was fortunate to have an interested and able father willing to further his ideas. The scene was set to go forward from engineering to a wider enterprise, and his immediate undertaking was to gather together workers to expand this aim. He was equipped with knowledge and desire for what he hoped to achieve. He was also young enough to experiment.

In his social life, he was meeting like-minded young people. Among his acquaintances was Francis Marshall Jones, Frank for short, who was a member of the party accompanying WJ in 1900 to visit the famous Paris Fair. Here he was able to make a close study of the craftsmanship which went into the products of manufacturers on the Continent, and return home to consider how he could make use of this expertise. Mr Jones, on the other hand, would have been looking at the work of continental boot and shoe manufacturers. He was the eldest son of Charles Jones, who, in 1879, with his wife Annie and her brother James Crockett (later Sir James) founded the well known Northampton boot and shoe firm Crockett and Jones, a business still running successfully more than 100 years on.

During this first decade of the 1900s, WJ began to have a more social life apart from business. His acquaintance with the eldest son of the Jones family developed into meeting others of this large menage of four boys and six girls, living in the spacious house Ravenswood, 20 East Park Parade, Northampton, overlooking the Racecourse. WJ met all ten of them and often went along to an evening meal.

It was my aunt's eldest niece who told me of these days before the Great War. She was Doris Hughes and her mother, Emily Ann was the eldest daughter of Charles and Annie Marshall Jones. Emily Ann's husband died at an early age and both she and Doris, then about 7 years old, came back to live in the family home. She related that Florence Jane was a pleasant girl with a good sense of humour and plenty of spirit, who had been known to slide down the bannisters! Eventually, this young lady went away to the Quaker School at Sibford Ferris to be guided into suitably grown-up ways. Florence Jane attended . Matters proceeded at a sedate pace, and it was quite a surprise when it became known that my father Harold, WJ's younger brother, had been more forthcoming in his wooing. He had become engaged to a charming girl, the only child of John and Alice Porteous, mine host and hostess of the Peacock Hotel, a well-known local hostelry in the centre of the town on Northampton's famous 400 year old Market Square. This hotel had its own stabling for horses, a large yard and comfortable warm rooms inside. The gentry of the surrounding district would come with their carriages; for John Porteous was a town councillor, well known for his council work, a very popular citizen, and interested in athletics and local sport. The Peacock Hotel prospered but sadly he, my maternal grandfather, died at an early age in 1907. Evidently his wife Alice was a sound businesswoman and continued to run the inn successfully with her staff for some years after his death.

Harold Austin Bassett-Lowke (author's father and WJ's brother) and Annie Mary Porteous (in the car) about to start off from the Peacock Hotel, Northampton, for their honeymoon. Standing are Annie Clarke and a family friend Bernard Douglas. The car belonged to my father who had the first car in Northampton. 1st Sept.1912.

J Bassett-Lowke Collection

Meantime, WJ's friendship continued with the Jones family and his interest in Florence Jane, their third daughter, flourished. His younger brother's engagement appeared to him overlong, two years with few signs of progress. Mischievously WJ, in his inimitable way, laid a wager with Harold that he would not marry Annie Porteous! The amount was £100, in those days a considerable sum and, for some months, it did appear that WJ would be the victor. However eventually, after nearly four years had rolled by, the banns were called, the wedding day was fixed and that was that! WJ sportingly accepted defeat and told my parents (to be) that he planned to spend the amount furnishing a room in their home, as a wedding present.

The room chosen was the drawing room, the lounge we would say today, and he swiftly set about his plan. The house was four storeys high and the first floor front room, which had a balcony looking out on to an attractive park, was completely restyled. The walls were covered in a pleasant light green paper with narrow, slightly darker, lines. The paintwork was reworked to represent light oak woodwork and the ceiling was hung with severe but attractive triple light fittings. The furniture, when it duly arrived from Germany, was also light oak, harmonising well with the room. It was constructed on modern straight lines, without any curves, and was eminently practical and exquisitely designed. The tall angular sideboard had a top two-door shelved display section, the doors of which contained panels of bevelled glass. Below, on either side, was a long shelved cupboard and, in the centre, an open area for display. There were also three long drawers below. The brass locks were marked Dittmar Model Fabr. The sofa, or chesterfield, was of typical oblong shape and finished in green cord velvet, and behind it, against the wall, stood an oak display unit into which it fitted. This unit had small glass display cupboards at either end, which would take crockery or silver items. There were two carving and two dining chairs and a tall straight grandfather clock of most modern design, which struck the hours and half hours with a deep booming sound. There was also a fireplace surround of the same attractive wooden construction which included a fascia above with a central mirror. At the sides were very long thin cupboards, reaching to the floor. Each item of furniture, made in solid oak, had a pattern of inlaid black bands and the various doors had a pattern of quartering with central oval inlay. Some of this fine furniture is still in the use of the family and is as perfect today as it was in 1913 when it reached my parent's home. Even after these years of usage all the adjustable shelves fit and doors open and close as they did 87 years ago. Today it is a truly remarkable

EARLY PROGRESS

The dining room at the Drive, the home of Frank Jones, brother of Jane Bassett-Lowke, with furniture and wall decoration by Mackintosh. The furnituure and wall decorations are virtually the same as that made for W J Bassett-Lowke's CANDIDA COTTAGE *at Roade. On the left, the modern grandfather clock which was part of the furniture suite which WJ gave to his brother Harold for his wedding in 1912.*

J Bassett-Lowke Collection

modern suite, in keeping with the 21st century. This was the first suite of really modern furniture that WJ chose and the early indication of how his preferences lay which, before long, were set to progress further in this direction.

To return to the business, there were developments ahead. He had met a number of Northampton citizens and one businessman, with whom he had become friendly through their mutual interest in model trains, was Mr John G (Jack) Sears (1870-1916). WJ would frequently visit his home at Collingtree Grange, Collingtree, near Northampton, to play with their mutual interest, the model railway. Mr Sears was founder of the well-known firm, the True Form Boot Co, and began to take an interest in WJ's growing business. It was he who encouraged the younger man to branch out and try his luck with a retail shop in London. Jack Sears knew London well as his own firm had shops in different parts of the capital. He set about finding a suitable property for WJ to enable him to open a retail outlet for Bassett-Lowke there. Jack Sears also promised that if this venture did not prove a success after a year, then he would take over the lease and establish another branch of his own boot and shoe business there. A suitable place on a short lease was found at 257 High Holborn. The rent was reasonable and it would be a start. The shop was small but immediately successful and opened in October 1908 with Mr E W Hobbs, A.I.N.A. as its first manager. In due time the promising business was transferred to larger premises at 112 High Holborn.

Mr Hobbs with his energetic personality and experience was the ideal person to be in charge. It was through his initiative that the Model Yachting Association came into being. Hours of service were 9.00 am to 7.30 pm and 9 am to 1 pm on Saturday and there was a staff of 6 plus a boy. In those early days, there was a small workshop at the back of the shop where urgent repairs and small jobs could be carried out. Also, at nearby places, the first meetings of model associations were held; for instance that of the Model Yachting Association. The Model Railway Club also held their inaugural meeting at The Bun House only two doors away from the High Holborn Shop at No.112.

This delightful photograph, with a young mother and her son, was used for publicity purposes. One can only wonder who these young Edwardian enthusisats were.
RailRomances Collection

Mr Sears continued his interest both in my uncle and his business. He was a wonderful mentor and was instrumental in persuading WJ to change W J Bassett-Lowke and Co. into a limited liability company. He became the firm's first chairman when the firm took the name of Bassett-Lowke Ltd in 1909. I knew he and my uncle had a solid friendship and he remained as Chairman until 1916, when sadly he died at the early age of 46. WJ was very grieved and throughout his life remembered him.

The first London shop at 257, High Holborn, which opened in October 1908 with E W Hobbs as Manager. Although the risk was underwritten by Jack Sears, of the True Form Boot Co., it turned out to be a great success for Bassett-Lowke.
RailRomances Collection

In 1912/13 the Bassett-Lowke policy of exhibiting at various exhibitions gave extra publicity and there was increased interest in models. The staff at No.112 were all experts and in 1908 Bassett-Lowke's first comprehensive model railway was sent out on tour. It was gauge 'O' and when fully assembled measured 20ft by 15ft and packed away into three large crates. The track was *Lowko* brass hollow track and there were three trains running. The power was electric, from accumulators, as at this time there were no such things as rectifiers. Automatic coupling and uncoupling was a feature that drew interest from the onlookers. The layout was taken to Bristol in 1913 and it ran there for a month, under the control of Bert Sell. Two brothers, George and Bert Sell, joined the firm at the time of the Franco-British Exhibition at the White City, London, where George was in charge of the B-L Gauge 2 model railway built for the LNWR railway company. Christmas trade was hectic and often the whole staff would have to work untill midnight. They all pulled together, salesmen helping the packers and again at stocktaking time the London shop would be at work over the whole weekend.

The business became well known for models of the finest class, with a staff of experts always on hand. WJ was at the London shop at least twice a week. There were many people well known in other walks of life who came regularly to this Mecca of model enthusiasts at No.112 High Holborn. Bert Sell listed some of them, although not necessarily in chronological order. Among their literary patrons were the writers John Galsworthy and Edgar Wallace, who favoured water line models; Rudyard Kipling came for Gauge 'O' equipment; Nevil Shute for steam equipment; Ethel M Dell, the authoress, whose husband was a Colonel Savage and the hero in her book *The Way of an Eagle*, wanted locomotives to half inch scale for her husband.

It is worthy of note that George Bernard Shaw visited No.112 on one occasion but the staff were unable to oblige his request. He wanted a mechanical and audible grasshopper for one of his productions!

J Bassett-Lowke
Collection

By 1910, the London shop had become too small and a move was made to larger premises at 112, High Holborn. Above, an early photograph of the interior of the second London shop, 112 High Holborn, which was a successful venture for W J Bassett-Lowke. . . . .

. . . . The extensive range of products is well illustrated. Whilst a large proportion was made in Northampton, products from other manufacturers were also sold although the emphasis was always on quality.
    RailRomances Collection

There were several motor racing men who also liked models. Prince Bira and Prince Chula of Thailand were both interested in different spheres of model railways and also water line models. In later years, Stirling Moss came to the London Branch and brought another American racing car customer to the firm. Sir Henry Segrave and Sir Malcolm Campbell were other welcome visitors whose interests were model railways. Americans who came included Vincent Astor and Mr Douglas (of Douglas Aircraft) who purchased a set of old time ships, made by E W Twining, who did a great deal of work for the firm on specialised models. Walt Disney was interested in all types of *perfection in miniature*.

Among well known actors who came into 112 High Holborn were Alec Guinness, John Clements, Jack & Claude Hulbert, the well-known *Mr Pastry* Richard Hearn, Stanley Lupino and Michael Rennie.

King Peter of Yugoslavia and his royal mother visited the showroom and after they had to leave their country, King Peter became an expert model maker, the London Branch suppling him with destroyer parts for a model. When they were boys, the Earl of Harewood and his brother, sons of Princess Mary the Princess Royal, were also interested visitors.

One very famous naval man who patronised the shop was Lord Louis Mountbatten. Bassett-Lowke made him a model of every ship in which he served and today this set of models is on view, I believe, at his family home of Broadlands in Hampshire. Lord Jellicoe, Admiral of the Fleet, used to call for yacht parts for the models in which he was interested. The Duke of Westminster, Earl of Moray, Lord Downshire, Lord Howard de Walden, the Marquis of Anglesey, Lord Cowdray and Lord Glenconner were peers of the realm from whom the staff were honoured to have visits. As mentioned elsewhere, several Indian Rajahs visited who were supplied with palatial railways for their estates along with other models and their royal custom was welcomed. The hobby of models had indeed taken a hold on many people.

The advent of war in 1914 inevitably caused changes with two members of staff being transferred to war work and one into the services. In 1915 Mr Hobbs was enlisted on war work making artificial limbs and left London. Mr John Wills replaced him for a short period, and made several structural alterations to the shop. In the same year WJ assigned Wills to Narrow Gauge Railways Ltd., initially to look after the newly acquired Ravenglass and Eskdale Railway in Cumbria and then the Fairbourne Miniature Railway in Mid Wales. Mr F I Underwood filled the management post up until 1919 when Mr H C Foreman took over.

In 1922, the opportunity arose to acquire an existing model shop at 5 Frederick Street, Edinburgh, whose owner, a Mr. Young, was experiencing financial problems. WJ seized the opportunity and came to an agreement with Young to take over the shop as an Edinburgh Branch for Bassett-Lowke. Young became the manager and James Walker was sent up from Northampton as his assistant. Trade proved to be good and in 1924 the move was made to a larger shop at 1 Frederick Street. This was a wrong move as trade dropped sharply and in 1930 the business was sold back to Mr. Young as a going concern!

WJ was thinking about the Common Market long before anyone dreamt up the EEC, and he was also conscious of the fact that your image, as a company, was of the utmost importance and in particular the extent of your empire. In 1912, M E P Malaret, who owned *Paradis des Enfants* in Rue de Rivoli, Paris, took on the Sole Agency for Bassett-Lowke *Specialities*. Bassett-Lowke was transformed initially from *London & Northampton* to *London & Edinburgh*, but could now pronounce themselves as

London, Edinburgh & Paris – Head Office : Northampton.

Manchester was the next target to cover the North West area and a new shop was eventually opened in 1927 at 28 Corporation Street, being managed by Cecil B Cox who apparently had no experience of models. He was literally just sent to Manchester and his only brief was to make it pay. James Walker was sent down from Edinburgh to assist him but after about twelve months Cox decided to get rid of him.

Amongst the medals I have of my uncle's prowess in different fields there is a very attractive silver one, which has the following surprising inscription on it : *International Kurverein Bobsleigh Race - Engleborg - February 1st 1912, W J Bassett-Lowke.* The reverse of the medal has an impressive image of a four-man bob-team. It was a revelation to learn that WJ had taken an interest in a strenuous speed sport like bobsleigh racing as he was not known generally as a sportsman, although a very active person and an excellent walker. Mind you, he did engage in regular tussles against friends at deck quoits in later life, when on his holiday cruises and made a point of 20 times 'round the block' before breakfast; rather different pastimes from the Cresta Run at St. Moritz! However, it does seem reasonable to hazard a guess that Mr Jack Sears may have been a member of that four man bob team. He was only seven years older than WJ and, in a description of his life in the *Dictionary of Business Biography*, he is described as a keen sportsman in his younger day and a supporter of many local sporting associations. My father was once invited to go to St Moritz with him in place of WJ who could not make the trip for business reasons. In our German Room as we called it, which contained uncle's wedding gift furniture, there was an attractively framed picture of my father in skating kit on the ice, and we children heard grown-up talk of how he enjoyed the trip to Switzerland, including the tobogganing. From my thought processes I surmise that Uncle had been a few times previously because the date, February 1912, was before my father's Swiss trip, which took place in 1913 after his marriage.

Jack G S Sears, grandson of Jack G. Sears, in writing to the author relates that :

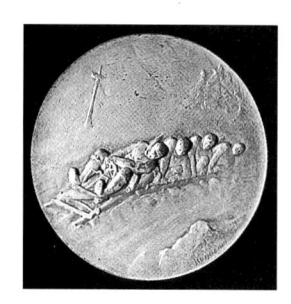

Above, Harold Bassett-Lowke, shortly after he was married, went with Jack Sears to St. Moritz for the winter sports in place of WJ who was tied up with the business. WJ did take part in a four man bobsleigh team at Engelberg, in Switzerland, in 1912 and received a medal for his participation.

J Bassett-Lowke Collection

My father (1903 – 1988) told me that your uncle filled him with enthusiasm for model trains and full sized locomotives and this great interest lasted all his life. They were clearly good friends and I know my father spent a lot of his pocket money in your uncle's shop. I was fascinated to learn that my grandfather was the first chairman of Bassett-Lowke. Sadly, I never knew my grandfather but his wife Caroline, my grandmother, lived until 1952 so I grew up knowing her well, although she could be quite a formidable old lady!

It was heartening to receive a letter like this confirming the comradeship and interest the first chairman of Bassett-Lowke Ltd had had in the new firm. He was, above all, a successful businessman in setting up the great boot and shoe firm, The True Form Boot Co., in the early 1890s. The Company with his brother, William Thomas Sears, trading in partnership, was converted in 1912 to a limited liability company.

Jack Sears was the architect of the rapid growth of his company. His clear business acumen was evident in all departments, along with his judgement and capacity for bold movement. He was never slow or timid and in big moves of the game; he had that kind of intuition for doing the right thing. In the details of management too, he laid the foundations of great success knowing that the secret of a favourable outcome was to delegate to competent managers. No doubt, this business acumen was of great assistance to my uncle who was probably given much good advice, which may well have contributed to WJ's professional approach at such an early age. My uncle was indeed a fortunate man to have had such a friend.

The young W J Bassett-Lowke, always imaculately dressed and complete with papers in hand in a typical pose.
J Bassett-Lowke Collection

Another friend of WJ's at this time was Dacre Gardam who was born in 1868 and eventually became a teacher. His younger brother, William, born in 1878 was apprenticed as a cabinet-maker and ultimately worked at Winteringhams on contract work for Bassett-Lowke.

John Wills was another ardent photographer, miniature railway enthusiast, and close friend of WJ. He was born in 1872 the son of John and Margaret Anne Wills of New Cross, Surrey, and first met WJ at the Society of Model Engineers in 1898. He assisted him on a part-time basis and joined the company in 1909 at the London shop. He had started out life in the legal profession and this legal training was invaluable to WJ. With the formation of Miniature Railways of Great Britain Ltd he became Secretary and heavily involved with the various miniature railways built. He followed on as Secretary of Narrow Gauge Railways Ltd and ended up running the Fairbourne Miniature Railway, as mentioned previously.

WJ and Lilley Greenly aboard the SS VIKING in 1911 on a Polytechnic tour of Norway, accompanied by his brother Harold, Kenneth Cullen, Stuart Turner and his wife, Robert Hardie, and Proctor Mitchell.
Henry Greenly Collection

WJ (on the footplate) and Henry Greenly in naval uniform on the Thunes 'Mogul' locomotive during the Norwegian cruise in 1911. They both travelled on the locomotive between Bergen and Vass. This visit to Norway was described as "the jolliest, if the wettest, trip on record"
Henry Greenly Collection

In the early 1900's, one could truly say that what was actually manufactured at Bassett-Lowke was hand-made, and with great pride in the work. The shelf at the back provided a test track for the locomotives once they were finished.
RailRomances Collection

WJ always kept in touch and visited him at Fairbourne in July 1943. Shortly afterwards he died.

Meantime, WJ and Henry Greenly were working together a great deal to promote miniature railways of all kinds; continuing together in their efforts to standardise scales and gauges of model railways and, in the process, attracting several interested and capable people to the company. One such engineer, James Mackenzie, originally from Scotland but then at East Hamstead, London, was appointed Works Manager in 1904. In 1903, his name appeared in the *Model Engineer* as a manufacturer and supplier of tools for the model engineer. The name of George Winteringham was brought to the attention of WJ in connections with a new model permanent way. It was good quality and WJ decided to take regular supplies. The first track was $3/4$" to the foot and, later on, a smaller scale was developed. Lowko track was another production and eventually WJ persuaded Mr Winteringham to come to Northampton. In 1908, he became Managing Director with James Mackenzie as Works Manager of Winteringham Ltd, an associate company, with all production being for Bassett-Lowke Ltd. Winteringham resigned in 1916. Thus, with Claret at Moulton and another skilled maker of standard steam engine parts, R Cornish, a sound foundation was formed for this side of the company.

Even as far back as 1909 companies strove against the high cost of advertising and were always on the lookout for cost effective gimmicks. One such company was the Great Central Railway who, in 1904, commissioned Bassett-Lowke to build a model in Gauge 1 of their 4-4-0 locomotive *Sir Alexander*. This was offered as a prize in a competition in their official timetable, complete with a corridor coach to match. The Caledonian Railway Company followed, likewise, in 1909 and engaged WJ and Henry Greenly to design a clockwork model of their Cardean locomotive in lithographed tinplate for $1^{1}/_{4}$" gauge, along with a West Coast corridor coach to match. It is thought that this was designed to run on the floor rather than on rails. The engine was advertised at 2/6d (12p) and the coach at 1/6d (7p). Bassett-Lowke supplied 30,000 sets to the Caledonian Railway! Whilst Bassett-Lowke took the credit, they were probably manufactured by Carette in Germany, as capacity was certainly not available in Northampton for these kinds of batches at this time.

Until 1913, the foundry of J T Lowke & Son had produced all the castings. Also at the rear of this firm's premises was a building probably the extension listed as 'under construction' in April 1899 and which WJ had been allowed to use. This was now fitted out with the necessary machine tools, a forge, and work benches. One of his father's men, Fred Green, was put in charge of this model department, and capably managed by him to WJ's standards for some years. Grandfather and Grandmother Lowke moved across the road to live at 13 Kingswell Street with room for their son WJ. The living

During this early period many special commissions were undertaken for customers, such as this Gauge 1 Great Northern Railway 'Atlantic' locomotive built for Roland Marens of Mannheim, Germany, c.1912. Notice the initials RM on the tender instead of GNR.

Henry Greenly Collection

space at number 18 became the office and stores for Bassett-Lowke. WJ and Franklin severed their direct involvement with J T Lowke & Sons.

The first meeting of the Directors of the new limited company, Bassett-Lowke Ltd (incorporated on the 11th March 1910), was held at the office of their solicitors Messrs Dennis and Faulkners, Northampton, on the 22nd of March 1910. There were three directors present, J G Sears, W J Bassett-Lowke and H F R Franklin with W A Harmer in attendance. WJ was then 32. The Memorandum and Articles of Association with the Certificate of Incorporation of the Company on the 11th of March were produced. It was resolved that Mr John George Sears be appointed the Chairman of the Company. It was also resolved that the registered office of the Company be at the Company's premises in Kingswell Street, Northampton. The Company Seal was produced being in the usual circular form, with the words *Bassett-Lowke Ltd, London & Northampton* round the rim and, on the inside, there were the words *Model Engineers* and a signal arm with the word *Lowko* on it. The latter was the adopted Registered Trade Mark of the company.

Initially shares allotted at incorporation were to W J Bassett-Lowke - 1, H F R Franklin - 1 and John George Sears - 1. Applicants for 3,375 shares were considered and it was resolved that 3,099 shares be allotted to applicants who included Mr J G Sears, Mr Edward Hobbs, Mrs Ada Jones (WJ's mother-in-law), H A Bassett-Lowke and Eliza Lowke (WJ's brother and mother). J T Lowke, his father and Henry Greenly were also allotted shares plus 9 other people. The meeting concluded with a vote of thanks to J G Sears, the Chairman.

WJ had great respect for his staff and in 1911 he reserved a complete coach on the LNWR train from Northampton to London, to enable his staff to visit the Model Engineering Exhibition.

When war broke out in 1914, supplies of model goods from the Continent naturally ceased and current orders for a lot of model railway goods were effectively marooned in Germany until after the end of the war. The Bassett-Lowke firm became engaged on war work, in the manufacture of screw gauges, work requiring a supreme degree of accuracy. Also, because for some time they had been making scale model warships, the Admiralty were prompted to place orders for miniature ships in very large numbers, models of both Allied vessels and those of the enemy. These were made for instructional purposes, and for use by naval officers for identifying ships at sea, and those working at Bassett-Lowke's were busy on these ships throughout the war, under the personal supervision of E W Twining. Some German ships were cast in white metal in moulds; the British ships were modelled in wood - a fleet from the super-Dreadnought down to a tiny submarine. In connection with the new concept of aeroplane warfare, these miniature ships were much used for instructional purposes. They were produced by workers in Northampton under the personal supervision of E W Twining, the work being to a very high standard to satisfy the Admiralty and other Government departments.

WJ, through Percival Marshall, had earlier been introduced to model maker E W Twining who at the time was at Hanwell making and selling model aeroplanes and parts. From then on WJ had taken various supplies of Mr Twining's work and even included them in an aeronautic catalogue in 1910. Twining was a fine model maker and also an expert mechanical draughtsman who did illustrations for the Bassett-Lowke catalogues.

Chapter Six
Pursuits and Interests

WJ's great boyhood interest in photography proved of benefit throughout his life. We first heard of it before 1900 when he cycled over to Wellingborough, with Harry Franklin, shortly after a railway accident and quickly took pictures of the wreckage, which were used in the local and national press, gaining financial benefit to help with the production of his first models catalogue. The hobby had started because of the availability of the dark room in the attic of the living quarters of No.18 Kingswell Street, a part of the business premises of J T Lowke & Sons.

There were further indications that my father, Harold, followed in his elder brother's footsteps when, as a schoolboy of 13, his diary showed that he too took pictures and developed and printed them and also toned them, obviously with previous tuition from big brother WJ.

In early 1914, the *Northampton Independent*, printed an article *Unique Photographs - by a Northampton Amateur - On Forbidden Ground*. Two pictures were shown : *Snake Charmers in Algiers snapped unawares* and *The Famous Vault of Mummified Bodies at Palermo* The article stated that the photographs were taken by Mr W J Bassett-Lowke of Northampton, and that they gave some idea of the fascinating interest of the lantern lecture he gave the week before to members of the Photographic Section of the Northamptonshire Natural History Society, describing a cruise in the Mediterranean. He exhibited over one hundred photographs he took on the tour, among them being some particularly fine pictures of the ruins at Pompeii and charming scenes in the lovely island of Sicily. Perhaps the most striking of the latter was the one reproduced of the Convento de Cappuccini, in the subterranean corridors of which were preserved the mummified bodies of wealthy inhabitants of Palermo.

Taken by WJ in 1914, the mummified bodies of wealthy inhabitants of Palermo, Sicily; a gruesome photograph that won him praise in 'The Northampton Independent'.
J Bassett-Lowke Collection

This, said WJ, *is a very melancholy but interesting sight. The vaults have the finest collection of bodies dried in Cappuccini fashion in the world - cardinals, nobles, court ladies, some of them in their robes and some in penitential garb, are fastened to the walls of the catacombs after being dried in sacred earth brought from Palestine. It is estimated that there are about 10,000 bodies in the vaults. The practice has now been condemned by law, and the most recent occupants have been dead about 40 years. Photography in the vaults was forbidden, but I managed by a bit of scheming to take some photographs. I propped a camera in a corner and left it there for a long exposure.*

WJ at Tunis secured another unusual photograph where he came across a picturesque courtyard with some native Arabs practising their art. They did not notice his presence, so he was able to get a natural picture free from the crowds that usually filled such pictures. At the close of the lecture WJ was heartily congratulated upon his splendid pictures and interesting descriptions of his tour.

Unfortunately most of the photographs WJ took on this occasion are no longer available. He did enlarge a few of them and had them framed to go in the room which he furnished as my parents wedding present; a good example of his photographic expertise. WJ used to provide photographs regularly for the *Northampton and County Independent* in the early 1900s.

Among the booklets he prepared as Managing Director of Bassett-Lowke Ltd he wrote the following on *Why We Use Photography*:

Photography is of incalculable value to us. Although many boys may think of us simply as makers of rather fascinating toys, the most important part of our work is the making of scale models of ships and railways.

This photograph, taken by WJ in Tunis, illustrates his professionalism in the field of photography.

J Bassett-Lowke Collection

> *In the making of these models, we work to a great extent, to drawings and details supplied by builders of the prototype; but often these are modified in small details during construction, and, therefore, the plans we use are not always strictly accurate and we have to rely upon photographs, taken during the progress of the work, to check up our model work and to give us final details.*
>
> *When we are modelling a locomotive, or any portion of railway equipment, we generally send a representative to take photographs of various details, and this saves many hours of studying of drawing and also has the merit of exactness. You may think that the camera lies sometimes when we take the family group, but we have never found it fail us in engineering details!*

Drawings of ships were much more complicated than those of railway equipment. It was practically impossible to obtain one drawing that contained all the details. Several different drawings had to be used and co-related. For instance, the rigging plan was separate from the ventilating plan. Therefore, armed with a camera and a Deck Plan, a visit was made to the ship and, with one press of the button, an enormous amount of detail was recorded which could only otherwise be obtained by laborious sketches.

When taking photographs for work on ships, the Deck Plan was marked with an arrow indicating the angle from which the photograph was taken and then against this arrow the number of the film. When the prints were completed, they were marked in the same way, and the craftsman working at the bench was then able to compare the plans and photograph; see the exact position in which the picture was taken and thus obtain the details of the various deck fittings required. Photography was also used extensively to assist with the interior models of ships, providing details that it would be almost impossible to reproduce by hand, such as lifeboat notices, small pictures, etc.

Photography was also extensively used in the making of architectural models of factories, public buildings, and often complete parts of cities. For modelling cities, the basis was an Ordnance Survey map, architectural plan, photographs of different parts and aerial photographs. A remarkable instance of this was in connection with a model of the City of Durban, made in Northampton, for the Wembley Exhibition:

> *In this case*, related WJ, *the model was made by model makers who had never seen the city at all, who worked entirely from Ordnance Survey maps and aerial photographs, and so accurate was the model that visitors to the Wembly Exhibition from Durban were able to pick out their own houses on the model!*

In conclusion, photography made the work of the model maker much easier and enabled better and more accurate work to be produced. WJ's interest in photography was of enormous use to Bassett-Lowke for their publicity:

> *Photographs of modelwork appeal to the prospective buyer better than pages of description*, said WJ, *and in addition to the use of still photography we also make use of the Ciné 'Kodak' and we have prepared several films to circulate*

among Public Schools showing the working of real railways and ships, and the making and working of their miniatures.

WJ was an ardent cinematograph enthusiast, producing 16mm films to professional standard. He produced numerous films such as *Real Railways and Model Railways* showing shots of the full size locomotives such as *Flying Scotsman*, *Royal Scot*, and *The Princess Royal* along with film of various garden railways including the famous Bekonscot Model Railway and Village; *Model Railways* featuring Cecil J Allen's 1¼" gauge and Victor B Harrison's 1¾" gauge railways. Other films featured Sir John Holder's railway at Broome; H F R Franklins 2" scale one at Radwell; production at Bassett-Lowke's works and the model of the *Queen Elizabeth*; the list is endless. He was innovative in his ideas. On the Beckonscot Model Village railway the camera was mounted on one of the wagons on a train and the result is that one is able to see a driver's view of this famous model railway; that is until a human hand gives the game away! All the films were very professionally titled with rolling titles, and very often a little bit of advertising for Bassett-Lowke.

His cine activities were not just confined to his railway interest. His friend Victor Harrison ran the family business of Harrison & Sons Ltd, who were printers of postage stamps, and in 1937 WJ made a film showing the stage by stage process of printing stamps, including the Coronation stamps. A unique record in its own right. Another film which he made, and one which has not been traced so far, was *The Making of Steel Plate at the Appleby-Frodingham Works, Lincs*. He also took the initiative in the production of a film depicting the historical, social and industrial features of his native town and it was exhibited to thousands of people at home and in the Midlands. The film was ultimately placed in the custody of the civic authorities for preservation.

One of his pet subjects was *The Progress of Transport by Water* and he used to give a fascinating lecture tracing the story of man's conquest of the waters from the Egyptians onwards, illustrating his story with 100ft to1 inch scale waterline ship models. Because of the delicate nature and intrinsic value of the waterline models, he always had to deliver this lecture personally, whereas other lectures he loaned the text and illustrations to clubs and societies for a nominal sum. He attempted to put this on to film but it was not really very successful.

WJ was awarded several medals for his photographic talents. Whilst there is no indication on the medals themselves, they were probably presented by the local Photographic Society.
J Bassett-Lowke Collection

W J Bassett-Lowke setting up his camera in 1925, with J N Maskelyne, Editor of 'The Model Railway News', to photograph the 10¼" gauge LNER 'Atlantic' on J A Holder's railway. This locomotive was originally 9½" gauge, named PETER PAN *and ran on the Treasure Island Railway at Wembley that year where it had the late King George V and Queen Mary as passengers.*

J Bassett-Lowke Collection

He usually took scores of photographs on holiday and when he attended a conference or social gathering. In fact when possible both his precious ciné and still cameras were his inseparable companions. On a Sunday afternoon, when I occasionally turned up for tea with auntie and uncle, as I passed the window of his study, I would see him bent over his splicer, which he used for editing and titling his cine films, or possibly with a cluster of photographs working out his Christmas card, or a composite picture for one of his books or catalogues. I used to go straight into the lounge and have a chat with my aunt who, as likely as not, was embroidering a cloth. She was an expert in this occupation and it was fascinating to watch her pattern and to see its various colours grow. Then, prompt at 4 pm, just before the trolley was wheeled in, he would appear at the door with a smiling face and sit down for his cuppa. That was usually 'it' as regards his work in the study for the day. His boyhood hobby of photography continued to provide pleasure, both to him and to his friends throughout his life.

Photography was the major leisure activity of his life and I cannot do better than to quote the notice which the Journal of the Northamptonshire Natural History and Field Club printed in their magazine at the end of his life :

> *He was a member of the Society for over 50 years. He was a man of amazing vitality and activity and his inventive ingenuity as a model maker won*

> him wide fame. In his earlier days he took a very prominent part in the programme of the Society especially the Photographic Section and was a pioneer in amateur film production and projection. In fact he was a keen and expert exponent of photography in all its branches.

Character Assessment

Among subjects in which WJ displayed an interest was, by varying methods, the assessing of character. Evidently he had his horoscope cast early in his teens. This is believed to give a prediction of a person's future based on a comparison of the zodiacal data from the period under consideration. Among his old papers is a page of typescript entitled *Horoscope of WJ B-L.* which reads :

> At this gentleman's birth the positions were not favourable amongst the Planets for early progress. His better prospects are after the 40th year. He has grit and energy and although in some points very changeable is able to adapt himself or make change in his environment if occasion requires with spirit and ambition that will keep him afloat. He is inclined to be stubborn, quick in anger, fond of argument and contention, ready to fight for justice, would make a good student for the sciences, inclines towards reading, yet has a merry side to the mind, jovial, quick wit, sharp and penetrating, shrewd, critical and alert, quite sympathetic yet at a time appears indifferent.

> Has mechanical ability, must avoid plunging with things for his rising sign is Scorpio, whose ruler is Mars, and being opposed by the Moon will give a tendency this way and cause him to be fond of freedom and adventure, very difficult to suppress but courageous. There is much latent power, but circumstances over which he would not have control and want opportunity have prevented the strength and ability showing to advantage. His best period is after 45. He need never be poor if he is discreet and looks after his belongings.

At the time I was at Bassett-Lowke he became interested in graphology, the assessment of a person's handwriting to obtain information about his or her personality. Although most scientists classify graphology as a pseudo-science (false science) its practice is widespread in Europe. Uncle placed a certain amount of reliance in graphology and every so often would send specimens of the handwriting of his friends and also of members of his staff to the Institute of Graphology and Psychology in London to be read.

Amongst his papersI found several readings and I believe the following to be one about his own handwriting :

> This script is strongly indicative of the unabated enthusiasms of one of many interests and unimpaired rapidity of thought and action. An interesting comparison may be shown with the earlier writing of this subject. In general attitude there has been no basic change in the period of 42 years, although the earlier script clearly indicates a rather over ingenious nature, apt too

quickly to enthuse upon and admire novelty in idea and expression without due proper consideration. With the passage of time this tendency has become mellowed and diluted by acquired scepticism, but there remains in the present script the characteristic shown also in the earlier specimen, which impels him always to resentment and sometimes active intolerance towards those who would endeavour to convince him of an error or a miscalculation of judgement.

Quick in thought and in his work, he is of those requiring independence of scope to permit him to give of his best, and he would be wary and cautious of any binding engagement. Friendly and generous by nature, he does not care to be led, and is much more content in a situation of prominence and leadership. He has lost none of the quite considerable personal vanity of his youth, would take much care in his appearance, and towards women his conduct would be gallant and considerate in the extreme.

With many interests, he has good taste, would be much diverted by theatrical performances, would have some leanings toward good music and literature, and would have much sympathy and pleasure in the beauties of Nature. A rather admirable spirit, adaptable and progressive in greater measure than many much younger subjects in these troublesome times.

The photograph submitted to The Weekly Despatch 'faces to be remembered' competition, August 1925, when WJ won first prize in that particular round.
J Bassett-Lowke Collection

The *Weekly Despatch* for August 9th 1925 ran a contest *Faces to be Remembered* which brought out another idea that *Your Face is Your Verdict* and gave the results of another kind of Character Comprehension. It shows 5 pictures of people who entered the contest and No. 1 is of W J Bassett-Lowke with his signature, gaining the first prize in that round with the description *Director and Engineer* and saying :

Here is a versatile, constructive and artistic type, very imaginative. His abilities are of a high order. He is quick to distinguish right from wrong. Rarely at a loss for a plan or idea. The writing shows strong will, reasoning powers, and kindliness.

The late Francis Parker, who was a close friend, commented that WJ was so full of fun and energy like a pea on a hot shovel. He recorded that WJ once said in the 1920s that if he could guarantee £600 per annum he would be quite content to continue with his many interests, unhampered by financial matters. He was also convinced that Britain's population was too great, there being no merit in numbers or material greatness. Francis recalled at the time that he would effectively demand attention in a restaurant by his continental method of raising his hands above his head and clapping loudly.

The Fabian Society

A more serious development in WJ's personal life was his decision to join the Fabian Society; the unofficial educational branch of the Labour Party. The founders chose the name for this new association after the Roman Consul and General Quintus Fabius Maximus Rullianus, known as Cunctator the *delayer*. Early members, Beatrice and Sidney Webb, Graham Wallas and George Bernard Shaw, with other young intellectuals had the object in view to attempt to reconstruct society in accordance with the highest moral possibilities and believed in *t*he inevitability of gradualness instead of outright revolutionary measures. In this they followed the plan of Roman Fabius, who against his mighty opponent Hannibal refused to be drawn into a pitched battle, and let the Romans, after the great defeat of Trasimene in 217BC, have time to recover their strength and their morale. His methods earned him the name of *delayer* and were not at that time appreciated, but later his wisdom came to be recognised and he played a useful part during the closing years of the war.

Early influential Fabians followed a strategy of advancing carefully with their developing plans and won interest in high places. The first Labour MP to join them was Ramsey Macdonald, who became Prime Minister in 1924 and another well known writer H G Wells, who also became a Design and Industries Association member. WJ joined in Dec.1916, when he was placed under the category of Engineer. The cost of membership was recorded there as 21/- annually and from 1919 until 1939 his membership was regularly paid by bankers order. In 1920 the Fabian Summer School was held at Prior's Field School, Godalming, Surrey, the directors being Sidney and Beatrice Webb and the school being attended by George Bernard Shaw and Henry Greenly, WJ's friend and consultant, and his wife at the end of July. Despite Greenly's leaning towards liberalism WJ managed to persuade him to attend.

WJ invited George Bernard Shaw to attend the Summer School in 1936 and the reply came back : *Too damned old now to go summer schooling nowadays .... I forget everything now in ten minutes but not the happy days at Northampton. Dotty and doddering but still able to write a bit.*

During his membership he took an active interest in various events and used to attend the schools at Dartington and Fensham. He also used his photographic talents to produce postcards of places of Fabian interest and he also helped in the layout of folders popularising the Summer Schools. In 1947 the Fabians broached the novelty of a Fabian School abroad at Hindsgavl, Denmark The Vice Chairman in 1947, John Parker MP, wrote a letter to WJ which included the message: *I very much like your Dartington Hall card and we shall be pleased to have 50*0. WJ was not the kind of person to leave any opportunity pass him by and it is not surprising to find that the official journal of the Fabian Society, the *Fabian News*, for many years carried an advert for Bassett-Lowke products.

The Design & Industries Association

WJ joined the Design and Industries Association as an early member. Raymond Plummer, who served on the National Council, became chairman in 1965 and two years later he was elected President. He researched the first 70 years of the D.I.A. and states that *nearly all the D.I.A.'s pre war records were destroyed when the Building Centre (who had given us office space) was bombed during the war. ……… Your Uncle first appears in the membership lists that I have, in one marked 'to March 8th 1917'. The member was in fact the Company Bassett-Lowke Ltd and he was their representative in the Association.*

The founding of the D.I.A. came from those who visited the Werkbund Exhibition at Cologne in 1914. Harry Peach (of Dryad's in Leicester), Harold Stabler (Silversmith and former director of the Poole Pottery firm Carter, Stabler & Adams, and artist Ernest Fellows, had been discussing the possibility of setting up a similar association to the German Werkbund here in Britain. Harry Peach went to the Cologne exhibition with Ambrose Heal (of furniture fame) and his cousin the architect Carl Brewer, and all returned enthusiastic. One other consideration was that some of them realised that strict adherence to William Morris' principles was going to be impossible in the machine age and that a new vernacular was really required.

The German *Werkbund*, unlike the D.I.A., benefited from much more Government support and a larger membership. It boasted 2,000 members in 1925, increasing to 3,000 in 1930, whereas the D.I.A. only had 602 in 1923 and 820 by 1930.

In May 1915 a working committee of eight consisting of Stabler, Heal, Brewer, Peach, Jackson, Mason and Hamilton Temple Smith, with Lord Aberconway in the Chair, established the Design & Industries Association. Other signatories with Lord Aberconway (then Chairman of the Metropolitan Railway) were Kenneth Anderson of the Oriental Steam Navigation Company, Artist Frank Brangwyn, Fred Burridge, Principal of the Central School, B J Fletcher, Principal of the Leicester School of Art, Sir John Hornby of W H Smith's, John Marshall of J Marshall & Snelgrove, James Morton of Sundour Fabrics, Frank Pick of the London Underground, Gordon Selfridge, Frank Warner the silk manufacturer and H G Wells the famous writer. Briefly the aim of this new body was to encourage a more intelligent demand among the public for what is best and soundest in design. Also to insist that machine work can be made beautiful by appropriate handling and to prove that many machine processes tend to have certain qualities of their own, emphasizing the example of the English Arts & Crafts movements and what could be learnt from the German *Werkbund*.

From its inception in 1915, the D.I.A. was developed widely over 84 years. Its intent was above all to improve British economic performance by making productive use of design, and giving a source of information and stimulus to those in industry, where the worlds of industry and design met on equal terms; in a sound working relationship. Membership was open to everyone: the professions, manufacturers, service industries, retailers, educational establishments and, not least, individuals.

The names of some of its presidents over the years showed well-known people concerned in generating interest in this most useful work; such names as The Lord Aberconway, Sir Clough Williams-Ellis, Sir Gordon Russell, Sir Peter Parker, and in more recent years Sir Montague Finniston and Sir Graham Hills. Sir Clough Williams-Ellis wrote:

> *Bassett-Lowke – yes indeed! When I took over the Chairmanship or Presidency, whichever it was, of the old DIA from Sir Lawrence Weaver, I found Bassett-Lowke, who I'd known before as a very active member, still endlessly enterprising. I think it was he who promoted and organised a trip round the northern capitals,*

> *in a chartered steamer, making contact with similar organisations wherever we halted.*

Amongst the 21 members listed in March 1928 is WJ, and as representatives of Branches and Groups is the name of Lewis Duckett, Principal of the Northampton School of Art, and Noel Carrington who edited the Puffin series of children's books published by Allen Lane. WJ worked on these attractive books with illustrators like F E Courtney, Paul B Mann and Lawrence Dunn and they were very popular sellers in the 1940s, and we shall look at his involvement later in our story.

Paul Mann did express an opinion about WJ as a person, which I consider very apt :

> *Whynne was such a Will o' the Wisp character that I doubt if many people, if any, really knew him. One thing I can say and that is he was a past master at getting other people to do all the work, especially research. However, he was one of the most delightful people I have ever met.*

At that time Miss Ethel M Pheysey, the D.I.A. secretary, was friendly with my uncle and aunt and she was a welcome visitor to new house *New Ways* in Northampton. The date 1928 is significant because it was then that a local group of the D.I.A. was formed in Northampton *largely due to the initiative of Mr Bassett-Lowke* says the editor in the D.I.A. Quarterly Journal recording this and adding *the group is already a vigorous child.*

WJ used to be the organiser of the D.I.A. summer tours that visited many countries in Europe. He was always anxious that members should look at new buildings and not at old masterpieces. When Noel Carrington told him that he had visited the Pont de Garde at Nimes, WJ expressed great enthusiasm : *but when he heard it was designed by the Romans he was no longer interested*!

With WJ's great interest in ships, the tours always had to be arranged on the latest liners where possible. On a trip to Sweden he did not just arrange a visit to the Town Hall, but would personally contact all the young architects and engineers. Whereas many cultural cruises were looking at the past, WJ was all for the present and the future in design matters.

My uncle was by no means everyone's 'cup of tea'. As mentioned earlier in this narrative he never drove or owned a car and therefore could be a difficult 'back seat' driver. But he travelled all over the place by train, bus or taxi, and, even in his latter years, went by air. I think he was at his best when aboard ship, conducting parties of his friends round the oceans of the world to 'foreign parts'. He took an interest in young people whose work showed promise. For instance it was through his advice that Ray Stutley, who worked in the ship model department, became interested in things to do with Northampton and took up amateur acting and joined the playgoers at the theatre.

Noel Carrington related that : *WJ had the Midlander's attitude of always going to London in his best suit .... he nearly always ate at the Trocadero and would ring up, say that he had much to discuss and we would meet at the Trocadero for lunch .... WJ would talk and I would listen.*

WJ was an exceptionally energetic and influential member of the D.I.A. and contributed articles to the D.I.A. *Quarterly Journal*, especially about visits to the Continent. He was very concerned and frustrated about the apparent slowness of Britain to respond to modernism, compared with the Continent, and he used the Journal as his forum for promoting modern design in this country based on continental developments.

Frank Pick of London Underground would often take a group of fellow D.I.A. members to look at his new stations and signal boxes and seek their criticism and comments, often making minor changes as a result. WJ's comments were nearly always of a technical nature rather than aesthetic. When WJ built *New Ways* he made the comment that nothing in the house was older than he was, when most of his neighbours were nurturing their antiques. Sir Gordon Russell pointed out that he did have a rockery in the garden, but this was probably for Mrs. B-L!

The Council of the Association held its January 1928 meeting in Northampton in order to inaugurate the local group and extended its visit over the weekend, with an enjoyable programme prepared by WJ. Actually the Council Meeting itself was held at his home *New Ways*, while other members of the Association, who had come for the weekend visit, toured the town with the guidance of Mr Reginald Brown, the Librarian and Curator of the Museum. The section of the Museum devoted to 'the Boot and the Shoe' earned commendation from all.

In the evening the members met for dinner at the Angel Hotel. The Mayor of Northampton presided and many local industrialists attended. The Chairman of the Association, Mr John Gloag, presented a clear address on the aims of the D.I.A. and its work to those who hitherto had known the association as just a name. Mr Lewis Duckett was elected Chairman, WJ became secretary and Mr H P Shapland's speech on the architectural possibilities and shortcomings of Northamptonshire rounded off an informative and enjoyable evening.

There was still time left for members to be taken to the nearby Opera House to see the Northampton Repertory Players in John Drinkwater's *Mary Stuart* and to compliment Northampton's producer, Herbert M Prentice, on the excellence of the show. An informal meeting on Sunday morning enabled interested members to view *New Ways*, the house designed for WJ by Professor Dr. Peter Behrens, and in the afternoon Sulgrave Manor and Brington Church were visited. Visitors ended up at nearby West Haddon, where members Mr & Mrs Shapland provided them with a welcome cup of tea; quite a full weekend.

The breadth of interest is illustrated in March 1928 by the D.I.A.'s involvement in the British Industries Fair staged in London and Birmingham, *Beauty the New Business Tool*, two furniture exhibitions, and the Amsterdam tour in April of that year led by WJ. A 3-day trip to Amsterdam, Leyden, Haarlem, Schveningen and the Hague, all meals, motor drives and gratuities cost £8.50 per person. Those travelling by another route from Southampton on the Friday morning by the Netherland R.M.S *Jan Petersen Coen*, a 1,200 ton steamer, berthing at Amsterdam on Saturday morning at 10 am, paid the extra sum of £11. In 1917 there would have been between 400 and 500 members when WJ's firm joined the D.I.A. and it stands at about the same figure today. WJ wrote several papers for the D.I.A. which, it is understood, are deposited in the R.I.B.A. library in London.

The Boy Scouts

Scouting began to develop in Northampton around 1909 and, 90 years on, it is still thriving. There was the Birmingham Rally in July 1913 at which Scouts from Northampton attended and gained prizes. They had to show proficiency in a variety of hobbies and a number of everyday jobs. Such was the demand on Scoutmasters for badge testing that many local personalities were invited to be badge examiners, amongst whom were Messrs Mackaness, Bassett-Lowke and Harvey Reeves, all well known public figures in Northamptonshire. At that time WJ would have been about 30 years old and known for being the 'model railways man'. On September 23rd 1913 King George V and Queen Mary visited the town to witness Army manoeuvres and in the Royal party was General Robert Baden-Powell, the Chief Scout. Northampton Scouts were in a privileged place lining the route at West Bridge and the Chief Scout spoke to many.

This was the first time WJ was featured performing a voluntary task for such a worthwhile activity for boys. Probably he had some model enthusiasts among the young Scouts he tested!

Uncle's Toys

One of WJ's leisure diversions was one that the younger members of his extended family were always delighted with and which has perhaps stayed longest in their memories of him. He had no children of his own and his common or garden hobbies did not touch extreme youth. He fascinated the youngest of his nieces and nephews, and continued to touch the hearts of his great nieces and nephews too, as they grew big enough to visit great uncle and aunt! It was simply *Uncle's Toys*. Today youngsters are transfixed and goggle-eyed playing with computers, but to little ones these simple toys gave immense pleasure.

The first toys to come out of *Pandora's Box* were two little plastic bottles coloured plain grey blue and about 2" high. These were named the *Mystic Bottles* which could do surprising things, unbeknown to us by way of magnets. With them was an explanatory leaflet and opening it we read *The Mystic Bottles will not stand together, with a twirl the Bottle will spin, and place the bottles on a flat surface about an inch apart and see the bottle roll away.* These bottles were of British manufacture (Prov. Patent No.4256/36).

Out of the next box came a fun ladder made of plywood rectangles joined together by tape and manipulated in the hand to get the slats to rattle up and down. I would spare a few minutes getting the knack and then trying to fathom how the tapes could cause the ladder to rattle up and down. Next there is a delightful little walking tinplate pecking bird, finished in bright colours. The leather wings flapped realistically as it hopped round in a circle, pecking all the time. When fully wound up it kept moving for an appreciable time, but more to the point it has, under one foot, the legend *Made in England*.

Another of his trick toys was a simple looking glass of beer that could be turned upside down without spilling a drop. This glass was always held by a grown up in the party, most times by WJ. No one was allowed to peer closely otherwise they would have spotted the secret; it was double walled with a brown liquid between the walls, which frothed on shaking to create a realistic head of beer! From Zurich, uncle also brought a small commemorative beer barrel, beautifully made in wood, which had printed clearly on it *WEISFLOG - BITTE - Zurich Schweiz*.

Another tinplate toy, *Express Boy,* is a little *Buttons* porter and his Express luggage, a brown cabin trunk. When wound up he runs along pushing the trunk and then jumps up on to it and has a ride and, after a while, jumps off again and repeats the process. This is of German manufacture and well finished, the lad dressed in a uniform of blue and grey and the trunk smartly brown with wooden bars. Words on the box say Geschopatent DRP 667474. It still runs well after all these years.

Perhaps the most popular of WJ's toys was a miniature train which was ignited by methylated spirit. It was small enough to be placed on the table and one lucky child was allowed by WJ to start up the engine. Applying a match there was excitement as steam came puffing out of the funnel and the train moved off. Certainly the grown-ups were also impressed!

One set of Christmas crackers came regularly from abroad each year and were I think Japanese. Inside the crackers were small envelopes and there was a central large bowl of water in the middle of the table. Opening an envelope one poured the contents gently into the water and then all watched fascinated as the little pieces gradually opened on the surface and became floating water lilies. This was a pleasure to the little nieces rather than the nephews, and to adults as well.

WJ went to a great deal of time and trouble to collect these novelties and to give fun both at parties and to his young relatives. He did not allow any rough play with such small miniatures and most times the little toys were packed carefully away in their boxes before the young guests left for home. But the fun enjoyed did help to bridge that tricky gap between youth and age. He was often called *The King of Lilliput* and, secretly, it was a title he enjoyed!

With a twirl of the hand Bottle will spin.

Charles Rennie Mackintosh (c. 1920), born in Glasgow on the 7th June 1868, established himself as an outstanding architect and artist. W J Bassett-Lowke engaged him to design the interior reconstruction and furniture for his new home at 78 Derngate, Northampton.

Courtesy Glasgow School of Art

Chapter Seven
78 Derngate and Mackintosh

There has been conjecture over the years since 1915 as to how, when and where WJ met the architect who remodelled his small house in Derngate, Northampton and accomplished something quite unique for its time. I remember I was in WJ's private office one morning as he sat going through his morning mail when I first asked him about Charles Rennie Mackintosh. There was a folder on his desk that he opened and started thumbing through the contents and, in a few minutes, took out a crumpled sheet of paper and said with a smile, *Read this*.

It was definitely old and dilapidated and had some typewritten words on it, with amendments in my uncle's own handwriting, which read as follows:

> *When I married in 1917 I had purchased one of a row of narrow Georgian houses in Derngate in the centre of Northampton. I wanted the house reconstructed and, having heard of the Scottish architect Charles Rennie Mackintosh through a friend, I got in touch with him. Thus it was to Mackintosh's ideas that I eventually made the reconstruction. The furniture in the hall of the Derngate house was made from Mackintosh's design by German prisoners of war in the Isle of Man. This furniture was afterwards transferred to my study at 'New Ways'.*

Here was the truth set out clearly and without ambiguity.

I was young - probably had only been in my uncle's office a year. Mackintosh was just a name to me, and through the years I had many other interests, including marriage and children. So it was not until after my uncle died in 1953 when my aunt and I saw more of each other and she talked of their life together and the people they met - also of Derngate and Mackintosh - that I became more interested. Some of the furniture had been left to me and I decided to find out about its history.

I am sure that uncle had no idea that his small Georgian terrace house which was bought during the 1914-1918 war, would ever prove to be anything more than a smartly modernised small comfortable home where he and his bride would start their married life. A 1948 sale catalogue for 78 Derngate contains information that the house was purchased by J T Lowke in 1916 for £250 plus £75 for an extra piece of garden.

Mackintosh was born in Glasgow on 7th June 1868, the fourth child of William and Margaret Rennie McIntosh. Beginning school at the age of 7, Charles went to Reid's Public School and then to Allan Glen's, a private establishment specialising in technical and vocational subjects. In 1884 he started work as an apprentice for an architect, John Hutchison, in St. Vincent Street, and also attended the

Looking up Derngate towards the Town Hall, with its small Georgian houses. No. 78 is the third house from the left. c. 1914

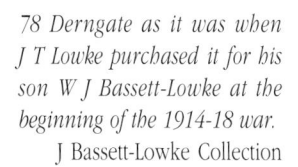

J Bassett-Lowke Collection

78 Derngate as it was when J T Lowke purchased it for his son W J Bassett-Lowke at the beginning of the 1914-18 war.

J Bassett-Lowke Collection

Glasgow School of Art. He was an outstanding student, succeeding regularly with top prizes, including a Gold Medal and Queen's Prize. Francis Newbery, the enlightened Headmaster, encouraged the young Mackintosh in his intended career as an artist-architect.

In 1889 Mackintosh joined the Glasgow firm of Honeyman and Keppie as a junior draughtsman and continued studying at the Glasgow School of Art. From 1891 to around 1911 he worked on at least 50 important buildings and interiors in and around Glasgow and designed over 400 pieces of furniture. The second significant phase was from 1916 to 1919 when he and my uncle worked together on this exciting commission - 78 Derngate.

The story of the first part of his working life, in Glasgow, has been well documented, and the city and its neighbourhood bear witness to the buildings and interiors he created. His pièce de résistance, the Glasgow School of Art, must head the list. *Windyhill*, the home he designed in Kilmalcolm near Glasgow for William Davidson, a Presbyterian businessman with modern tastes, and *The Hill House* at Helensburgh, looking out on the Clyde, for the publisher Walter Blackie, are both outstanding for their time. He designed two

The well known door of 78 Derngate, as Mackintosh designed it, with the owners W J Bassett-Lowke and his wife Jane.
J Bassett-Lowke Collection

schools, a church hall, two newspaper buildings, and Queen's Cross Church in Garscube Road, where the Mackintosh Society is now housed. Incorporated within the Hunterian Art Gallery at the University of Glasgow, are the principal interiors from 78 Southpark Avenue, Glasgow, where Mackintosh and his wife Margaret Macdonald lived from 1906 - 1914, and which they decorated and furnished together. This is an outstanding reconstitution of interiors, saved from demolition by the University in 1963. The salvaged fixtures were kept in store until the 1970s and then carefully reassembled as *The Mackintosh House,* an integral part of the University's Hunterian Art Gallery, being completed in 1981.

For Miss Catherine Cranston, Mackintosh designed the fascinating and imaginative tearooms in Glasgow. These were in Buchanan Street (1896/9), Argyle Street (1898/9) and Ingram Street (1900/11) and the one surviving Cranston tea room *The Willow* in Sauchiehall Street. The latter was painstakingly restored in 1980 to the original Mackintosh design, complete with its original wrought iron work and gesso panelwork by Margaret Macdonald. Notable too that the Glasgow architects, Keppie Henderson and Partners, Mackintosh's reconfigured partnership, were the consultants. The atmosphere of the great architect lingers.

Until around 1909 there seemed to be no end to the commissions received by his firm, but then slowly the pattern began to change as the economic situation in Glasgow declined. Gradually, over the next four years, Mackintosh lost recognition and this state of inactivity brought on depression. He took to drink, his work suffered, and eventually in 1913 he resigned from his firm. He appeared tired and ill and not long afterwards he and Margaret Macdonald travelled south to Suffolk and the little village of Walberswick for a rest and change. There he convalesced and developed a quiet interest in sketching and painting plants and flowers. He never returned to Glasgow to live but, with Margaret, found another great city in which to begin again.

The Great War had broken out. The couple settled in Chelsea in 1915 and were living there when, sometime that year, my uncle contacted Mackintosh. 78 Derngate was a remarkable commission and the last major piece of work Mackintosh received. He brought new energy, interest and dedication to this small Georgian house in the town centre of Northampton, in the Midlands of England. The real rest cure in Walberswick which, in his wife's words, he had so badly needed, had prepared him for work again and paved the way for a revival of his architectural work.

The rear of 78 Derngate, with Jane Bassett-Lowke, showing the alterations made by Mackintosh. The verandah was open to the south west and provided a fine view over the Nene valley.

J Bassett-Lowke Collection

At this crucial time it was obvious that my uncle had deliberately sought out Mackintosh. Roger Billcliffe in his book* describes WJ's search for Mackintosh which evidently took him to Glasgow, because Mrs Newbery Sturrock (daughter of Francis Newbery, the head at the Glasgow School of Art when Mackintosh attended) remembers him staying with or visiting the Newberys. Typically, when he came to a decision, he lost no time and obtained the necessary details of the whereabouts of the architect and his wife, and one must assume that this was Chelsea, London - the perfect spot to which my uncle, who loved the City, would go to meet him.

What did WJ want? Letters survive in the Mackintosh archive of the Hunterian Art Gallery from uncle to CRM but sadly none from Mackintosh in return. Meeting, probably every week when my uncle was in London, they presumably developed an excellent working partnership, without need of correspondence.

Mackintosh's work for 78 Derngate was both stylistically progressive, visually striking and a contrast to his better-known white interiors of the Glasgow years, adorned with delicate touches of colour and

The dining room at 78 Derngate. The lanterns with their concealed lights, on each side of the fireplace, and the centre light gave a very pleasing lighting effect to this room. Note the Mackintosh clock with its ten columns on the mantle shelf.
J Bassett-Lowke Collection

A view of the dining room looking towards the window recess, which Mackintosh introduced to increase the size of the room. Facing south, it was a spot in which to relax. In the foreground are the Mackintosh designed dining table and chairs.
J Bassett-Lowke Collection

organic motifs. He saw a room as a unified work of art, in which the designer should be responsible for every detail from cushions to architectural design.

As for No.78, excellent articles appeared in the *Ideal Home* magazine in 1920. They appear to have been written by the magazine's Editor, with the assistance of WJ and with his photographs, and can therefore be relied upon to present the salient facts of how a delightful modern home was created out of a ramshackle little Georgian terraced house in the early years of the Great War.

To remodel a house from top to bottom may seem, on the face of it, a somewhat doubtful form of

---

* Opposite : Roger Billcliffe - *Charles Rennie Mackintosh - The Complete Furniture, Furniture Drawing and Interiors.* Lutterworth Press, Guildford & London, 1979.

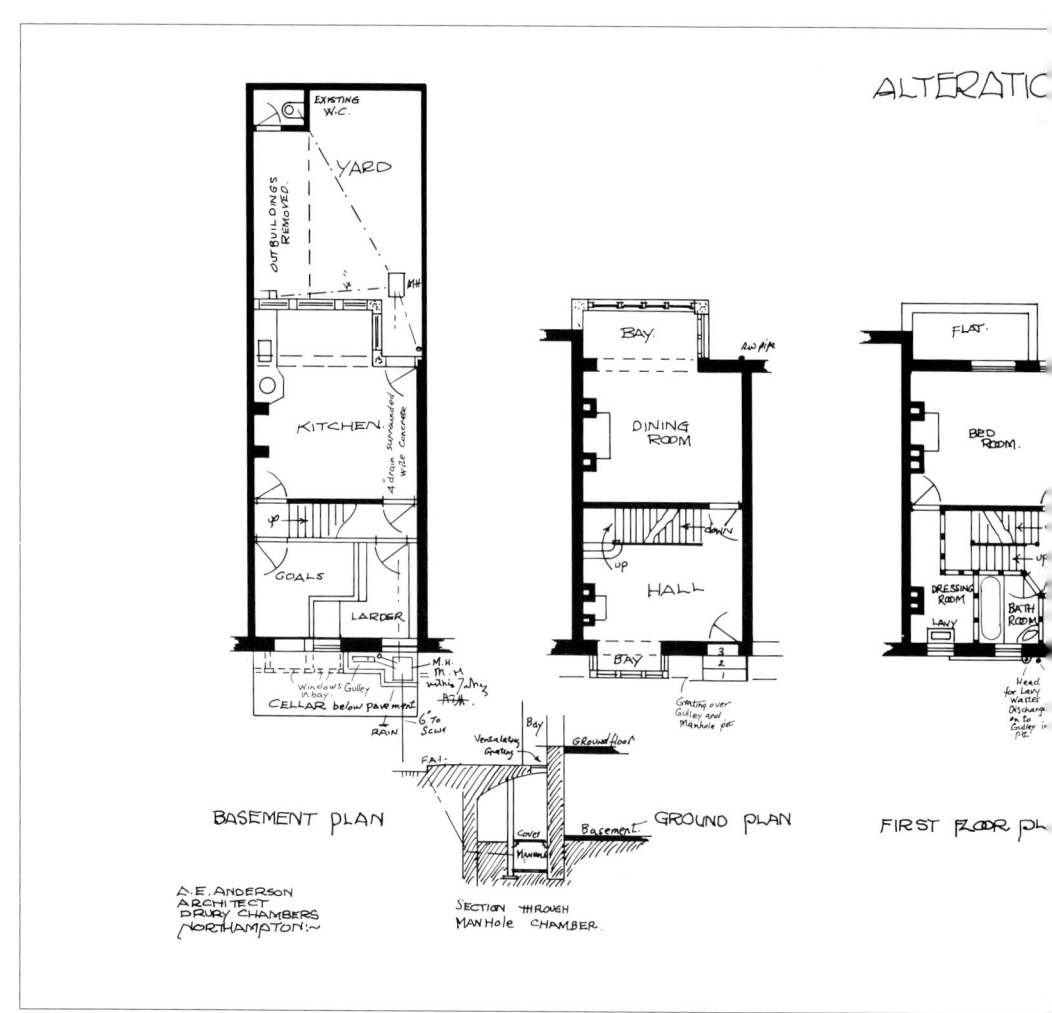

Retraced from original in Northamptonshire County records by John Milner 1998

economy. But when, in those days of dearth of housing accommodation, an old cramped, dilapidated, and more or less uninhabitable dwelling was transformed, by the simple expedient of renewing its 'inside' into a charming and up-to-date miniature residence, there is economy indeed, as a modern house has then been produced with a minimum of building. The house being one of a row with no front garden, the opportunities for improvement were limited, so that it was only possible to make an extension at the back, and just add a small bay at the front.

Whether such adjectives as 'up-to-date' or 'modern' adequately serve the purpose of describing the unique transformation that WJ effected at No.78 Derngate is open to question, as in some respects it was a house of the future.

Prior to the alterations, the front door opened into a narrow passage, which was carried out through the house, with the flights of stairs one above the other in stereotyped fashion. One of the most complete changes effected was to turn all the stairways round at right angles across the centre of the

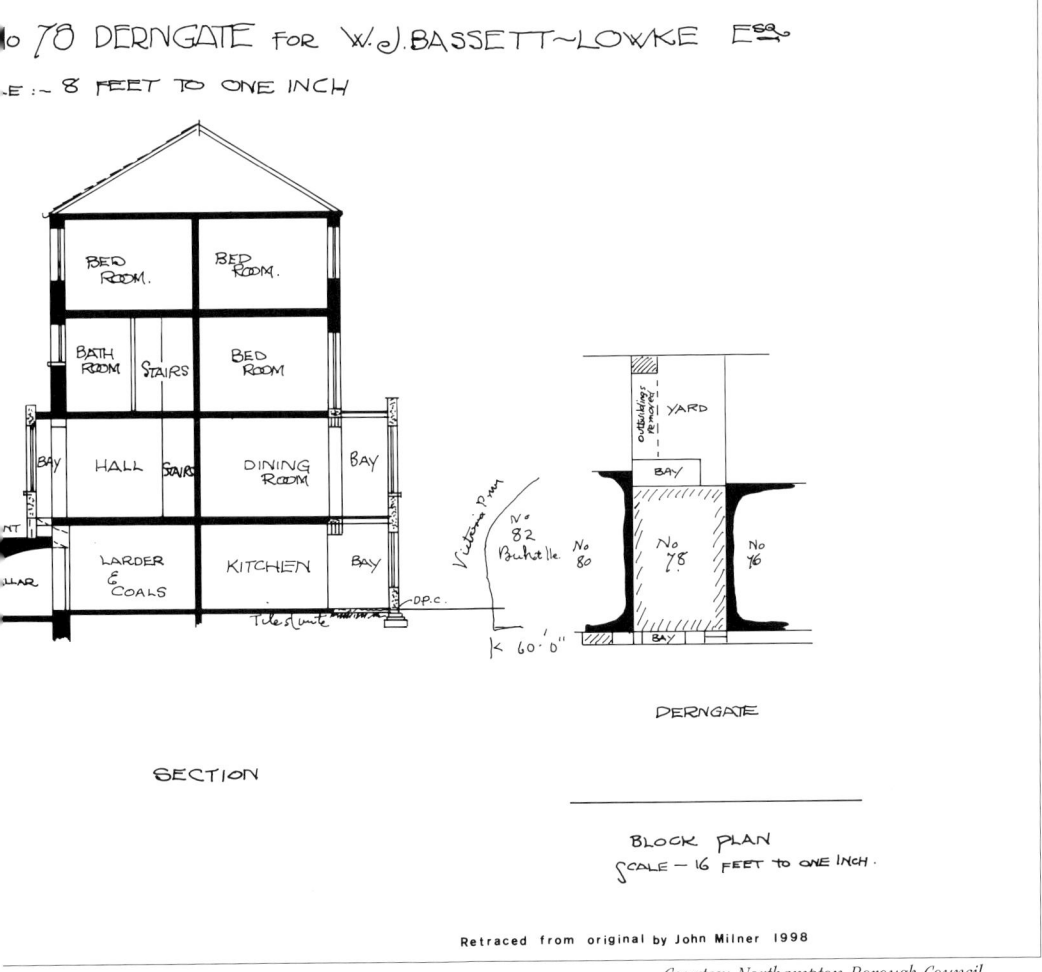

No 78 DERNGATE for W.J.BASSETT~LOWKE ESQ.
SCALE :- 8 FEET TO ONE INCH

SECTION

BLOCK PLAN
SCALE - 16 FEET TO ONE INCH.

Retraced from original by John Milner 1998

Courtesy Northampton Borough Council

house, so that space was now left for a cosy lounge hall. Thus, instead of turning immediately to the left on entering the front door in order to ascend the staircase, one walked diagonally across the hall to do so and ascended behind an inviting screen to the floor above.

The decorations in the hall were distinctly futuristic in character. The result of taking away the partition between the entrance passage and the front room, opening up the whole of the area, added to the spaciousness of the hall, although still quite modest at 12ft by 9ft. A projecting bay window with heating coils under the window-seat further extended the floor space. The general colour scheme was black, yellow and petunia.

The floors were stained black and wax polished and were partially covered with horsehair carpet, black centre with broad black and grey chequered border. The stair carpet was grey and of the same material.

The walls and ceiling were painted a dull velvety black and all the woodwork and furniture was

The hall looking towards the road. There is a comfortable recess with a settee brightened by petunia coloured cushions. The colour scheme was black, yellow and petunia.

J Bassett-Lowke Collection

A family party in the hall, with several brothers and sisters of Jane Bassett-Lowke's, which shows the screen extended on the left which acted as a divider between the room itself and the front door which opened straight into it. The photograph clearly illustrates the darkness of the decoration. The curtains were also a Mackintosh design.

J Bassett-Lowke Collection.

stained ebony black and polished. The walls of the room and stairway were divided into panels by bands of stencilled white chequer work which returned on the ceiling and terminated in square panels of stencilled chequer.

All around the room, at a height of 5ft 9ins from the floor, the walls were decorated with a frieze (about 3ft deep). This was a rich, geometric design of V-shaped leaves stencilled in rich golden yellow and out-lined with silver grey, enriched at regular intervals by subsidiary V-shaped leaves stencilled in rich, bright colours - emerald green, vermilion, cobalt blue and petunia purple. This, with the black background showing through, gave an effect that was at once rich and gay and yet quiet and peaceful.

All these colours were echoed here and there in the various fitments; the black and yellow in the smoker's cabinet, the green, blue and petunia in the silk shade of the standard lamp, and the petunia cushions of the window settee. The door screen, which was made of ebonised wood, was panelled in

The unusual fireplace with its variety of compartments, each one with a specific purpose in mind. Visible in the photograph is the fireback with 'B-L 1916' cast into it.

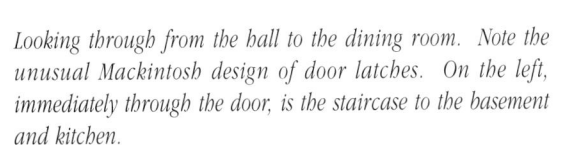

J Bassett-Lowke Collection

Looking through from the hall to the dining room. Note the unusual Mackintosh design of door latches. On the left, immediately through the door, is the staircase to the basement and kitchen.

J Bassett-Lowke Collection

The verandah from the main bedroom showing the magnificent view which Derngate enjoyed at that time, the verandah furniture and built-in bedding trough.

J Bassett-Lowke Collection

The kitchen was basic but well designed. The walls were finished in white tiles with just a black border near the ceiling and the floor was tiled in green and white. The door on the right gave access to the staircase and, beyond, the boiler room. The door on the left was the larder.

J Bassett-Lowke Collection

petunia tapestry with triangles in golden yellow at the top of each fold. The overmantel was of a special design, and at the side of this and in the stairway screen were semi-circular niches for flowers lined at the back with leaded silver lights enriched with squares of gold and yellow. Natural light for the kitchen stairs was provided through leaded lights in mirror and yellow, and these in return helped to give effect by the transmitting of artificial light from the staircase into the lounge/hall. One particular feature was a pair of wardrobe cupboards for hats and coats with a clock in the centre having a face of astrological design. The doors of this wardrobe were latticed with a mirror back.

In using black on the walls and ceilings, the idea was to get a sense of mystery and spaciousness, and it was claimed that this result was certainly achieved.

The hall was artificially lit by a centre circular candelabra, made of brass and decorated woodwork, with eight electric candles and one centre electric light. On the ceiling over this was a square decorative piece of special design, finished in white matone.

Through the swing door and across the head of the stairs leading down to the kitchen, was the dining room. This had been improved by an extension which was built on the back of the house, and which rendered possible the provision of a large window recess, adding considerably to the size and appearance of the room.

Another structural alteration was made by building cabinets into the recesses on each side of the fireplace cabinets. The upper parts were glazed and were for the display of silver, china, etc., the lower part being fitted with drawers, and also special pivoted boxes to hold wood and coal; thought being given to every little detail.

Lighting was described as a large 'semi-direct centre light' of a very novel design, consisting of two hardwood rings joined together by spacing lengths of similar wood. The rim was lined with fabric and an opal bowl formed the bottom, the whole being suspended by a series of short lengths of chain hanging vertical. The effect of this fitting when illuminated was said to be most pleasing.

On each side of the mantelpiece there was a form of lantern cupboard with three faces divided into small squares and glazed with ground glass. These novel fittings contained concealed lights and, when in use, radiated a pleasing glow sufficient to read by at night, as well as giving a particularly attractive appearance. With the exception of these two projections, the whole of the wall was finished flush across the fireplace with walnut woodwork, including a large mirror in the centre of the overmantel. The fireplace was finished in cream Dutch tiles throughout, with armour-bright grate. A deep bright-white frieze ran right round the walls, below which there were flat vertical strips of walnut, forming panels, which were papered with a tapestry design. The furniture was made throughout of walnut, the dining table being oval, 6ft. x 4ft. with 4 inch square legs. Two easy chairs of a square tub

The guest bedroom as seen from the doorway showing the curtains, made in striped cotton edged with untramarine harness braid, and with silk bedspreads to match. The top of the bedspreads were in ultramarine blue and both the curtains and the bedspreads had blue silk squares edged with bright emerald green.

J Bassett-Lowke Collection

pattern were provided for the window recess, plus a coffee table.

The table top was fitted with translucent green erinoid*, which enclosed an electric lamp for light effect or bowl of flowers. The centre of the window was a large sheet of plate-glass, giving an unimpeded outlook onto the garden. Two square footstools on each side of the fireplace were meant to serve a dual purpose - their other function being to act as workbaskets, the tops being made removable for that purpose.

The floor in this room was covered with thin oak boards, fastened on the top of the old deal floor. The general appearance of the rooms both by day and by night was very quiet and restful.

Descending to the kitchen in the basement the extension at the back of the house provided a large window recess similar to the dining room, making the kitchen quite spacious.

Although below the street level, the floor of the kitchen was level with the garden, and was therefore very light and airy. The old kitchener was removed and a modern range fitted in its place. The floor was tiled throughout in green and white tiles, grouped in 9 inch squares. The walls, right up to the ceiling, were finished in white glazed tiles with decoration only just by a 1 inch band of black tiles near the ceiling. The wall tiles were carried into the floor tiles by means of a concave tile, so there were no corners for the accumulation of dust and dirt. A large dresser occupied one side of the kitchen and was flanked by cupboards going right up to the ceiling.

Opposite the range (and in addition to the range), there were both electric and gas cooking arrangements. Two electric ovens, together with other electric appliances, were placed on a specially designed bench, with tiled top and pull-out shelves. On the stove was the motto *Fais ce que dois, advienne que pourra* which, translated, means *I do what I have to, come what may*.

All the woodwork, with the exception of that which was left plain, was finished in light green enamel, and the ceiling in white matone. The lighting consisted of two watertight ship's ceiling lights, which were neat in appearance and, owing to the ceiling being low, more suitable than the ordinary hanging lights. Leading from the kitchen, and occupying part of the space under the hall, was a large pantry. The other space under the hall was reached by crossing the foot of the stairs, where there was a coal cellar and boiler room, from which was supplied the hot water for the radiators, bathroom and bedrooms.

On the first floor were situated the bedroom, bathroom and other offices. In the first floor bedroom advantage was taken of the extension of the back of the house, previously mentioned, to form a balcony or covered verandah reached by opening the French windows, glazed with plate-glass, the full height of the room. The verandah was open on two sides, south and west, and commanded a magnificent view of the valley of the Nene. It afforded a desirable venue for light breakfasts and suppers in the summer time.

It was furnished with one table and two chairs, finished in white enamel. The floor was tiled in white encaustic tiles, with an oblong black and white border.

---

*Eriniod was a material made by Erinoid Ltd of Strand-on-the-Green, Middx., and was made from casein, a protein product from milk, and was supplied in a variety of colours.

In the bedroom was a neat washing recess at the side of the fireplace, which had been porcelain glass tiled, and fitted with a washing basin with hot and cold water supply. The cupboard here was glazed with three mirrors, and was illuminated by a centre electric light. The room was papered in light grey with a narrow-figured mauve edging. The carpet was mauve, and the furniture was all in grey sycamore of severe design, quartered and relieved by black inlay. Twin bedsteads were also in the same wood and finish. The dressing table and bed-side pedestal cupboards were covered with plate glass, which added considerably to the lift of the furniture. The lighting was a semi-direct electric light, and the general effect of the room, especially when the French doors were open, was delightfully cool and refreshing.

Opposite the bedroom there was the bathroom, finished in white enamel and papered with grey mosaic paper. On the left hand of the pedestal basin was a drying cupboard, and the fittings were most modern in character, including the Kohler bath, with all fittings nickel-plated, glass shelves, etc. The floor of the bathroom and landing was covered with blue-grey Jasper lino.

Ascending to the second floor, use was made of the recess in the stairs for a linen cupboard, which was kept aired by a small hot water coil.

A further view of the guest room showing the extent of the striped design, following on from the ceiling and down the wall. The furniture was in light waxed oak. Reflected in the mirror is the fireplace and note the louvre panels in the door, for ventilation.

J Bassett-Lowke Collection

The first floor landing with the stairs up on the right and the bathroom immediately on the left. The door facing up the short flight of stairs was a heated linen cupboard. . . . .

. . . . The bathroom, finished in white and papered in grey mosaic, was fitted with a Kohler enamel bath with nickel plated fittiings. An airing cupboard was provided and the floor was covered in blue-grey jaspe linoleum.

J Bassett-Lowke Collection

Mrs. Bassett-Lowke, with WJ's cousin Alice Lovejoy, sit and enjoy the benefit of the verandah.

J Bassett-Lowke Collection

The guest bedroom faced south, and was situated immediately over the first floor bedroom, and from point of view of decoration was perhaps the most daring in the house. The general finish of the ceiling and walls in this room was white, and from the back of the twin-bedsteads a design of corresponding width in black and white vertical striped paper was carried up to the ceiling, and continued over the beds in the form of a canopy, terminating with a transverse piece of the same design exactly above the foot of the bedsteads. From each side of this canopy two strips of about 18 inches wide were prolonged to the window. These turned round at right angles and joined each other across the head of the opening. This design was edged with ultramarine blue harness braid, fastened with black drawing pins. The curtains were made of black and white striped cotton material, also edged with the same braid, and decorated transversely at the bottom. The bedspreads were of black and white striped silk, the centre ultramarine blue, and both the curtains and bed-spreads had an addition in the shape of square patches of blue silk, edged with bright emerald green.

The furniture was of simple design in light-waxed oak with a narrow edging in black, on which was stencilled ultramarine blue squares, effecting thus an ensemble with the other arrangements.

The back and top of the washstand was covered with blue silk, over which was placed plate-glass. The knobs on the furniture were in ebony, inlaid with mother-of-pearl. The carpet was plain grey Brussels. There were no pictures on the wall and the lampshades were bell shape pattern, covered in ultramarine blue silk edged with pink, with round, blue wood beads suspended to the edge by ribbons. The general effect and colour scheme were striking in the extreme, and unique for the period in bedroom decoration. The French windows in this room opened on to the top of the open verandah formed by the reinforced concrete roof of the verandah below (not as per the original drawings). French louvred wood shutters were also provided for this room. Opposite this room, on the same floor, was a small study.

Above this was an attic, or maid's room. The furniture here was of simple character, all enamelled white, and the floor was covered with blue Jasper lino.

The top panels of the bedroom doors were fitted with louvred ventilators. These formed a very efficient method of ventilating bedrooms without the necessity of leaving the door ajar.

The Editor of the *Ideal Home* magazine commented at the time that *Mr and Mrs Bassett-Lowke are to be congratulated on the result of their efforts.*

My uncle and aunt did indeed merit praise and I must say it is surprising to me that the name of Charles Rennie Mackintosh is not mentioned in this context. It is a matter of mystery that his name did not appear on early articles on the house. My uncle was obviously pleased and asked him to carry on with other consultative work for him after his marriage; furniture design and alteration of colour schemes, graphics for the firm, and so forth.

Another article on 78 Derngate, written in the 1920s, relates the story of 'New Insides for Old Homes', again illustrated with similar pictures, did however end with the words: - *The whole scheme of furniture and decorations for the hall and guests' bedroom was the work of Mr C.R. Mackintosh, an artist architect of Chelsea who, in pre-war days, practised in Glasgow and was responsible for the charming and unique tea rooms for Miss Cranston in various parts of the city.* This magazine was *Berger's Mercury* and the article was on two pages, dilapidated and old, but readable. Attached to the article was the original, written in a hand unknown but amended in places my uncle's handwriting.

An architect living in Northampton submitted the drawings for the alterations by Mackintosh to 78 Derngate. Dated the 31st May 1916 they were headed *Borough of Northampton, Notice of Intended New Building – F250*. The extension and alterations to the building cost £650; two and half times the cost of the house.

The architect was Alexander Ellis Anderson, brother of a well-known young architect at the Glasgow School of Art, William J Anderson, who coincidentally was the first winner of the Alexander Thomson Travelling Studentship in 1888. Mackintosh was the second successful candidate in 1890. I further discovered that Alexander Ellis Anderson had been architect previously to my grandfather, Joseph Tom Lowke, for various alterations to some of his works' buildings and later on in the early 1920s he had assisted my father, H A Bassett-Lowke, with additions to his home. He was obviously the family's architect and was also a colleague of the architect Keightly Cobb, my uncle's family friend, who lived four doors away from WJ in Derngate at No.70. In fact, in the list of folk living in Derngate in 1920, I was interested to see the name of Alexander Ellis Anderson as living in No. 72 Derngate, very near to both the Bassett-Lowkes and the Cobbs. Thomas Howarth, in his book on Mackintosh*, states that the rear of 78 Derngate, to the best of the author's knowledge, presents more than any other work in this country, the characteristics of the modern movement and Roger Billcliffe also, on page 218 of his book (previously mentioned), writes that *the whole rear of the house - with its sharp angles, broad openings and use of sunblinds, seemed prophetic of the International Style*.

Be that as it may, WJ and Mackintosh appear to have worked very well together and they must have met many times in London during the 10 months between the plans for No.78 being submitted and passed. In fact it was early July before the plans were approved, which allowed a time span of only 8 months before WJ's marriage on March 21st 1917. A great deal of preparation with Mackintosh must have taken place beforehand, and those working on the building must have moved with fair speed. One has to consider that after their brief wartime honeymoon, uncle and his bride were able to cross the threshold of No.78, find everything in order, and take possession of a marvellous modern home.

Of the few letters that WJ wrote to Mackintosh, which are, together with many other documents and pictures, in the care of the Hunterian at Glasgow, I am so glad that the first, written on July 31st 1916, has survived. It shows the optimism and pleasure at the start of a great adventure. It starts by thanking Mackintosh for the drawings safely received and goes on:

> *I have obtained possession of the house today and my friends are commencing the work, and should be glad if you would let me know about the floor of the hall.*

The letter is incomplete but it is full of questions. *The hall?*

> *It appears from your drawings of the carpet it is hardly necessary to have this covered with oak and so little to be seen. I presume you advise the base mat being sunk but would not the stair carpet be better the standard 22" wide as you cannot get it in 2ft. Personally I am not keen on hair carpet for the stairs but thought of something of a Brussels, like the <u>enclosed</u>, which I think can be obtained*

---

*Thomas Howarth - *Charles Rennie Mackintosh and the Modern Movement*, London, 2nd Edition, 1977.

in black..........doubt whether we are doing right by having a curtain across the hall. I still think it would be better if you design a screen for the door about 3ft long and 7 ft high and re-hang the door so it opens back against the wall.

This letter could well have been a formidable one if there were as many items discussed in the missing

WJ and his new wife leave Abington Avenue Congregational Church after their marriage ceremony on the 21st March 1917. Being wartime, it was but a simple wedding with a short honeymoon of a few days in Bournemouth.

J Bassett-Lowke Collection

page or pages as in this first single one! Some months later - November 2nd 1916 to be precise - WJ writing on his company letterheading, with the heading 'Government Controlled Establishment' displayed plainly but conspicuously across the top, goes straight in:

I have decided to have the radiator originally ordered and same is being fixed today. He gives dimensions and then requests : *I shall be glad to hear from you with reference to the screen and also the cigarette box as soon as possible. I am getting one of my draughtsmen to make you a 1" drawing of all the walls of the hall so you can proceed with your decoration scheme. I am enclosing exact details of the dining room cupboards to enable you to let me have drawing for the lanterns. I want a stand lamp for the dining room, would you recommend me to have a <u>plain brass</u> one in antique finish or one in walnut similar to the table lamp you are designing for me.* [He finishes in cordial terms] *Kindest regards, yours sincerely.*

January 1917 produces a batch of 3 letters in 4 days.

On the 11th I have arranged with Messrs Heal to reduce the size of the Hall carpet as agreed and also to have the centre of same black. With reference to the runners from the door to the kitchen stairs, have you any objection to my having these in

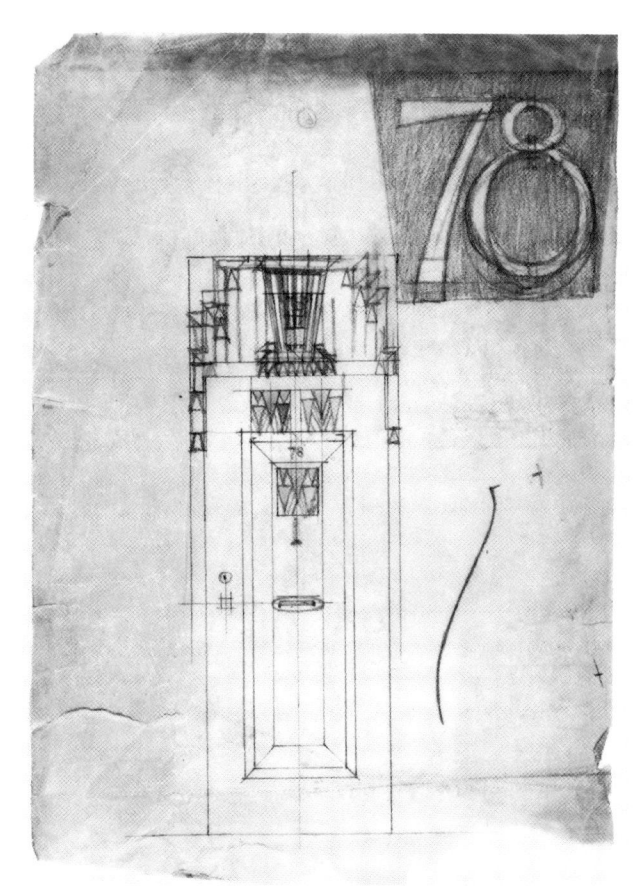

The original sketch by Mackintosh for the front door of 78 Derngate. This was a preliminary study but the general design was adopted for the finalised drawing.
©Hunterian Art Gallery, University of Glasgow, Mackintosh Collection

the natural grey hair colour as they would show less dirt than plain black. He adds a footnote. *What idea do you suggest for the Bed Spreads of the Oak Bedroom?*

The next day, January 12th, he follows with a short note enclosing a pattern of the material for the Hall Screen, and it is in this letter that he raises an interest in plastic. Evidently Mackintosh had made use of a synthetic material in 1911, for niches between latticework panels in the Chinese Room of the Ingram Street tea rooms, he designed for Miss Cranston . It was called Lactolith or Balalith and was a product patented in 1899 by a German professor.

With the Great War intervening, it became difficult to obtain supplies from abroad. In this particular letter in January, WJ mentions a new material:

I presume the material you mention is similar to Erinoid, which is now made in England and which I can obtain in almost any colour, an unpolished sample of which I enclose. Have you ever thought of using this in the decoration of furniture

The finished front elevation showing the new bay window and alterations finished. Taken in 1917, Mrs. Bassett-Lowke stands at the door of her new home.

J Bassett-Lowke Collection

> *instead of wood inlays or enamel stencil? He then switches to My cabinet maker has the dining room overmantel nearly finished but I notice he has not made the mirror quite square but has worked to your 1" drawing which shows it about 19" wide x 22" high, but I presume this will not spoil the design.*

He looks forward to further drawings and only signs the letter, *Yours faithfully,* but this may simply have been dashed off with a pile of other letters in haste. Sure enough, on January 14th, he is back to the usual *Kindest regards* when he encloses booklets about Erinoid and patterns of yellow silk for the Hall Screen, and then continues with his view that the Dining Room Door is out of keeping with the style of the room and requests Mackintosh to send him a 1" scale drawing of what he suggests. He says:

> *I will get a price from my contractor in both ordinary wood and walnut and see if I can afford it. Do you consider it should have glass or Ventilators in it; in any case, the design must be severe and plain.*

I think these five letters give a vivid insight into WJ's character, pertinent and bustling, and also show the meticulous detail which he seems to apply to everything - a necessary attribute for success in his own model business. Although he was a demanding client, I feel there is politeness and cordiality (although we have nothing on paper to judge from Mackintosh) in a business relationship between two men who have respect for each other.

According to the *Northampton Independent* of March 24th 1917:

> *The wedding of W J Bassett-Lowke, elder son of Mr & Mrs J T Lowke of Northampton and Miss Florence Jones, third daughter of the late Mr C Jones and Mrs Jones of 20 East Park Parade, Northampton took place on Wednesday at Abington Avenue Congregational Church. The happy event was accompanied by many handsome gifts and good wishes, for the respective families are well known and highly respected. The bride's father was one of the founders of the great shoe manufacturing firm of Crocket and Jones, and the bridegroom is the Managing Director of the famous firm of model engineers bearing his name. As lecturer, photographer and lanternist he has rendered useful public service, and since the war started his firm has been busily engaged day and night on contracts for the Admiralty and War Office. The ceremony was conducted by the Rev. C S Larkman assisted by the Rev. R M Stanley MA and the bride, who was attractively attired in a light grey travelling costume, was given away by her brother, Mr Frank Jones. The best man was Mr J Flinton Harris JP. Owing to the war the ceremony was a very quiet one and afterwards the newly married couple left for a few days at Bournemouth. The presents to the bridegroom included a case of silver teaspoons and forks from the London Office staff and his firm, a writing case from the Young Men's Senior Class at Doddridge Chapel, and a silver tray from the employees of Messrs Lowke's works department.*

While uncle and auntie lived in Derngate, friends and relatives came from near and far and enthused over the house with its modernistic comfort and original decor; the hall lounge and the guest bedroom being the main points of conversation.

Gradually, signs were emerging of his motto of *Fitness for Purpose*, an ideal which was pursued by him both in his personal life and in setting the standard in his business of *Perfection in Miniature*.

An early group who came to visit on July 8th 1917 were WJ's Doddridge Young Men's Class, from the Chapel where, prior to his marriage, he was a regular attender. These young men each signed the flyleaf of the choice Morocco-bound Bible they presented to him, headed by Chas H Battle, a personal friend, who was closely linked in his later life with the Northampton General Hospital. A family group gathered there one evening from my aunt's family, which was not small as she had four brothers and five sisters who came with their spouses. On the Lowke side of the family, we very small children with our parents visited another time with Grandpa and Grandma Lowke. I thought about the strange and wonderful room we saw as we stepped through the front door! As we went round I was impressed to the point of silence and open-eyed wonder but managed to eat a sandwich or two of the scrumptious tea that Auntie Floss provided. Of course, as usual, I was chided about my appetite; Vivian on the other hand was steadily watching uncle and the magic toys he brought out.

A famous visitor who stayed twice at No.78 in the 1920s was George Bernard Shaw, when he came to address political meetings in the town. One visit became generally known to Northampton's public when the story was narrated about a young reporter who asked a question of the great man which had little to do with politics. Several versions of this have been told but the one I heard from my uncle in later years was that the young man had dared to ask GBS how he had slept, having heard of the rather startling decor in the visitor's bedroom. Shaw replied in his dry, quick manner *As usual, with my eyes shut.*

About 1920, it was decided to change the somewhat dark and extreme decoration of the hall. It has been suggested elsewhere that the original decoration was beginning to affect WJ and my aunt, but there is no positive proof of this. Initially, the hall reverted to plain walls and Mackintosh was again approached to devise a suitable scheme. The result was less harsh, the screen being painted grey in lieu of black with a new smaller stencil frieze based on the original design. This design was repeated again in the study of WJ's later house *New Ways*.

Tea for members of the Jones family at 78 Derngate c 1920. WJ is seated on the left and on the right is Mrs. Annie Marshall Jones, Mrs. Bassett-Lowke's Mother. The photograph shows the interim decoration of the lounge/hall before the new Mackintosh designed freize was applied.
J Bassett-Lowke Collection

The young couple settled in happily and enjoyed the novelty of everything and meeting many new friends. Long standing friends, Keightly and Evelyn Cobb, lived close by at No. 70 Derngate. WJ was at school with Keightly and was best man at his wedding. After three or four years my uncle began to be concerned about his young wife, as it was evident that she was not her usual fit self. He prevailed on her to see the doctor and later a specialist was called in. She saw several, and during this time Uncle took her to Baden Baden to consult a well-known German specialist, Dr. Schwartz, to see what could be done. Rheumatoid arthritis had been diagnosed. The consensus of opinion, from the experts consulted, was that it could be helpful if they left the lower ground of the town, with its proximity to the river Nene, and perhaps moved to live in a spot towards the higher ground approaching the Wellingborough side of the town.

So of necessity and with much regret, they began to consider the next enterprise in their lives; the building of another home to my uncle's standards and suited for their future needs. This project was one in which my aunt took an equal part and it did help her to be outward looking and to do her share to be the helpmate which she continued to be, all her life.

Since 1926, 78 Derngate has had several owners and, apart from that transferred to *New Ways,* much of the original furniture has been dispersed, although some major items are on display in the Central Museum, Northampton; the Victoria and Albert Museum, London and the Hunterian Art Gallery in

Glasgow. Nevertheless there has been an ever-increasing interest in this important later work of Mackintosh for his patron W J Bassett-Lowke.

In 1997 the house and its neighbour No. 80 were acquired by Northampton Borough Council from the Church Commission on a 99 year Lease, for a new charitable trust, the *78 Derngate Trust*, which was established in 1998 to oversee the restoration of No. 78 and to create a visitor/design centre in Nos. 80 and 82 (acquired 1998) to form an integral part of the project.

Let us hope this spirit shines through for the two of them in that the Trust may be able eventually to open the doors of 78 Derngate to the public and reproduce again, with its work and goodwill, the sparkle of Mackintosh and WJ which was present when he lived in Derngate over 80 years ago.

One famous visitor to 78 Derngate, in the 1920s, was George Bernard Shaw seen here with Mrs. Bassett-Lowke at the front door.
©Hunterian Art Gallery, University of Glasgow, Mackintosh Collection

Chapter Eight
Candida Cottage

There were changes that Mackintosh was asked to make after Uncle and Aunt had lived in No.78 Derngate for a few months. The first furniture for the guest bedroom was made of mahogany inlaid with mother of pearl. By 1919 this had been replaced with a light oak suite, edged with black and blue, and set in a dramatic black and white striped setting. It is not known why the room was changed; perhaps the first scheme was installed so that No.78 was ready to receive guests straight away. This first set of furniture was duplicated for WJ's friend Sidney Horstman of Bath and that suite is now in the Victoria and Albert Museum.

During this time, my uncle was busy on a pair of old cottages he had acquired in 1914 in the small village of Roade just outside Northampton. Why my Uncle and Aunt wanted a second home is not known. Alterations had been going along gradually to convert the two into a single building. The architect is unknown but could have been Alexander Ellis Anderson who was responsible for work for the Lowke family for some years. Windows and casements had been altered and a stone loggia added with access to its roof through new French windows from the bedroom above. In honour of his friendship with George Bernard Shaw, uncle named the house *Candida Cottage* after his play *Candida*. WJ and his wife had been host and hostess to Shaw in the early 1920s and *Candida* was one of uncle's favourite Shaw plays.

Mackintosh designed some of the furniture and decorations for the cottage. An interesting letter relating to the furniture survives dated June 29th 1918. The first sentence confirms his appointment to see Mackintosh in London and continues :

> *I agree with you, we ought to talk the matter over on the dining room suite before you proceed with the detail drawings. I shall also want a Gramaphone [Gramophone] Cabinet of the same style and enclose you herewith details of one that our Works made for me when I was married which gives you important measurements internally. With reference to the top well, this must not be less than 4" from the underside of the lid to the face of the box and if designed deeper the lid should be split in the same way as shown in the enclosed drawing as otherwise the well is too deep to handle the needles etc. properly. With reference to the overmantle I think you ought to allow for a standard of 3' 6" which is about the size of the tile surround of the average grate. I also require a design for a service table, this I think should be about 2' 6" by 20" wide about 28" high, and a pullout shelf each side and underneath similar to sketch. Perhaps you could let me have your advice on these 3 items when we meet.*

CANDIDA COTTAGE (*as it was to become*), in the village of Roade, near Northampton, was a pair of cottages prior to being renovated and altered by W J Bassett-Lowke during the 1914-18 War.
J Bassett-Lowke Collection

The interior during renovation. It certainly needed some imagination to take it on and WJ was certainly not short of that!
J Bassett-Lowke Collection

The cottages after renovation and conversion into one residence. Externally, apart from new enlarged windows, a stone loggia was added and French windows which gave access to its roof from the main bedroom. WJ named CANDIDA COTTAGE *after George Bernard Shaw's play 'Candida'.*
J Bassett-Lowke Collection

A letter very much to the point and which reveals Uncle's close attention to detail. It closes with an intriguing sentence:

> *I am pleased to hear the rivets did for Mrs Mackintosh and I have some more if she requires any. Yours sincerely.*

This letter puts me in mind of the one surviving letter from Mackintosh to uncle, written just before his wedding.

> *2 Hans Studios, 43A Glebe Place, London S.W.3*
>
> *Monday 19th March 1917.*
>
> *Dear Bassett-Lowke,*
>
> *I have today sent from Mrs Mackintosh and myself to you and your soon to be wife a little book of Plays by George Bernard Shaw. I should have sent this to Miss Jones but I have no knowledge of her home address. Will you both please accept this token of our best wishes for your united happiness?*
>
> *Yours sincerely,*
>
> *C R Mackintosh.*

It certainly reveals a charming and thoughtful side to a brilliant man that is not usually seen.

There are no records of Mackintosh visiting Northampton. Much of the communication seems to have been done through letters and uncle's London visits, and perhaps through photographs or drawings of the sites at Derngate and Roade. The *Candida* furniture was simple and practical, in dark stained oak and highly appropriate for a country cottage. Plastic was used for the decorative red and turquoise blue inlays (according to Brighton Museum) and the chair seats matched up with blue rexine covers. The walls were covered with a dark brown paper brightened with a stencilled border in blue, black and red. Simple coco matting, dark blue and grey in colour covered the floor. WJ had made a rough sketch of the service table (trolley we would call it today) and Mackintosh's design for it was in keeping with the chairs. The oval dining table was also of oak and decorated with blue

The dining room, showing the transformation. The restoration had been completed before Mackintosh was consulted in 1918 to design the dining room furniture and wall decoration seen here.
    J Bassett-Lowke Collection

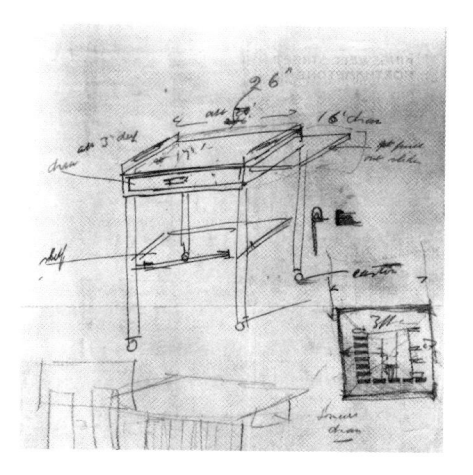

A rough sketch by WJ of his idea for a service table which he sent to Mackintosh. The finished result is seen in the previous photograph of the dining room.

J Bassett-Lowke Collection

Radolith, and the stencilled border pattern was repeated on each wall. Local craftsmen may have made some of the furniture but some was certainly made by German prisoners of war interned on the Isle of Man.

My uncle was a pacifist but, when war arrived, it is evident that the firm went quickly on to war work. The whole firm was keen to help the war effort, and although a pacifist, WJ was no war profiteer. However, several of his German friends and business contacts were in London at the outbreak of war and they were interned at Knockaloe just on the outskirts of Peel on the Isle of Man. WJ secured a permit and regularly visited them until the time of their release.

The story of how German prisoners of war came to manufacture furniture for WJ really starts with James T Baily. He was a carpenter and became a teacher of crafts, being eventually recognised as a leading authority on craft teaching in schools. He was a Fellow of the College of Handicrafts, at one time Secretary of the National Union of Manual Training Teachers, and a devout Christian. He became a Quaker, using his craftsmanship and organisational abilities at the Quaker school at Ackworth but, during the 1914-18 War, he became involved in the introduction of craft work for prisoners held in the internment camps, including the one at Knockaloe.

Charles Matt, who before the war was a foreman in a London furniture factory, was a craftsman who found himself at Knockaloe with the many other internees and he gathered around him some skilled cabinetmakers. Woodworking and carving was thus developed and some less skilled were taught the craft. Some fine carving work resulted and the internees manufactured some of the modernist furniture, which Charles Rennie Mackintosh had designed for my uncle's home at 78 Derngate.

This pleased James Baily and it also allowed the internees to earn something during their years of captivity. WJ was sympathetic towards the Quakers and sometimes attended their meeting at Northampton. In fact, years later, I accompanied him on one occasion to a meeting. WJ may have met James Baily at some time, and may have known other internees, but would certainly have been appreciative of the teaching bestowed on these lonely men. In addition to the furniture made for WJ, he also brought back carved bone napkin rings, buckles, and other decorative items also made by the internees.

Candida Cottage was completed by 1919. Photographs show the finished rooms and my aunt and

CANDIDA COTTAGE 107

Above, the opposite view of the dining room showing the long window, with its window seat, the Mackintosh oval table, chairs and sideboard and, below, the lounge, which opened out on to the loggia, and the new staircase; there is no 'modern' influence here except perhaps the wall light on the extreme right.

J Bassett-Lowke Collection

uncle in the new stone loggia. Some of the furniture was transferred to *New Ways* when WJ and his wife left Derngate and eventually it went to the Brighton Museum. The vivid colours of the inlays have faded over the years, but that is all.

WJ's brother-in-law, Frank Jones, owned a plot of land in Wellingborough Road which had an established garden, and on which he intended at some time to have a house built. He and his wife were then living in the Drive in the Kettering Road area of the town. Mrs. Jones was uncertain about moving, in fact she and her husband chose to ask Mackintosh to repeat the *Candida Cottage* dining room furniture and décor for this house.

Mackintosh designed three remarkable clocks for WJ: one with ten columns and now in a private collection; a domino clock (Glasgow Museums); and the guest bedroom clock (British Museum). Each was a marvellous example of modernism. Mackintosh did other small commissions for my uncle, including designs for advertising labels and his Christmas card for 1922.

Left, the upstairs, prior to renovation, was no better than the ground floor. Note that there is a staircase up into the roof space; the roof having a very high pitch and, below, the bedroom after restoration, showing the French windows leading out on to the balcony over the loggia.

J Bassett-Lowke Collection

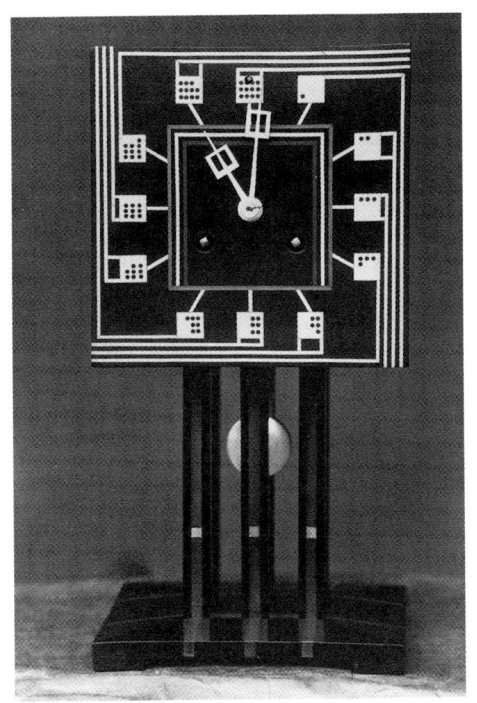

CANDIDA COTTAGE 109

Mackintosh designed two clocks for WJ which were made by German craftsmen at the Knockaloe internment camp, in the Isle of Man, during the 1914-18 war.

Hunterian Art Gallery, University of Glasgow

J Bassett-Lowke Collection

Certificate 1

No. of Certificate 123
Number of Shares 20

BASSETT-LOWKE, LIMITED.
INCORPORATED UNDER THE COMPANIES (CONSOLIDATION) ACT, 1908.

CAPITAL £20,000, divided into 20,000 Shares of £1 each.

This is to Certify that Mrs Florence Jane Bassett Lowke of New Ways, Wellingborough Road, Northampton is the Registered Proprietor of Twenty Fully Paid Shares of One Pound each, numbered 13273 to 13292 both inclusive, in the above-named Company, subject to the Memorandum and Articles of Association and the Rules and Regulations of the said Company.

Given under the Common Seal of the said Company the .... day of 1952

C.J. ....
R H Lilley .... } Directors.
K C Turton .... Secretary.

No Transfer of any of the above-mentioned Shares can be registered until this Certificate has been deposited at the Office of the Company.

RailRomances Collection

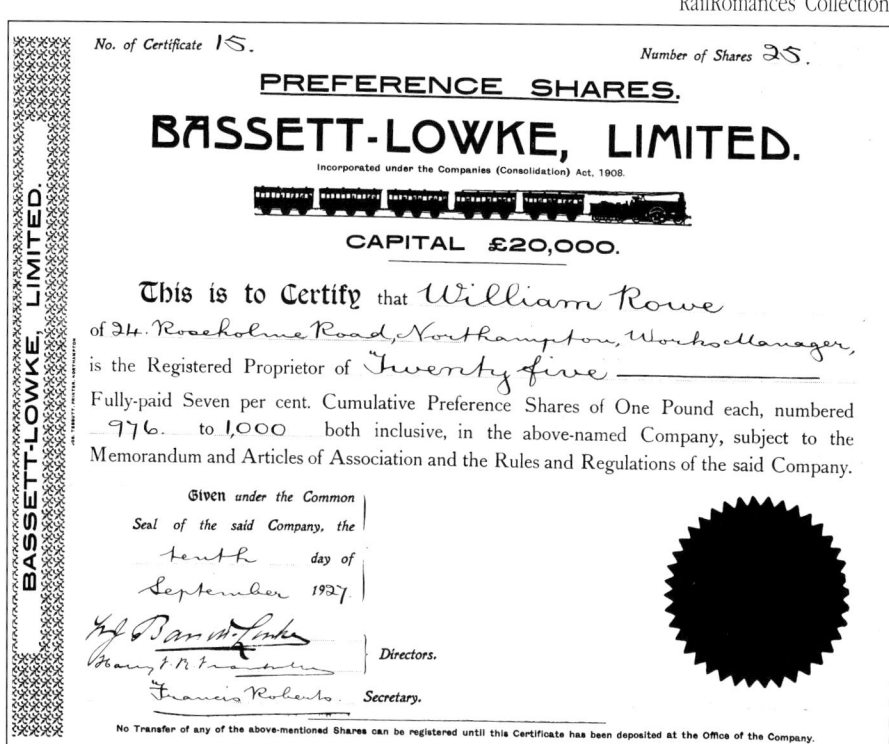

Certificate 2

No. of Certificate 15
Number of Shares 25

PREFERENCE SHARES.
BASSETT-LOWKE, LIMITED.
Incorporated under the Companies (Consolidation) Act, 1908.

CAPITAL £20,000.

This is to Certify that William Rowe of 24 Roseholme Road, Northampton, Works Manager, is the Registered Proprietor of Twenty five Fully-paid Seven per cent. Cumulative Preference Shares of One Pound each, numbered 976 to 1,000 both inclusive, in the above-named Company, subject to the Memorandum and Articles of Association and the Rules and Regulations of the said Company.

Given under the Common Seal of the said Company, the tenth day of September 1927.

W J Bassett-Lowke
Harry F M .... } Directors.
Francis Roberts. Secretary.

No Transfer of any of the above-mentioned Shares can be registered until this Certificate has been deposited at the Office of the Company.

Chapter Nine

Post War Rebuilding

After the 1914-18 war, plans were made for the Ship Models Department of the firm to become a satellite company of Bassett-Lowke Ltd under the management of Harry Franklin. This subsidiary business went through with the same two partners who had created the first business in 1899, Harry Franklin and W J. Harry Franklin wished to develop the range of ship models from what the firm had been doing previously. He called on E W Hobbs, the marine expert who pre-war had been for a time manager of London Branch, but was now back as a freelance. Mr Hobbs designed six model ships to a standard length of 60cm individually boxed and superior in style and detail to what had been produced before, with the aim of attracting customers looking for better quality. Not all were successful. Certainly the tugboat and the lifeboat succeeded but others, being narrower, rolled badly and a revision of the range had to be worked out. Actually, with the addition of 2 more types and removing those not successful, this range continued in production until the beginning of the Second World War. One metre models were later introduced - the T.B.D. and various liners - White Star *Doric*, Blue Star *Arandora Star*, Cunard *Mauretania* and the Royal Mail Steam Packet *Asturias*, each supplied in a polished wood carrying case. Mr Whynne, as the ships models' craftsmen called WJ, was still the spearhead salesman for the exhibition quality models produced for the big shipping lines, many of which are still to be seen in museums 80 years or more since they were made.

There were four main departments in Ship Models Ltd, each with their own foreman. George Shaw, a model maker who came from the North managed the metal department; Arthur James was the man in charge of the paint shop; Leo Halford managed the boiler department that also made the small brass fittings. A new man was introduced in 1919 to take on the woodworking department. His name was Percy Claydon. He was a craftsman who came from Glenns, Northampton's well-known builders. WJ knew Mr Herbert Glenn, his previous boss, and was aware of his skills in woodwork.

At sometime during his long service with WJ my uncle sent Claydon's handwriting to be analysed and I do not think he would be averse when he read the result: *an industrious and ambitious personality - a fast and reliable worker - the product of self-education and self-discipline*. He was all of these things and proved an excellent servant during his long years with Bassett-Lowke. Many a time he would accompany WJ to consider the work on some special model job for which they were quoting. He produced small furnishings for New Ways including, I believe, a nest of tables, a cake stand, a standard lamp, and a chest of drawers to go in the lounge. Percy Claydon served the company over 40 years and recalled that a characteristic remark of WJ at Board Meetings, which would infuriate the Financial Director, was: *assuming these figures to be correct*.

When working on the first boat he was designing ,Percy Claydon pushed a 2-wheeled barrow up to Abington Park with the *Streamlinias* in it to test on the lake. There were steam and electrically operated versions of this model and it was a popular addition to the model boat side of the business.

The '0' gauge DUKE OF YORK *model introduced and manufactured by Bassett-Lowke in 1927 and* ....

.... *above, the LMS* MOGUL *which was introduced in 1925 and available in clockwork, electric and steam versions.*
Bob Burgess Collection

Some enthusiasts had extensive garden railways in the smaller gauges, such as this gauge '1' railway at Bishops Stortford which belonged to Victor Harrison, of Harrisons the stamp printers, and a very good friend of WJ. Victor Harrison is on the right.
Bassett-Lowke Society

The post war period presented a new challenge, that of rebuilding the business after the turmoil of war. The return to normal business was, as one would expect, a slow process. War work suddenly came to an end and firms had to be usefully employed during the interim period in order to retain their workforce. Various contracts, towards the peace effort, were issued and Bassett-Lowke received one such large contract for the manufacture of high-grade cinema projectors. As a result of the war WJ had to resort to producing the models hitherto manufactured in Germany as Continental trade with the UK virtually ceased. In 1919 he embarked upon reorganisation of the business to manufacture a wider selection of goods at a competitive price in this country.

After the end of the War orders which had been placed with Bing in Germany prior to the start of hostilities, and which had been completed and held in store, were now released and delivered. WJ assumed that everything would now settle down to normal business as it was in 1914, but this was not to be so. He misjudged the market and overstocked with model railway goods, some of which remained on the shelf for many years thereafter.

WJ's other German supplier, Carette, closed in 1917. G Carrette, who was French, had fled to France at the start of the War and his partner, Paul Josephthal, was called up into the armed forces. After the War WJ made contact with them both and was able to acquire all the tooling for the products that Carette used to make for Bassett-Lowke. These were now transferred to Winteringhams for them to manufacture in Northampton.

The Chairman of Bassett-Lowke Ltd., Jack Sears, died in 1916 and his place was taken by Edward Lewis who served until 1927.

In 1921 the whole of the mass production of tinplate rails, '*Lowko*' track, steam locomotives, vertical engines, the wooden stations, signal boxes and engine sheds, and a whole host of associated products, were handed over to Winteringham Ltd. They had the same Board of Directors as Bassett-Lowke Ltd, with the exception of J D Riley, MP, who was Chairman. All specialist modelling such as architectural and industrial models, glass case models of locomotives, etc., were made by Twining Models Ltd and for whom Bassett-Lowke was sole concessionaire. At this time, there were close on three hundred employees engaged on model work in Northampton, and that is not counting the sub-contractors who supplied detail parts. With Ship Models and Winteringhams as separate entities, Bassett-Lowke did no manufacturing and concentrated on marketing.

WJ always recognised that he had to move with the times. In 1923, he advertised the Oracle Wireless Receiver. *Made throughout in Northampton* the advert proclaimed, price £6. 6s. 0d (£6.30). For an extra £4. 10s. 0d., a Loading Induction Unit could be added *enabling Paris to be heard*. It all came in a polished mahogany case with an Ebonite panel and brass fittings. It would appear that it was marketed in conjunction with A W Bond of Euston Road, London.

An associate of WJ at the time was local model railway enthusiast Phipps-Walker who was related to Pickering Phipps, MP, who ran the family business of P Phipps & Co., Northampton Ales. He was one of the partners in Walker & Holtzaphell of 61, Bond Street, London, a well-established firm model engineering suppliers. It was Phipps-Walker and WJ who were instrumental in creating *The Model Engineering Trades Association* (META).

WJ was nearly always one step ahead of his competitors, and the market. He really surprised the market unaware in April 1925 when he exhibited the first '0' example of a 2-6-0 *Mogul* locomotive at the Model Railway Club Exhibition; No. 13000 painted in L M S livery. The reason that he caught the market on the hop was when the L M S were six months off revealing the actual full size locomotive; WJ had obtained copies of the drawings from the L M S! It was produced in clockwork, electric, or steam, in both gauges '0' and '1', in a variety of company liveries, and also in kit form. It is thought that close on 20,000 had been produced up to 1968. He obviously had good contacts within the L M S company as it is known that he was present on a special run in early 1934 to Llandudno in North Wales of their famous *Royal Scot* [*] locomotive, built in 1927, and the subject of another successful model. WJ recorded this occasion on cine film.

Like the Caledonian Railway Company, mentioned earlier, Godfrey Phillips the cigarette manufacturers also saw the virtue in model railways as an advertising gimmick and, with His Royal Highness the Duke of York then being a popular figure, they ordered a batch of 30,000 *Duke of York* 4-4-0 locomotives in 1926. Later on, in 1932, the Kensitas Cigarette Company promoted a similar batch, but this time something a little up-market by way of a *Princess Elizabeth* locomotive. One wonders where they all are now? How many of these substantial orders were attributable to the marketing expertise of WJ we shall probably never know.

On the 8th December 1926, the national newspapers carried an official warning from the Home Secretary about the dangers of model railways designed to work off the mains electric supply. WJ was quick to point out that *none of Bassett-Lowke's models were designed to do so and that most of these dangerous railways come from abroad!*

The subject of the range of model railway equipment both sold and produced by Bassett-Lowke, somewhat like the ship modelling and architectural side of the business, is outside the scope of this book. Taking the *Royal Scot* as a typical example, we will follow WJ's own description of the building of this model locomotive.

From Steel Sheet to *Royal Scot*

George Holland, Lecturer and Dramatic Critic commented (1949) that *to go over the Bassett-Lowke works is to be particularly impressed by the tone, the interest and the prevailing spirit of pride in quality.* It was not a mass production factory in the true sense although somewhat dependant on machines. *In these workshops artist and artisan join in happy co-operation .... therein lies one of the essentials of the firm's success.*

> *Have you ever visited a model railway factory?* Wrote WJ, *It's one of the most fascinating places in the world for anyone who is the least bit mechanically minded.*
>
> *Locomotives, coaches, vans and wagons, stations, signals, points and track; you've seen them all shining, spick and span in toy shop windows, but haven't you ever wanted to know just how they were made, how the huge masses of raw material in a factory warehouse are magically transformed into models you admire so much?*

---

[*] This was not the original *Royal Scot* 6100 but 6152 with the original plates and numbers from 6100 as it was in better condition for the tour.

Let us take a special trip round a well known scale model works during the Autumn season. Noise and motion are everywhere, long lines of heavy power presses perpetually throbbing, overalled workers bending over their intricate jobs. At one end of the factory the raw material is stored .... stack upon stack of steel sheets,, huge rolls of aluminium alloy, thousands of rods of brass and iron, and countless piles of wood and metal waiting to be consumed by the hungry presses .... your favourite locomotive was once just a handful of metal, a couple of rods and a lithographed sheet.

The well-known scale model works that WJ described was, of course, Bassett-Lowke Ltd. Of all the mass-produced models made, a locomotive is by far the most complex and interesting item to study. To give the reader a feel for this side of the business in the late 1920's we will follow the manufacture of the Gauge '0' model of the famous *Royal Scot* locomotive, as described by WJ.

For the making of this model the actual working drawings of the full size *Royal Scot* were obtained from the London Midland & Scottish Railway Company, and these were reduced to Gauge '0' size being then modified by an expert draughtsman with a wide knowledge of model manufacturing limitations and difficulties. The resultant design was then submitted to the manufacturing department for their approval and, this obtained, the highly skilled workers in the model-making department would hand make a sample model. As the sample model was made the blanks or flats (the terms given to the tinplate parts before they are folded or shaped) would be developed, the information thus obtained being used to produce the multitude of press tools required. In the *Royal Scot* there were over 400 different operations all requiring tooling; no light job and always, at that time, the manufacturer's heaviest production cost.

The '0' gauge model of the LMS ROYAL SCOT, No. 6100, was introduced in 1929 and was one of the early lithographed models to be built solely by Bassett-Lowke.
Bob Burgess Collection

The *Royal Scot* was produced in lithographic finish. Early locomotives were spray finished after assembling but the lithographic process, which reproduced the designs of the locomotives, carriages and wagons, in the right colours on the tin-steel sheets before any manufacturing operations were started, was a production revolution. With the design complete, tooling made, presses set up and lithographed sheets to hand production was ready to roll.

Each tinplate part is first blanked, then the edges are beaded over to take off any sharpness, assembling holes pierced, windows embossed and cut, and it is finally shaped ready for assembling. This is press work, done in four or five of the heavy power presses (40 ton) at the rate of 1,200 pieces per hour. When sufficient of one part are finished, the presses are stopped, out come the tools, new ones are fitted up and another part goes through in mass.

All the tinplate parts, the boiler, cab, firebox, and underframes were finished in this way and, on the assembly table, they met the heavier motion parts, such as the valve gear, which had been pressed out of thicker metal on more powerful presses, and also the solid parts such as chimneys, domes, buffers and wheels. These were cast in a special anti-friction aluminium alloy in steel moulds and were finished and polished on lathes and polishers. In the assembling room the locomotive bodies moved round, gradually nearing completion until only the mechanism and driving wheels were missing.

The manufacture of the clockwork motor was far more complex, with the steel side-plates being pressed out on the heaviest presses. Gear wheels were pressed out as discs from hard brass sheets and then the teeth were cut on a special machine, the gear blanks being arranged on a mandrel in groups of 30 to 100 at a time depending upon the size of the wheel. Once all the parts were made the mechanism was assembled and one of the last operations was putting in the spring, inserted by a special winding machine. Finally :

> *The six-coupled driving wheels are attached to the mechanism and it is tested on the track for freedom of run and ability to pull a load. Having passed all the tests satisfactorily it is fitted into the locomotive body, the valve motion adjusted, and the complete locomotive goes through the hands of the finishing department, who touch up any little chip or scratch, which may have been made during assembling. The whole body is now sprayed with varnish and placed in a special drying oven, which permanently hardens the finish.*
>
> *Before boxing, each locomotive must also undergo tests and any one found unsatisfactory in power and speed of run and ability to negotiate curves, is rejected.*
>
> *So now you know that before your model locomotive reaches you, through the medium of the toy shop, it has been through a pretty rough time!*

Today, these and all the other model railway products of Bassett-Lowke are now truly collector's items, they are much cherished and exchange hands for large sums of money.

In 1933 the full size *Royal Scot* was exhibited by the LMS Railway Company at the Chicago World Exhibition. Having seen it, Mr. C Norvin Rinek, of Pennsylvania, could not rest until he had a replica of it in his own garden! He commissioned Bassett-Lowke to build a $7^1/_4$" gauge, $1^1/_2$ inches to the foot, scale model of this famous locomotive. It was designed by Henry Greenly for Bassett-Lowke.

The *Father* of Table Top Railways

Up to about 1918 a gentleman named Leon Rees was a partner in Eisenmann and Co., a company involved in the toy trade. After 1918 he left that company to start his own business L Rees & Co. Ltd, based at Pinner in Middlesex, and in so doing acquired the agency for Bing of Nuremberg products for the United Kingdom and the British Empire, excluding Canada. How this came about is not known but there was a close working relationship between WJ and Leon Rees, especially with regard to improving the range of gauge '0' and '1' traditional British models. There was a positive demand for better realism. Frank Rees (Leon Rees' son), who worked at both Bing and L Rees & Co. Ltd from 1926 until 1964, recalled that :

It was about this time (1922) that WJ came up with the idea of a table top railway which was immediately given the gauge '00'. This was then manufactured by Bing's, both in clockwork and electric, and the range was supervised by WJ .... I can well remember going with the rest of the family and my father, driving his first Model T Ford, to visit WJ at Northampton.

WJ was thus the father of '00' gauge railways but sadly the name of Bassett-Lowke was not to be behind the exploitation of this new concept and spiralling demand in later years. This first system is said to have been designed by Henry Greenly. In the late 1920's, WJ's German friends Stefan and Franz Bing experienced severe business problems and they had already lost their manufacturing for Bassett-Lowke. They set up a new toy manufacturing company, in association with Oppenheimer & Erlanger, trading under the name if Trix and WJ persuaded them to produce a new '00' gauge table top railway system, more comprehensive than the first one. Bassett-Lowke, as sole concessionaires, placed this on the market in 1935. It was an enormous success and sales exceeded all WJ's expectations, helped enormously by the fact that the product was linked to the name of Bassett-Lowke. There was a problem in that the Germans favoured heavy flanged wheels whereas the UK market was moving towards a much finer scale. WJ failed to convince them to change their outlook but nevertheless Trix-Twin as it became known was a great success. The new system made up for the decline in Gauge '0' and the period up to 1939 was a profitable one as a result.

With the onslaught of war looming and with WJ's friends Franz Bing and S Kahn (who worked for Trix) both being Jewish, WJ was able to use his contacts on the continent and get them both over to this country. Business was set up in Clerkenwell Road, London, as Trix Ltd with WJ was a Director. With the Trix range being of continental prototypes, WJ persuaded them to produce a range of British trains marketed as *Bassett-Lowke Scale Models* being manufactured by Precision Models a wing of

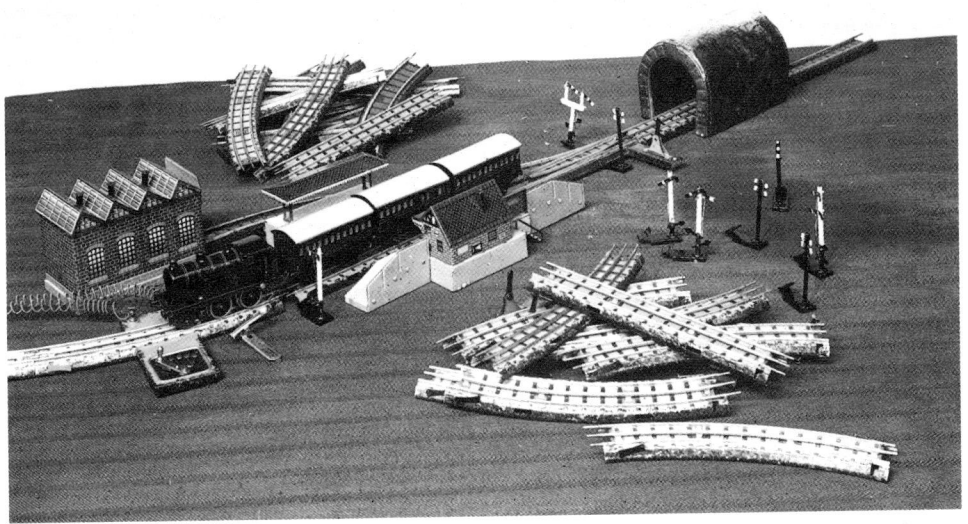

The first stage of WJ's idea of producing a table top railway, designated '00' gauge, came in 1922 when Bing produced the first train set of this size, in both clockwork and electric. The above set was advertised in the Toby magazine in 1925 for 8/- post free (40p).

RailRomances Collection

A photograph of the prototype '00' gauge Trix-Twin German 4-6-2 Pacific locomotive, being developed in 1936. At this stage it still had a lot of details missing including the spoked wheels. It was far away from the superbly detailed models which were to be made by other manufacturers in later years.

Bob Burgess Collection

Trix Ltd and Bassett-Lowke. After the War there was a failure by Trix, despite WJ's attempts, to recognise that a change to a more scale appearance was required to compete with their rivals Hornby. Precision Models ended up in liquidation and despite attempts by three other purchasers Trix died leaving the market open to Hornby.

Most model railway enthusiasts of the era will at some time have bought a copy of *The Model Railway Handbook*, the first edition of which came into being in 1906. WJ decided that there was a need for an inexpensive small book covering all aspects and with up-to-date guidance for the hobby, mainly to avert the large amount of correspondence that he had started to receive from amateurs seeking advice. He said at the time :

> *No apology is either required, or tendered, for the publication of this brochure, since the majority of manufacturing firms, in dealing direct with amateurs, find their correspondence seriously increased in courteously replying to the large number of queries arising out of the goods they supply.*
>
> *During the early years of the writer's connection with model engineering thousands of communications bearing on the subject passed through his hands, and had this book been available, much of the correspondence they entailed would doubtless have been saved. Therefore, within these pages, such required information on the subject of model locomotives and railways is freely accorded in a generalised and instructive form.*

WJ's principle was simple; tell them the answer to everything they are likely to ask, they will stop writing to you and at the same time they generate a profit instead of taking up the firm's time! Although written in his own name, it did contain contributions from other experts in particular

Henry Greenly, who also signed the earlier copies alongside WJ. It was published by Bassett-Lowke.

The first edition was stapled with a thin cover and cost 6d (2½p). The next three editions were also stapled, and then it was decided to enlarge the fifth one from 96 to 142 pages with plenty of photographs and additions to the text. Cecil J Allen, the author and well known model railway expert, designed the first four covers with the next four being designed by Kenneth S Cullen and with these the distinctive Bassett-Lowke style of lettering came into being. Another artist who did covers for this popular little book was E W Twining. In 1940, the 13th edition was issued and was a totally revised version with the collaboration of Cecil J Allen and Roland Fuller. It was re-written post-war in 1948 when WJ commented that :

> *It is most gratifying to find after the long standstill caused by the war that the interest in the hobby is even greater than in pre-war days, not only in England but also in the U.S.A. and on the Continent.*

He also expressed his opinion at this time that despite the increasing popularity of the smaller gauge '00', it was having no effect on the gauge '0' market. In the very near future this situation was to change with increased competition from Hornby in both the gauge '0' and '00' markets. What would have pleased WJ was that the name Bassett-Lowke has always been associated with quality, right up to the present day.

WJ was a prolific writer and producer of sales literature. Over the years individual catalogues were produced for *Model Railways '0' and '1' Gauge*, *Model Railways 2" and 2 ½" Gauge*, *Garden and Miniature Railways 3 ½" to 15" Gauge*, *Stationary Engines*, *Model Engineering*, and *Ship Models*. Their design and layout was what you would expect from a man of perfection and today they are very much collectors items. The covers were well designed and colourful, conveying WJ's philosophy of *fitness for purpose* in design. Apart from sales literature numerous brochures were written by WJ on various aspects of model railways, all helping to ensure that his name and that of Bassett-Lowke was always at the forefront of what was going on. The ultimate production was perhaps *Fifty Years of Model Making*, the booklet produced in 1949 to celebrate the 50th Anniversary of the Company.

> *Perhaps the best-known name in the world of model railways is that of Bassett-Lowke and any book written by him is sure of a warm welcome.*
>
> Woodworker, December 1940

In 1913 a fleet of nine large scale model battleships were constructed for the Imperial Services Exhibition held at Earls Court, London. The fleet was tested on the river Nene, at Northampton, on the 17th May of that year and was reviewed by the Mayor. Each one was 30ft long and was controlled by two men.

RailRomances Collection

Colour Supplement

This colour supplement has been sponsored by Northampton Borough Council, the 78 Derngate Trust, RailRomances and other anonymous sponsors.

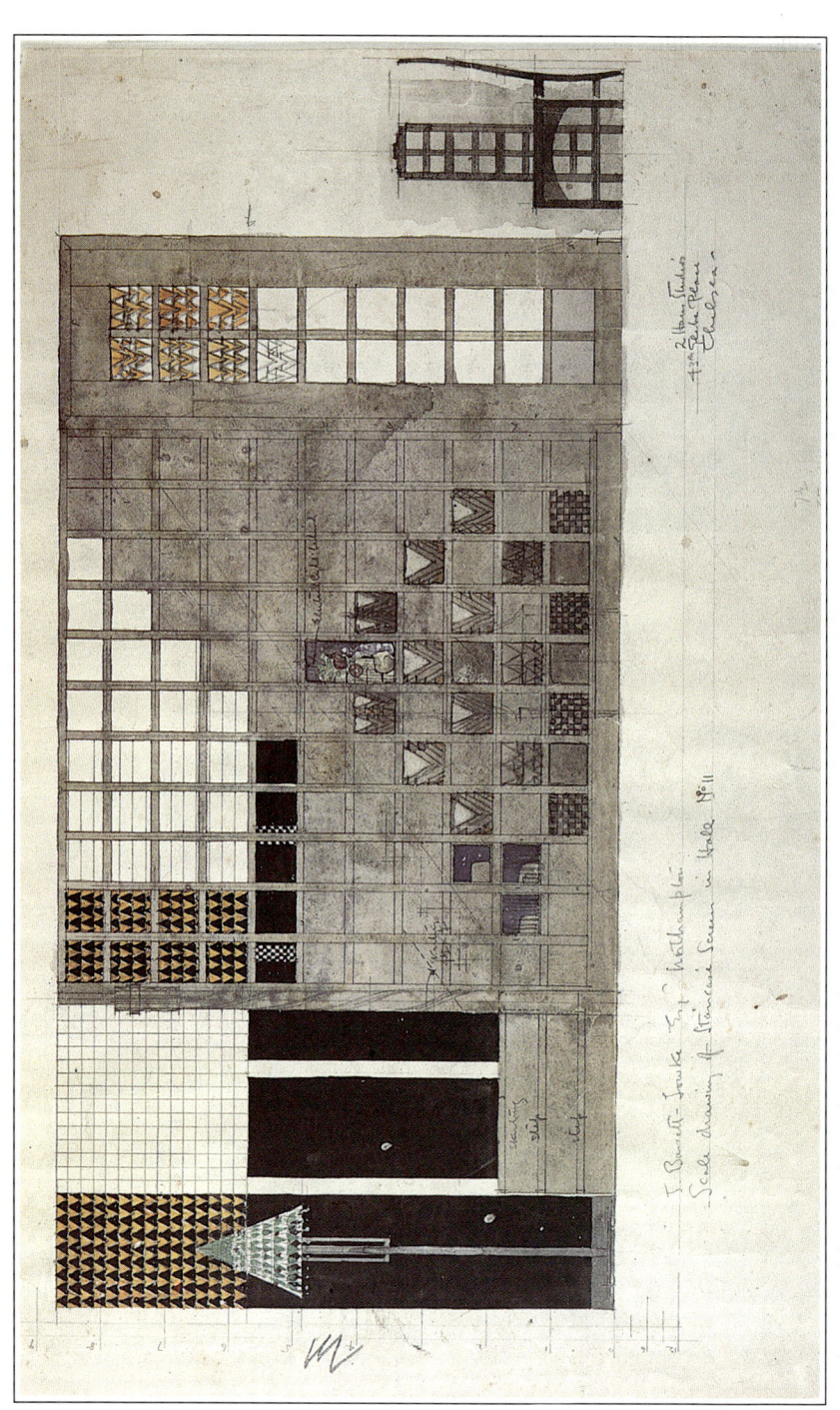

The original drawing, by Mackintosh, for the staircase screen in the lounge-hall of 78 Derngate. © Hunterian Art Gallery, University of Glasgow

The reproduction of the lounge-hall at 78 Derngate, showing the staircase screen as it appeared when built. The design by Mackintosh was distinctly futuristic in character for 1917. The walls, screen and ceiling were described as dull velvety black, with the floor stained black and polished and furniture to match. For such a small room, it was a very bold decision but, about three years later, the decoration was changed to a less harsh design.

Glasgow School of Art Collection

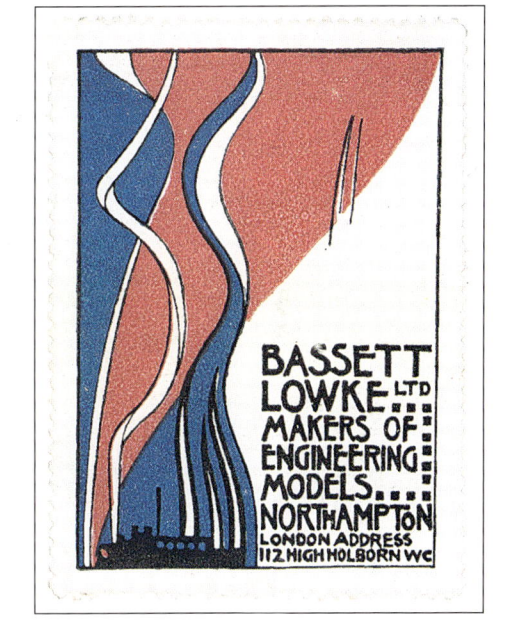

Advertising label designed by Mackintosh for Bassett-Lowke c. 1921

© Hunterian Art Gallery, University of Glasgow.

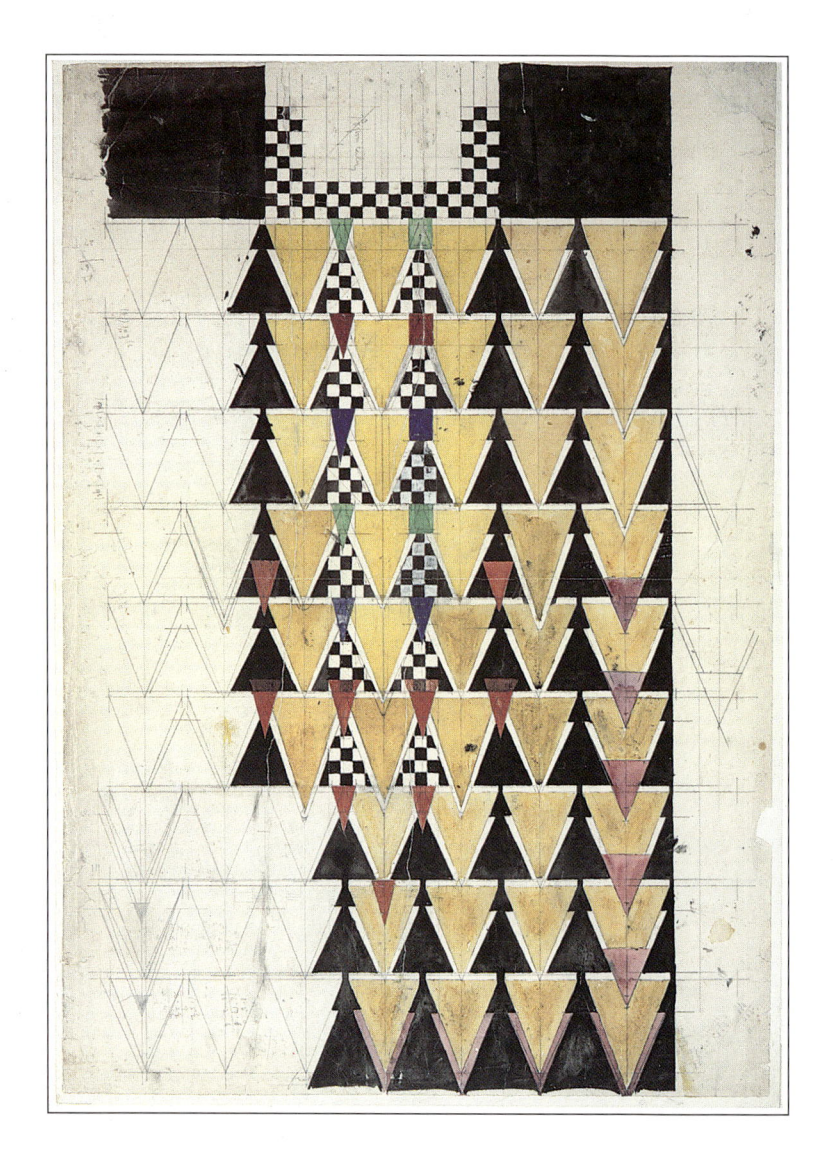

The design, by Charles Rennie Mackintosh in 1916, for the wall frieze stencil in the lounge-hall of 78 Derngate. Set against black walls, it was richly coloured with triangular motifs in gold, vermilion, blue, green, grey and white. The effect was at once rich and gay and yet quiet and peaceful.
  © Hunterian Art Gallery, University of Glasgow, Mackintosh Collection.

The reconstruction of the guest bedroom at 78 Derngate, with the original furniture designed by Mackintosh, currently on display at the Hunterian Museum and Art Gallery, Glasgow. It vividly illustrates the boldness of the wall decoration and richness of the furnishing.

© Hunterian Art Gallery, University of Glasgow, Mackintosh Collection

Wenman Joseph Bassett-Lowke
1877 - 1953

Janet Bassett-Lowke Collection

John G (Jack) Sears (1870-1916), who was founder of the True Form Boot Company, Northampton, became a close friend of W J Bassett-Lowke through their mutual interest in model railways. He encouraged Bassett-Lowke to expand and open a shop in London. When Bassett-Lowke became a limited company in 1909, Jack Sears became its first Chairman and remained so until he died in 1916 at the age of 46.

Courtesy Jack G S Sears

A painting of the front elevation of 'New Ways', Northampton, designed for W J Bassett-Lowke in 1924 by Professor Dr. Peter Behrens, the celebrated German architect.

Private Collection

A characterization of W J Bassett-Lowke for his 1935-36 Christmas card, by artist Ernest Noble, depicting the always smartly dressed WJ, never a thing out of place and wherever he travelled his cine camera at the ready to record events.

Janet Bassett-Lowke Collection

What the Engine Driver Sees!
FROM W.J.BASSETT-LOWKE & Co
NEW
WAYS
1927
WITH THE SEASONS GREETINGS FROM W.J.BASSETT-LOWKE NORTHAMPTON
1825
1925
100 YEARS CANNOT IMPROVE ON THE OLD WISH A MERRY CHRISTMAS & A HAPPY NEW YEAR
FROM W.J.BASSETT-LOWKE, NORTHAMPTON.
A CHRISTMAS TIME GREETING
from Mr & Mrs Bassett-Lowke New Ways · Northampton
WHYNNE
'NEW WAYS' greets you in the Old Way
A MERRY CHRISTMAS AND A HAPPY NEW YEAR
This crazy WORLD
this is the festive season
-mills standing idle
greetings from W.J. BASSETT-LOWKE NORTHAMPTON
W.J.BASSETT-LOWKE & Co.
MODEL MANUFACTURERS
NORTHAMPTON ENG.
SPECIALITIES
"NEW-WAYS" WESTON ROAD NORTHAMPTON
CHRISTMAS 1944
WJ BASSETT-LOWKE AND Co.
NORTHAMPTON.

A selection of the many Christmas cards, business cards and labels, designed for W J Bassett-Lowke over the years by several prominent artists. The earliest is the 'What the engine driver sees' order acknowledgement card which is pre 1909.

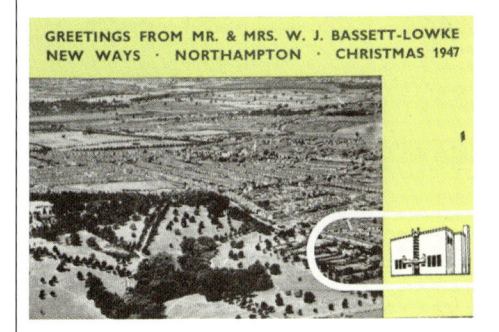

Janet Bassett-Lowke Collection

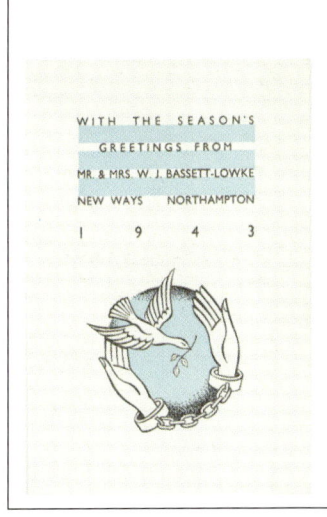

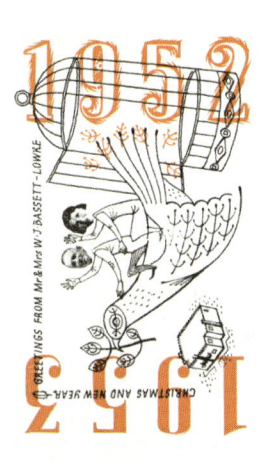

Wenman Joseph Bassett-Lowke

A triptych portrait of W J Bassett-Lowke painted by John Archibold Alexander Berrie.

Courtesy Northampton Borough Council
Central Museum

'Travel'

Executed by Philip Green, May 1928, specially for W J Bassett-Lowke and depicting the main elements of travel.

Janet Bassett-Lowke Collection

In 1909, Miniature Railways of Great Britain Ltd., an associate company of Bassett-Lowke which specialised in building miniature railways, exhibited the 15" gauge 'Atlantic' locomotive ENTENTE CORDIALE *at the International Exhibition, Nancy, and were awarded a gold medal.*

Janet Bassett-Lowke Collection

Above, a line was opened at Rhyl, North Wales, in 1911 (see page 44). Here 'Little Giant' locomotive PRINCE EDWARD OF WALES is seen with a full load of holidaymakers. Below, W J Bassett-Lowke's attention was drawn to a derelict narrow gauge railway in the Lake District in 1915. This was taken over and rebuilt as a 15" gauge line to become the Ravenglass and Eskdale Railway. Locomotive COLOSSUS is seen here at Prospect Point with a train of Bassett-Lowke 4-wheel carriages and a capacity payload. c 1918. Both lines are still running.

RailRomances Collection

Bassett-Lowke 7¼" gauge Great Central Railway locomotive IMMINGHAM *drawn by Viennese artist Joseph Danilowatz in 1938. The drawing was originally used on the front cover of the book 'Liliputbahnen' by Ing. Dr. Walter Straub, who was assisted by W J Bassett-Lowke.*

Chapter Ten

Wonderful Models

*Let no man that intendeth to build settle his
Fancie upon a draught of the works on paper,
without a Modell of the whole structure*

Sir Henry Wotton 1664

It is outside the context of this book to write about the thousands of models made by Bassett-Lowke, but there were some marvellous and out of the ordinary ones which I will single out in this chapter to illustrate the versatility of the business over the span of WJ's lifetime.

From Blackpool to Port Sunlight

The first major architectural model was made in 1912 for the Corporation of Blackpool and was displayed in the Bureau of Information, High Holborn, London. Built to a scale of 40ft to one inch, it showed the town and sea front, including the famous piers, the great wheel, and of course Blackpool Tower. The central pier contained 10,800 separate parts to reproduce the detail of the ironwork alone. To complete the scene, all the buildings were internally illuminated with electric light, in the sea was a model of a Corporation boat approaching the pier, and in the air was one of a Bleriot monoplane.

In the middle of constructing this model, WJ's architectural modeller decided to emigrate to the USA. At the time, Ernest W Twining's business was not doing very well and WJ put a proposition to him to carry on with the model of Blackpool. The success of the Blackpool model led to a fully detailed architectural model of Lever Brothers', the soap manufacturers, famous Port Sunlight complex and village, followed by an equally impressive model of Immingham Docks near Grimsby built for the Great Central Railway's stand at an exhibition in Ghent in Belgium. WJ found Twining a permanent studio for his needs at the rear of the J T Lowke yard, and here he took control of architectural modelling for the firm, although he was never to become part of the Bassett-Lowke Company. Twining worked for the firm on the production of a large number of very fine models, right up to the 1940s when he joined the Bristol Aeroplane Company.

The Battleship Fleet

The first contract which merits attention as possibly one of the largest the firm carried out in the early days, was a fleet of working model battleships constructed for the Imperial Services Exhibition held at Earls Court in 1913. The fleet was tested on the river Nene at Northampton and was reviewed by the Mayor of Northampton on May 17th 1913, the day before their despatch to London. My father told me he had been the manoeuvrer of one of the front vessels on that day.

There were nine large vessels, some over 30 feet in length and each one controlled by two men. Electric motors and accumulators supplied propelling power, and the controls enabled the ships to be moved about just like the real vessels. The big guns could be fired, flag signals made, and searchlights shone and moved across the water.

Edward W Hobbs, A.I.N.A., the firm's naval architect, who was at that time a member of staff at the firm's London branch, carried out the whole of the design work. This was one of the most important pieces of model work Bassett-Lowke had yet undertaken and the task was completed and passed by the clients in just 8 weeks. The *Fleet* was transported by Pickfords to Earls Court, its movement being reported in the *Commercial Motor* for the 29th May 1913.

Certainly, the publicity generated in connection with the realistic display at Northampton was said, at the time, to be unique in the annals of the press. Practically every national paper printed photographs and reports of this spectacle. For the duration of the Earls Court Exhibition, this *Fighting Review* was the highlight of the whole show. What a feather in the cap of Edward Hobbs, who designed the majority of the firm's model sailing and power boats and work of a similar nature at that time. This particular enterprise was a mighty commission to have been carried out during the early formative years of Bassett-Lowke Ltd.

The Queen's Dolls House

A special assignment in which Bassett-Lowke Ltd played a small part was in supplying certain items for the world's most famous Dolls House built for Queen Mary in 1924. The idea of presenting a Dolls House to Queen Mary was conceived by Princess Marie Louise, first cousin of King George V. This monumental project was designed and carried through by the famous architect Sir Edwin Lutyens. He was architect of the British Pavilion of the celebrated Paris Fair of 1900, the City plan and Viceroy's House in New Delhi (the most extensive British building constructed since Christopher Wren's St Paul's Cathedral) and the Cenotaph in Whitehall, three peaks of excellence, besides the exquisite Dolls House. His life was crowded with notable architectural works accomplished during the years of this century up to 1943.

This wonderful Dolls House was created in a room in his own home and was being made there for the best part of two years. It must have been the project of all projects that he tackled and may possibly prove to have been the most popular commission of his life.

Sir Edwin consulted and enlisted the help of 1,500 experts and was the ultimate perfectionist in deciding that so many of the tiny artefacts should be working models. The electric lights switched on, there was hot and cold water, the lavatories flushed, the clocks ticked, and there were miniature keys which opened the many doors in the model building. One very special item was the miniature gramophone, which could be wound up and which played *The National Anthem, Rule Britannia* and *Home Sweet Home*.

There were 40 rooms, and in the nursery was the tiniest model railway in the world made by Bassett-Lowke. It was on an oval track with a 4-6-0 tender locomotive, two bogie carriages and a station, named appropriately *Windsor*. The firm also supplied, as concessionaires for Ernest Twining Models,

WJ was amongst the 1,500 people who contributed towards the world's most famous Dolls House, which was built for Queen Mary in 1924. This is part of the Day Nursery and shows the model train set, built to $^1/_{12}{}^{tb}$ scale, together with a station aptly named WINDSOR. *It was undoubtedly the smallest train set Bassett-Lowke ever made.*

The Royal Collection © 1999 Her Majesty The Queen

model cars to Daimler and the Lanchester Motor Co. who presented these for the garages attached to the Dolls House. They were a 40 HP 1922-23 Lanchester Limousine and a Daimler Station Bus with a shooting brake body. Much work was done on the Dolls House by Twining Models, including a miniature of a fully rigged ship of war named *Royal George*, and possibly one of the smallest models he ever made. Twinings also supplied a model of a Sunbeam 20/60 HP open tourer and a 40/50 HP Rolls-Royce Silver Ghost limousine-landaulet for presentation by the manufacturers.

Bassett Lowke also made 33 household items of equipment and furnishings and was honoured to be among the chosen few to help in the creation of this lovely gift for the Queen. In the first place it was a special present to Her Majesty by a number of well wishers who hoped it would benefit the charities helped by Queen Mary. In this respect the Dolls House was exhibited at the British Empire Exhibition at Wembley in 1924, and later at the 1925 Ideal Home Exhibition. It was then moved to its special room in Windsor Castle, where it has been on regular display to the public ever since, giving much pleasure to visitors, the children particularly, but also to the many of all ages who value perfection in miniature. A painting competition for children was organised by the British Charities Association, in conjunction with the unveiling of the Dolls House, to help hospitals and they offered 100 prizes. The prizes were dolls houses for the girls and a Bassett-Lowke train set for the boys!

After the Dolls House was completed, the head of each company participating in the building of the Dolls House received a letter from Queen Mary thanking them personally.

A Railway for a Rajah

In the early days after the Great War, the London Branch reported that H H The Maharajah of Patiala had visited them with an entourage of three cars, Indian ladies and secretaries, and that they had dealt with an order.

East mingles with West, as in WJ's words:

To that well known address, 112 High Holborn, WC1 came the two young Princes of Patiala with their Father to order a complete model railway - no elephants or a cavalcade of horsemen, nor dressed in flowing robes (but certainly with an entourage!) as His Highness had decided there was no finer gift one can make to a son than the gift of a real railway.

The choice lay between three types. In $7^{1}/_{4}$" gauge there was the well known London & North Western Railway *George the Fifth* 4-4-0 express locomotive, which would haul 8 adults or as many as a dozen youngsters, and *Immingham* a 4 - 6 - 0 Pacific type based upon J G Robinson's design for the erstwhile Great Central Railway. In $9^{1}/_{2}$" gauge, 2" to the foot scale, there was the popular Great Northern Railway 4 - 4 - 2 Atlantic type combining a particularly handsome appearance with proven performance and which could haul loads of 25 passengers or more.

This latter model was the Princes' choice and two *Atlantics* were ordered plus two sets of castings, presumably to build two more in India. The locomotive and tender, designed by Henry Greenly, were nearly 10 feet long, whilst the whole model weighed three-fifths of a ton.

The rolling stock supplied consisted of four replica open 10 ton goods wagons each fitted with two seats and two high capacity wagons with bogie wheels also fitted with seats. The Princes would thus be able to carry 16 passengers at least. Half a mile of track with six points operated by hand levers was supplied but no sleepers were included as these could be readily obtained out in India. The track was to be laid in the grounds of the College at Lahore, where it was anticipated the Prince would still be studying. Afterwards this track was taken up and re-laid by local labour, supplied by the State Railway Company, in the grounds of the Maharajah's palace in Patiala State where he hosted his Royal garden parties. Two tracks were laid in a circle on the huge lawns. The wagons were modified in such a way that serving dishes could be placed on top with burning coke beneath to keep the food hot. The trains would be driven round in opposite directions and anyone wanting food would stop it and be served. Similar, but on a larger scale, to the Maharaja of Gwalior's silver table top railway and perhaps even inspired by it. It is interesting to note that the Maharaja's son called at the London shop several years later and advised the staff that the railway was still running well!

The railway was at the Palace until 1948 and in 1955 it was sold to a rich businessman in Kanpur, Mr. S M Bashir, who re-laid it around his own home. The railway ran until 1960 after which it was put into store and in 1997 the two locomotives were sold, still boasting their original paintwork but in a bad condition, to another resident of Kanpur who now hopes to fully restore them.

The task of making the complete train, and also a model of the battle cruiser H.M.S. Hood, is reputed to have been completed by Bassett-Lowke in just over three weeks. Thus East and West met, as sometimes they do, with real understanding and the result was a railway fit for the son of a Rajah! Other Indian Rajahs who came to Bassett-Lowke's were the Maharajahs of Jodhpur, Mayerbhang and Cooch Behar; a high honour for the firm at the time. In December 1925 the Maharaja of Jodhpur ordered a $9^{1}/_{2}$"

H.H. The Maharajah of Patiala visited the London shop (c.1920) to purchase a miniature steam railway for his two young Princes. An order was placed for two 9½" gauge Great Northern Railway 'Atlantic' locomotives, plus castings for another two, and rolling stock to match. Above, one of the locomotives is seen at the Bassett-Lowke works minus its tender. Both locomotives still survive in India.

Bob Burgess Collection

gauge railway to run over a half mile circuit in the palace grounds and connecting with a lake. It was reported that *the lakeside station is to be modelled on Kings Cross*. Very ambitious for 9½" gauge I would think!

The Wembley Exhibition

The great Wembley Exhibition of 1924 and 1925 merits special mention. WJ with his wide experience of creating varied and striking exhibits said that never before to his knowledge had so many models been on display together at the same exhibition.

Ship models at the Exhibition made by Bassett-Lowke included for the White Star line the *Majestic*, *Olympic* and *Cerannic* and for the Royal Mail Steam Packet, the *Ohio*, *Almanzora*, *Oraca* and *Ordana*. The Canadian Pacific Railway Co. had a model railway track laid on elevated shelving around the inside walls of their large pavilion. Two trains were running continuously all day. For the Whisky Distillers Association a large model showed the method of production of their famous spirit. There were the Cardiff docks of the G.W.R., the town and harbour of Durban, the Hayes Works of the Gramophone Company, the Hornimans Tea Plantation, the Chloride Electrical Company at Clifton and the Boots Pure Drug Company.

The Down Special

The General Post Office commissioned Bassett-Lowke to build a large working gauge '1' model railway, based upon the *Down Special* Postal train from Euston to Aberdeen. It was intended to illustrate the working of the Travelling Post Office.

It was first shown at Radiolympia in 1934. It was 120 feet long and consisted of double track arranged for continuous running, with 12ft diameter loops at each end. Most of one loop was in the form of a hill tunnel giving scope for artistic scenic effects and a modern type station occupied the centre of the track. At two positions on the track, scale model pick-up and delivery apparatus was fitted, enabling the model train to deliver and collect the mail sacks automatically. The locomotives, rolling stock, signals, and railway buildings were all built to 10mm scale. The locomotives L.M.S. *Royal Scot* and *Black Watch*, fitted with special electric motors, ran a distance of over 125 miles at Radiolympia and created immense public interest.

Also in 1934, a working scale model of the London Underground system was produced for the then newly formed London Transport Board. It was exhibited at Charing Cross Underground Station and was designed by Henry Greenly.

The Grand Union Canal

A working model of a canal was built for the Grand Union Canal Company for their stand at the 1936 British Industries Fair. This was over 17ft long and represented a typical canal scene, from green fields and hedges and suburban villas to a canalside factory and its loading activities. The canal contained nine gallons of real water, a working motor barge, and hand-operated lock, automatically changing the level of the canal by means of a concealed centrifugal pump. The model was planned to demonstrate to the public the advantages of canal transport and the facilities available for cargo transportation on the English canal system.

The Coal Mine

Another tribute to Bassett-Lowke workmanship and design was the giant model coal mine that was made in the workshops of Bassett-Lowke Ltd under the direction of Captain A Lockhart, R.N. It was built to the order of the Mining Association of Great Britain, for exhibiting in the Government Pavilion at the 1938 British Empire Exhibition in Glasgow. The whole model, built in the amazingly short period of four and a half months, was housed in a very large shed, the roof of which had to be raised to accommodate it.

The working model constructed to a scale of one inch to 4 feet, represented 700ft of geological strata below ground with two coal seams being worked to demonstrate all the latest and most efficient methods of mining. The surface workings, reached by a gallery, were laid out to represent 11 acres with everything from shower baths to coal trucks, and was illuminated and worked with perfect realism. It was in fact the dream model of every mechanically minded man or boy, as well as being of interest and value to the engineer as a practical model of a utopian mine. The largest of its kind in

WONDERFUL MODELS   143

In 1934, Bassett-Lowke built a working model, in gauge '1', of the General Post Office's travelling Post Office for display at the Radio Olympia Exhibition. It had two positions on the track with pickup and delivery apparatus to demonstrate the automatic collection and delivery of mail. Two L.M.S. locomotives, ROYAL SCOT and BLACK WATCH were supplied to operate the trains.

J Bassett-Lowke Collection

A working model for the Grand Union Canal Company was made in 1934. Much ingenuity was needed to create a realistic model with real water, working locks, and moving barges. Built to a scale of $1/48^{th}$, it was over 17ft long and demonstrated the facilities for cargo transportation on the English canal system.

J Bassett-Lowke Collection

the world, this exhibit must have been regarded, apart from its technical value, as an important achievement in model engineering.

Glass panels set into the side of the seams and strata gave sectional and longitudinal views of the general layout and working of an up to date coal mine. The first panel showed board and pillar workings by which the coal is cut out of intersecting tunnels, the whole making a honeycomb of cutting so that the remaining squares of coal act as supporting pillars to prevent subsidence under the colliery workings or any other buildings on the surface. The other panels showed the more usual method of advancing along the coal face and allowing the roof rock to fall in behind the workings except where there were connecting galleries.

A view of part of the surface workings of the $1/4$ inch to the foot working model of a coal mine, built for the Mining Association for their display at the Glasgow Exhibition, 1938.
RailRomances Collection

The four methods of conveyance were all demonstrated in working form, namely by a belt conveyor, shuttles, an endless ropeway to which the trucks are hooked and pulled along, or by pit ponies. One of the cleverest and most fascinating points was the shaft with its express truck lifts and the mass of railway points converging on the bottom shaft. Other views below the surface include the transformer housing, water pumps, pony stables and such intricate details as ventilation screens, notice boards and even the thick rubber gloves which had to be hung up near all electric switchboards or controls. The surface level was up a high flight of steps, where there was an 11 acres colliery field, beautifully laid out, with every type of plant modelled and the buildings looking exceedingly lifelike. An intricate network of rails, carrying 90 assorted coal trucks and two model locomotives interlaced the whole area.

The huge bath house with the roof sliced open showed row upon row of perfectly finished shower baths and each floor was fitted with 650 lockers. From the pit-head the coal could be followed through its final stages. First in the tippler house where the best and cobbles are sorted out and shot into trucks and then up into the washery where the smaller coal is water-washed and graded right down to peal and duff, the latter being little more than a coal powder. Not only was this model the most intricate and interesting in layout and design but in coal mining it was this last factor, the ability to sort and wash for use the finer grades, which made all the difference between profitable or loss making workings.

The work was carried out under the supervision of Mr P F Claydon, Works Manager, who went with WJ to Germany to see a similar but smaller model at the Dusseldorf Exhibition, to ensure a successful working model by their own firm. After it had been disassembled the model was transported in sections by train to Glasgow and after the Exhibition there, it toured the country starting at Charing Cross Underground Station in London.

The Silver Train

A solid silver train was made in 1906 for the Maharajah Sir Madhava Rao Scindia of Gwalior who ruled over one of the best run states in India. His passion was railways from full size down to models.

It was said to represent the State Railway of Scindia (North West India). In all, 250 feet of 3-rail electric solid silver rails, fixed to sleepers of polished teak, were laid out on the exceptionally large dining table in the centre of the banqueting hall of the palace. It ran up one side of the table within reach of guests, around a loop at the far end, and returned up the other side so that each and every guest had access to it. At the other end of the table the tracks disappeared into two tunnels and hence into the Royal kitchens. The Maharaja sat at the head of the table presiding over his guests and a complex control panel that bristled with switches and levers. He was effectively in total control. He could, with a flick of a switch, deprive a guest of his drink or dessert, in which case the trains went speeding past his waiting glass or plate. The silver train headed by a silver 4-4-0 engine with a 6-wheel tender having the letters G L R on the side (presumably standing for Gwalior Light Railway) pulled along seven wagons each holding a cut silver decanter filled with liqueur, or whatever the course might be. Each of the wagons bears a letter of the family name SCINDIA. It stopped automatically when a guest lifted out a dish or a decanter, moving on again when the article was replaced.

The then Prince of Wales (later Edward VIII), who was in the middle of an eight-month tour of the Orient, went to Gwalior in February 1922, as his father George V and his grandfather, Edward VII had done before him, to shoot tigers for a few days. Gwalior was to tigers in those days as Scotland is to grouse today. The Maharajah of Gwalior was unquestionably the greatest tiger impresario of all time.

In 1906, a solid silver train was made for the Maharaja of Gwalior and this was laid out on the banqueting table. The wagons were fitted with dishes or decanters and served each guest around the table according to his or her needs. In the 1930s, it was returned to Bassett-Lowke for overhaul and it still resides, in working order, in the Palace to this day.

J Bassett-Lowke Collection

Gwalior's imperial visitor was the most important that he had ever entertained, and the Prince arrived at Gwalior on the narrow gauge railway which had been among the Maharajah's improvements to his state and which continued to be one of his simple passions. He enjoyed driving the locomotive himself whenever possible. He died in 1925 and was succeeded on 5th June 1925 by Sir George Jivaji Rao aged 8, so it would have been during this reign that the silver train was sent back to England for a thorough over-haul. According to Bassett-Lowke records, it still runs around the Maharajah's banqueting table on the same silver rails on sleepers of polished teak, carrying foodstuffs and drink in the casket carriages.

At the time in the 1930's that the silver train came back to England for its spring-clean, both Ray Stutley and I were working at Bassett-Lowke Ltd. It was kept securely locked up except while the renovation work was being carried out, and only a few had the chance to see it for there was a man from the Indian Embassy on duty to keep watch over this valuable object. He was based at the Grand Hotel at the top of Kingswell Street, but most of the time was on guard over his precious charge, and saw it locked up every night.

Sir George Jivaji Scindia died in July 1961 and was succeeded by his son Mahav Rao Jiwagi Rao Scindia at that date, but at the end of 1970 the Maharajahs had been stripped of their Privy Purses. In 1988 there was a splendid marriage; an alliance between two of India's most powerful families Jyotiradityyarao Scindia, the 23-year old son of the Maharajah of Gwalior and Rajkumari Priyadarshini Raje, the 19-year old daughter of the Prince of Baroda. It was a splendid ceremony lasting nine days, three of which took place at Gwalior, and at the first banquet the silver train was still operating!

So the silver train of 1906 is still with the latest Maharajah of Gwalior and the passion for trains still lives on. May the liqueur laden Silver Train live on in the annals of the Scindia family; perhaps the most unusual model my Uncle's firm ever made.

Railways, Aeroplanes, and Cars

Bassett-Lowke built a very large quantity of scale model locomotives and rolling stock for the various railway companies and manufacturers, for both exhibition and design assistance. Beyer Peacock & Co. Ltd of Manchester, builders of the articulated Beyer-Garratt locomotive, were amongst the firm's best customers in this field. Numerous large-scale models were built for this company over the years, including an electrically operated fully detailed $1/16^{th}$ scale 4-6-4 + 4-6-4

A glass case model of the Harwich-Zeebrugge Train Ferry, built in 1925 for the London and North Eastern Railway Co. For the Antwerp Exhibition, in 1930, a much larger model was made where the trains were loaded on to the ferry which, when fully loaded, drew away from the quay.

Bob Burgess

Rhodesian Railways Beyer-Garratt for exhibition purposes. Aeroplanes were built for many of the airlines and cars for most of the manufacturers. An unusual model was one of the German *Graf Zeppelin* built for the Science Museum, London. The list is endless.

Many very finely detailed scale models were manufactured over the years for the locomotive manufacturers. This model, completed in July 1946, is a ³⁄₄" scale working model of a 4-6-4 + 4-6-4 Rhodesian Railways Beyer-Garratt locomotive, and is just one example of numerous such models built for Beyer Peacock & Co. Ltd. of Manchester.

RailRomances Collection

The full size LOCOMOTION No. 1, which was over a century old when this model was made, was still an imposing figurehead at Darlington station. This model is a 1¹⁄₂" scale, 7¹⁄₄" gauge, model built in 1934 for Robert Stephenson & Co., the makers of the original.

Bob Burgess Collection

Bassett-Lowke model railways were not just used for the pleasure of the enthusiast. Railway companies soon realised that they could be used for instructional purposes, such as signalling training. This 2" gauge layout, complete with comprehensive signalling, was built for the London and North Western Railway Company in 1908.

Bob Burgess Collection

Another model electric layout, gauge 2, under construction for the London & North Western Railway Co. in 1912.

RailRomances Collection

WONDERFUL MODELS   149

Training to be an engine driver? A Bassett-Lowke 9½" gauge 'Atlantic' locomotive with Captain C F Ward-Jones and his son, on their garden railway at Harness Grove, near Worksop. c. 1930s.
RailRomances Collection

Harry Franklin, WJ's partner, built this 10¼" gauge railway around the grounds of his home at Radwell, Bedfordshire. It was ¾ of a mile in length and had a station, tunnel, viaducts, bridges and even signalling. WJ related that 'a speed of no less than 25 miles per hour had been achieved on this line'.
RailRomances Collection

In 1938, a 10¼" gauge LMS 'ROYAL SCOT' 4-6-0 locomotive was built by Bassett-Lowke for the Marquis of Downshire for his railway at Easthamstead Park, Berkshire. Above, John Braunston, who was head of the boiler department, is seen working on the chassis . . . .

WONDERFUL MODELS 151

.... WJ views the progress as it is nearing the stage of final assembly. In the lower photographs, the locomotive is seen on test, prior to being painted, on Harry Franklin's railway at Radwell. WJ, as usual, is immaculately dressed for the occasion.

RailRomances Collection

Models in time of War

During World War I, the facilities of the Company were engaged principally in the production of master gauges for munitions manufacturing and models for war services such as training media, recognition or planning procedures. Starting in 1912 waterline models of warships of all the worlds' navies were supplied to the British Admiralty for recognition training. In 1939 the quantities ordered were increased substantially and supplemented by contracts with the Air Ministry, for whom the models were equally useful as an aid to identification from the air.

Soon after the outbreak of World War II Winston Churchill, then First Lord of the Admiralty (which was responsible for many service innovations), instructed that a special secret workshop should be established for constructing a working model of a special machine. This was later known as *White Rabbit*, a high-speed digger for digging trenches 15ft deep by 25ft wide, intended to stop tanks from passing. Bassett-Lowke were requested to install suitable equipment in the basement of the Pump Room at Bath (home town for a large Admiralty establishment) and to provide two men, who would be sworn to secrecy, to work there on the project and complete a model in six weeks. Work carried on, long enough for the model to demonstrate that the design was practical but, in the event, May 1940 showed that this kind of warfare was a thing of the past and the idea was scrapped. When it was tested, it was said that John Innes garden compost was used and this was purchased from various sources in small quantities so as not to arouse suspicion!

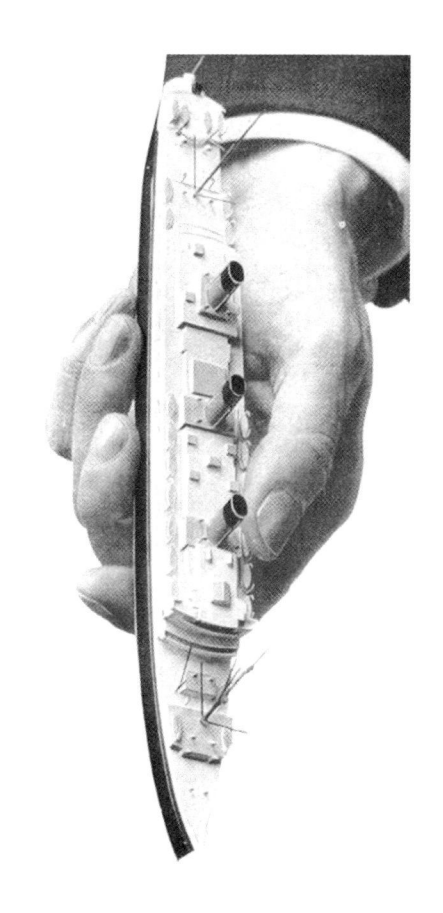

A talk by W J in 1945, at the close of the second World War, gave an interesting and remarkable review of how models had helped in time of war. This talk was transmitted over the Pacific service on September 6th 1945 and over the North America service on Friday and Saturday the 14/15th September of the same year. At this time I was married with a small child but was still working part-time for him and recall this talk being prepared.

The Navy used miniatures in the 1914-1918 war. Coast guards, submarine crews, and lookout officers on all the warships studied their own, the Allies', and the enemy ship types from models.

> *I stood at the door of what was once a ballroom, but on this occasion it was not filled with dancers and a swing band, but with quiet men in navy blue, grouped round a large glass tank filled with water, and intently watching the 15 foot model battleship floating there. Besides navy blue, there was quite a display of*

During the second World War, waterline model ships were manufactured in large quantities for the Admiralty and Royal Navy, being used for identification training and such like purposes.

J Bassett-Lowke Collection

Women were employed on the waterline ship models, working under the instruction of a skilled man to monitor their work. During the War, everyone was on overtime of two hours extra each day, including the office staff.

Ray Stutley Collection

gold braid, for the watching officers were senior ranks in the Senior Service and this was the only school of its kind in England - The Damage Control School.

The instructing officer was giving a demonstration. He touched a knob on the deck and said 'the ship has been holed in No.4 Compartment on the port side. What is the best action to take?' And as he spoke the vessel took a list to port. Pressing another knob he showed how the list could be best neutralised, and than went on to explain other points of technical interest.

The hull of this battleship was built of heavy gauge brass sheet, beaten and moulded to a skeleton wooden former. Bulkhead, valves and decks were riveted and soldered in the correct positions inside the hull and all joints made absolutely watertight. Special care was taken to scale the weight of the ship correctly and each compartment contained a watertight box equal in cubic capacity to the amount of machinery and stores contained in that particular compartment on the real vessel.

Every compartment on the model was separately controlled by an inlet valve from the deck, so that each could be flooded at will. The value of such a demonstration was that it could illustrate in miniature what happened if any one or more compartments on a ship were damaged and exactly which corresponding compartments it was necessary to flood in order to keep her on an even keel. In a real incident, correct counter action would mean the difference between sinking with all hands, or keeping afloat, maintaining fighting capacity and slowly getting to port for what might be only minor repairs. This is but one of the ways in which models, and model-makers, assisted in the war effort.

There is a tendency to regard models as *toys* and working models as *luxury toys* but that is a long way from the truth. Practically the whole of the invasion of France, in its early stages, was planned with models, down to the last detail. Before the invasion, the then Prime Minister, Winston Churchill, was provided with models of the enemy defences to enable him to discuss last minute preparations for D-Day, and many senior officers and admirals also used models to familiarise themselves with the details of the many types of landing ships and craft employed. Combined Operations Headquarters are said to have had the most up-to-date fleet of models of landing ships and craft in the world, including every type that had then been built.

The landing craft modelled for the planning of the invasion ranged from small fast craft used by officers and men only, to large carrying craft with opening bows carrying tanks and other heavy equipment, also converted liners for troop carrying. Of special note were the models of the Mulberry Harbour, with its caissons, pier head pontoons and blockships, all built to a scale of $1/48^{th}$ actual size. After the War in 1950, a further model of the Mulberry Harbour was made for the Arromanches Museum in France at a cost of £8,000.

With the project in miniature before them, Service chiefs were able to test their ideas and see where any weakness lay and where plans could be improved. The capacity of each type of craft was worked out and the method of loading. Amphibious warfare presented some completely new problems to those responsible for training. Sailors had to make themselves familiar with tanks, field guns, ambulances and all the paraphernalia of a military operation, starting by sea, and the army had to be trained in making the best use of all available ship space without interfering with the handling of the craft!

Bassett-Lowke played an important part during World War II in the preparations for the D-Day landings. Apart from supplying scale models of all the landing ships, they built a $1/48^{th}$ scale model of the Mulberry Harbour complete with its caissons, pier head pontoons and blockships.

Bassett-Lowke Society Collection

The models for this job were not what we would call exhibition or museum work. Great detail was not necessary; so long as we put on all the gear which might project and make loading difficult, the models were serving their purpose. The scale for them was for the most part $1/48$" to the foot. There must have been hundreds of types of craft and literally tens of thousands of models made just for this operation.

In World War II models were ordered by all branches of the Services for training and recognition purposes, for planning, for exhibition to inform the public and also for experimental work. The Navy, the Fleet Air Arm, and the R.A.F. all had to recognise a ship on sight, and they did not always have the chance to get a close view or make a leisurely examination. For weeks and months trainees were taught *recognition* by studying waterline models built to a scale that would approximate to a ship from say, three or more miles away.

These *recognition* models were usually made from hard wood with metal details. They were all made by hand and the chief tools used were the chisel, plane, saw, files of different sizes, pliers and that useful asset the safety razor blade! If the model was very tiny, for some details paper was used. For the funnels of ships the modeller often used thin tubes, but for the smaller ones paper was wrapped around a shaped template glued together and thoroughly dried, but before painting the Admiralty Inspector examined each one of the fleet lined up on the work bench. They then went to the paint shop for spraying in the correct shade of grey, and were finally packed, each in a separate box, with a label giving full details of scale and the boat inside. The success in producing each one of these small models depended on the skill and practice of the craftsman or woman, but they were generally made in batches of anything from six up to thirty models, the average time taken being three days per model.

The army was not behind in the use of models, in its training bases. One of its most important jobs was to build bridges; bridges to carry railways, motor transport, men and supplies. Many of the army's engineers were trained to build bridges by using models.

Most are probably familiar with the Bailey Bridge. It had only been developed during World War II, and was a valuable asset to our motorised forces. Models of this bridge were sent to nearly one hundred Army Training centres and to fighting fronts all over the world. Numbers were shipped to Burma and the Pacific.

Another large project undertaken by Bassett-Lowke, for the Ministry of Supply, was for the Railway Bridging School. WJ relates that :

> *In 1942 for the first time I visited an army training establishment in the north of England. It was a cold, wet windy day and the sappers were assembling a huge 150 ft steel railway bridge. Some of the joists they were handling weighed as much as three tons. I asked how long it took to erect this type of bridge '14 days' was the answer. Well that seemed pretty fair to me, especially in view of the weather conditions, which, after all, were probably not unlike actual field conditions.*

One of the most familiar developments during World War II was that of the Bailey Bridge. To facilitate and speed up training, Bassett-Lowke were commissioned to construct about 100 sets of miniature bridges in kit form, seen here in manufacture at the Northampton works with WJ inspecting the work (1942).

Bassett-Lowke Society Collection

Also in 1942, a different type of bridge called the Inglis Bridge was constructed by Bassett-Lowke for the Ministry.
Bassett-Lowke Society Collection

A large scale development project was undertaken by Bassett-Lowke for the Railway Bridging School during 1942/43 . . . .

. . . . to assist with the development of railway bridge erection, and to speed up training. WJ always took a very keen interest in this kind of work.
Bassett-Lowke Society Collection

This training takes a long time, but you can hardly expect the men to take as keen an interest in this wet and cold weather. It was therefore decided to try and speed up the men's training by the use of scale models.

A special large hall was built and a section of the railway line laid. A gap was left in the line to represent the river over which they would have to construct the bridge. Detailed scale models of each component of the bridge were made, so that the huge steel joist became a small replica that could be held in the hand, studied, then fitted and bolted into position.

The training procedure was that the parts comprising the complete bridge were loaded on to a model train in the correct order for building. At the site the components were unloaded in proper sequence

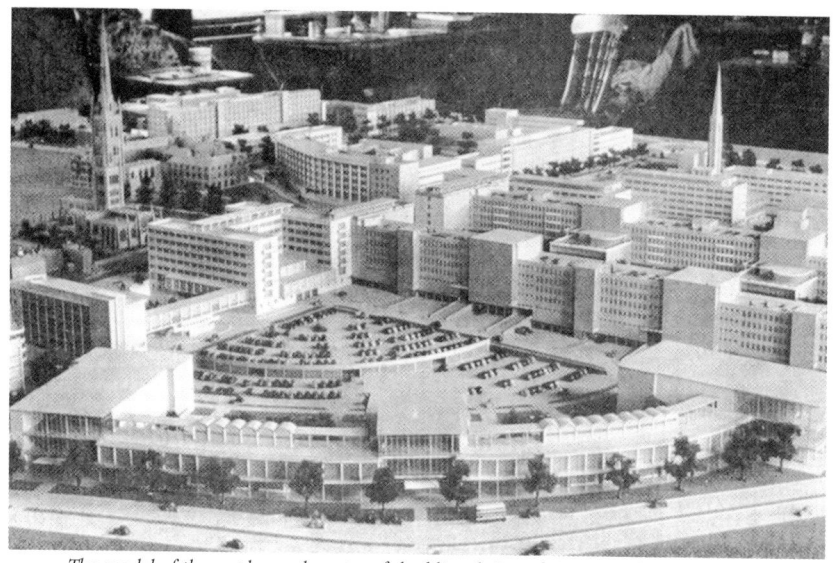

The model of the re-planned centre of the blitzed City of Coventry, built to a scale of 24ft to one inch, which was presented to the City by the MIDLAND DAILY TELEGRAPH.

J Bassett-Lowke Collection

and the bridge erected. Working in ideal dry conditions with miniature sections, producing a bridge 25ft long, the model bridge was a success and cut down the period of training considerably.

After VE Day production was switched over to models for post-war planning, such as the layouts of housing estates, town improvements, prefabricated and permanent houses, kitchen units and many new ideas for making the post-war world a more pleasant and easier place in which to live.

A new plan for the blitzed City of Coventry was modelled in all detail. It showed the proposed new shopping centre, cultural centre, car parks with miniature cars in them, playgrounds, trees and gardens; in fact, every little detail that can be shown to a small scale. Coventry was the first blitzed English city to be re-planned in detail after the war. Built to a scale of 24ft to the inch, the model was presented by Lord Iliffe, Director of the Midland Daily Telegraph, to the City of Coventry.

The firm had the honour of receiving thanks from two Prime Ministers for work done in the two World Wars. A letter from 10 Downing St. was sent on 6th September 1918.

> *Dear Mr Bassett-Lowke,*
>
> *I am exceedingly obliged to you for the submarine and standard ship models which you were good enough to send me, and beg you to accept my sincere thanks for the trouble you have taken in the matter.*
>
> *Yours very faithfully,*
>
> *D Lloyd George.*

Mr Winston Churchill wrote (c.1945) to Bassett-Lowke Ltd, acknowledging the presentation of a series of $1/192$nd scale models representing all types of landing craft used in the D-Day landing on the Normandy coast on June 6th 1944, the start of the Allied Invasion of Europe.

As you know, Commander Hunt brought to Chartwell the very fine landing craft models which you so kindly prepared for me and I now write to express my thanks for all the trouble you have taken in this matter.

Mr Churchill also sent to WJ, as a gift, a box of his well-known cigars.

To conclude this brief look at the model making activities that my uncle developed, one realises that it would have been difficult to visit any large company's headquarters or exhibition without seeing the name Bassett-Lowke somewhere! Finally, one model of particular interest to my sisters and me was a modern sunbathing lido, which was a particular pool in Northampton we used to frequent. In complete contrast was a scale model of the luxury swimming pool on the Canadian Pacific Railroad liner *Empress of Britain* scaled at 1" to the foot.

W J Bassett-Lowke examining the $1/8$ inch to the foot model of H.M.S. ANSON made for Swan Hunter & Wigham Richardson and completed January 1947.
J Bassett-Lowke Collection

All works of taste must bear a price in proportion to the skill, taste, time, expense and risk attending their manufacture. Those things called dear are, when justly estimated the cheapest. They are attended with much less profit to the maker than those things which everyone calls cheap.

John Ruskin

The Bassett-Lowke office outing to Harry Franklin's miniature railway at Radwell, Bedfordshire. Left to right are Joan Garrard [WJ's secretary], Ethel Wakelin, Miss Daniells ['Danny'], and the author in the white beret.
J Bassett-Lowke Collection

WJ driving one of Captain Holders 'Atlantic' locomotives [c.1930]which may be PETER PAN, used on the 9½" gauge Treasure Island Railway at Wembley in 1925 and, afterwards, converted to 10¼" gauge.
RailRomances Collection

Mrs. Bassett-Lowke and WJ with Captain Holder's re-built 10¼" 'Pacific' locomotive named AUDREY, seen here on Holder's railway at his home 'Keeping', near Beaulieu, Hampshire.
RailRomances Collection

Chapter Eleven

A Whirlwind Life

WJ in his personal life became interested in the Rotary movement. On April 12th 1921 he was present at the preliminary meeting with Northampton worthies C W Phipps, W P Cross, A E Marlow, M B Fullerton, Major J C Lewis, ex-Mayor of Northampton and Councillors F Kilby and S Adnitt. Dr P S Hichens and Colonel (later Sir) John Brown K C B, D S O, were unable to attend but had expressed a wish to join the Club. In June 1923, Vice President J H Marlow and Rotarian Bassett-Lowke attended an International Conference in Ostend. The Northampton Rotarians, as members of the Doddridge Travel Club, visited Zurich in June 1926 and it was reported that the arrangements were admirable in every way *in the hands of Mr. Bassett-Lowke*. On August 14th of that year, WJ organised another trip for Rotarians to visit the Northern Capitals calling at Stockholm, Bergen, Oslo, Copenhagen and Rotterdam. They sailed from Grimsby on the new 20,000 ton Orient liner *Otranto*, and returned to Tilbury on the 4th September. WJ was a prolific organiser of trips for the various organisations to which he belonged. It is said that one of the reasons for his high profile in the area of arranging trips was that in so doing he either secured a free place or a concessionary rate for himself – true entrepreneurial spirit!

In June 1928 WJ, with fellow Rotarian Ralph Smith, sailed on the transatlantic liner the *Baltic* for the United States, where they attended the Rotary International Conference at Minneapolis.

In 1935 the number of representatives of the Northampton Rotary Club at Margate must were led by their president WJ and secretary H Musk Beattie, along with Rotarians C F Allen, J L Holland and 11 other members, and all accompanied by their wives; perhaps a record attendance. Also under WJ's presidency, the first Ladies Night was held at the Masonic Hall, Princess Street, Northampton.

In 1932 the Rotarians founded an International Committee, the first chairman and secretary was WJ, who at that time must have been the most widely travelled man in Northampton with regular contacts in nearly every European, Australasian and American Country. Committee members were C H Battle, W P Cross, H Musk Beattie, W York-Groves, J Mills and the Reverend Lloyd Ellis.

In tandem with Rotary, the repertory movement was advancing. A book entitled *Adventure in Repertory* was written by Aubrey Dyas, a well-known Northamptonshire solicitor enthusiast, with a foreword by J B Priestley and published in 1948. In the preface, thanks are accorded to Bernard Holloway, the editor of the *Northampton Independent*, and to Miss Betty Reynolds, the secretary during formative years. He also lists being indebted to Alderman W J Bassett-Lowke *for encouragement and help, particularly with the illustrations*.

As expected, the Rotary Club welcomed the idea of the repertory movement and enthusiasts approached the Mayor of Northampton. He promptly agreed to call a public meeting to discuss the launching of

WJ was President of the Northampton Rotary Club during 1934/35 and is seen here wearing the Presidential chain of office.

J Bassett-Lowke Collection

a repertory theatre in Northampton. This meeting took place on June 18th 1926 and successfully started the ball rolling with two committees. The first committee voted Councillor Harvey Reeves in as Chairman, Mr Bascomb as Deputy, Mr Donaghey and Mr Holloway as joint secretaries and as members Councillor H W Dove, Mr Reginald Brown, Mr W J Bassett-Lowke, Mr H Musk Beattie, the Rev. J B Dollar and a representative of the Northampton Rotary Club. The second committee consisted of Mr Compton James, Miss Wallace, Mrs Frank Panther, The Rev. J E Evans, and the Rev. J Trevor Lewis, RD. Meeting followed meeting, and ultimately the first committee devised a concrete scheme.

There was the question of where the company would be housed. The Opera House was the obvious choice as its atmosphere and tradition, Mr Aubrey Dyas said were ideal. But the place was due to be demolished! Could they save it? Initial enquiries were sympathetically received by Lieut. General Sir John Brown, KCB and Mr W Pepper Cross, OBE, the directors of the Northampton Syndicate, owners of the theatre. Eventually, a company known as Northampton Repertory Players Ltd was formed with a capital of £2000 divided into 2000 ordinary shares of £1 each. But raising the capital necessary proved an anxious business. A substantial amount was subscribed by interested people but left a balance to complete. At a final meeting held in Mr Francis Graves' room at the *Northampton Echo* offices, the whole concept hung in the balance. After alternate hope and despair, the amount was raised. The Board of Directors consisted of Sir James Crockett (Chairman), Mr H Horton (Deputy Chairman), Mrs Helen Panther, Mr W J Bassett-Lowke, Mr Francis Graves (of the Northampton Echo) and Mr H Musk Beattie (Secretary). One seat was reserved for a representative from the Playgoers Association. As usually happens when a new project is going forward there were dismal Jonahs but the first play, chosen because it was a strong with broad appeal, was *His House in Order* by Sir Arthur Pinero. Frances Graves, the editor of the *Northampton Independent* left the town and went to live in Windsor but used to call to see WJ when he came to Northampton. He was there in 1937 and 1938 and still interested in the Repertory Theatre.

The first night was Monday January 10th 1927 and His Worship the Mayor (Councillor James Peach J.P.) with the Mayoress were present to give the adventure in repertory a start in the Borough. The Royal Theatre, as it is now called, has passed through many ups and downs, but during my uncle's life time he remained an interested and hard-working director almost up to 1953 when he died.

One young man in whom WJ took an interest was Tom Osborne Robinson, who throughout his school days had been fond of art almost to the exclusion of all other subjects. He was employed by the Bonaventure Press in Fish Street, Northhampton, as a commercial artist and was then earning 5 shillings a week. In the evenings, he attended the Northampton School of Art and came under the tuition of the principal, Mr Lewis Duckett. As it happened, the Bonaventure Press was the printer of the Bassett-Lowke catalogues at that time and Osborne Robinson was designing the covers for several of these. WJ approved of his style. In fact, Osborne Robinson designed the firm's logo *Lowko* while still an art student.

After a year's smooth sailing, there was an upset behind the scenes and the scenic designer was dismissed. What to do next? WJ had a brainwave and put forward to his fellow members of the Board of Directors the name of Tom Osborne Robinson. Tom accepted the challenge and started off by completing the half-finished sets for John Drinkwater's *Mary Stuart* and, on the strength of his work on this play, he was offered the post of scenic artist, which he filled with distinction for 48 years. He became consultant designer and eventually a member of the Board of Directors. He was invited to go to other theatres and in the 1930s designed productions for Stratford-on-Avon and for the Old Vic theatres, but he remained loyal to his home town and turned down offers which would have meant more than a temporary period away from Northampton. The School of Art also benefited from his talent as a tutor and he did special work in America, lecturing at Vanderbilt University, Nashville, Tennessee. He also gained a commission for a giant mural in the Douglas MacArthur Academy of Freedom at Howard Payne College, Brownwood, Texas. In consideration of his achievements, Sir Sacheverell Sitwell wrote to the *Chronicle & Echo* early in January 1976 supporting Osborne Robinson as a candidate for the honorary freedom of Northampton. Unfortunately he died that same year. Throughout his life, WJ maintained a great interest in his early protégé's career and Osborne Robinson continued from

Mr. WHYNDE (Founder of BLOW-KO, LTD.)

An ENGLISHMAN by birth   A FRENCHMAN by temperament
A FABIAN in politics   An AMERICAN in appearance
A COSMOPOLITAN in habits   An IDEALIST in outlook
A GERMAN in philosophy   A FUTURIST in art
An INTERNATIONALIST in thought

READ HIS UNREADABLE WRITINGS : -

"A Life on Wheels ; or, The Cities of Europe from a Railway Carriage Window."
"England, by one who is sometimes there."
"Business as a Pleasure ; or, Pleasure as a Business."

TO THOSE WHO WISH TO TRAVEL :-

Place yourself in the hands of "The Whynde." Versatility guaranteed.
Archaeological Lectures attended.   The Dansannts preferred
Railway Stations the principal attraction.
Hotel expenses avoided - nights spent in express trains.

TRAVEL TRIPS FOR TIRED TOURISTS :-
Whynde's Typical Tours
NORTHAMPTON—NURNBERG——NURNBERG—NORTHAMPTON
just long enough to eat a *Bratwurst*.

NORTHAMPTONLONDONNEWHAVENDIEPPEROUENPARIS
PARISROUENDIEPPENEWHAVENLONDONNORTHAMPTON
Full 20 minutes in the Gay Capital —— seeing all one *should*

Favourite Books - Baedeker's Guides.   Continental Tiime Tables
Shaw's Plays.
Telegrams—   Phone—
Wanderlust, Europe.   "0" Unsettled
Motto —"Keep Moving!"

time to time to do commissions for him.

Often on a Monday night WJ used to walk along with me to the Repertory Theatre, which was on my way home. He liked to watch the first act of the show each week and would say: *Like to come in?* We would creep quickly into Box A, having first asked the Box Office lady if it was free, and sit down as silently as two mice. I began to realise he had that uncanny sense of being right about the appeal of a play with already a wide knowledge about them and their authors. As a Director he would suggest certain plays that might be tried out. Through his friendship with George Bernard Shaw, WJ secured the right in April 1930 for the theatre to put *Fanny's First Play* on the Northampton stage, and several plays of GBS received popular acclaim at the Theatre. These Monday night trips would only take in the first act, so when it finished he would get up and say: *Time I must be off* or *I'll be late for your aunt's nice supper, but you can stay*. I soon became known as Mr Whynne's niece and did occasionally stay. Altogether, I became interested in my job and my new but gradually developing interests. Uncle and I became friends.

This chapter contains a lot of names, which I have given in detail to try to illustrate the wide variety of activity and contacts in my uncle's life at this time of the 20s and 30s of the century. Add to this that he had not long been married and also that he and my aunt were planning their new home over the first seven years, with much time and thought being spent on it. His life was very full; he worked hard at business as well as at his hobbies and interests.

To describe him as a *whirlwind* is not far from the point!

Christmas Cards

Early in the 1920's, WJ started to design his own personalised Christmas cards. Today we have *personalised cards,* which usually means a mass-produced card with one's name printed on it. WJ's were very different and, as one would expect, very much ahead of their time.

Charles Rennie Mackintosh did the earliest one for 1922 and it is clever and attractive. You have to look carefully to see the trains sweeping along with white blobs of smoke coming from their chimneys. You can imagine the white cliffs of Dover, the triangular ridges of waves and the two charming sailing ships on the blue sea. Uncle treasured this and I think it is by far the best of the 1920s cards. The one for 1925 shows all types of locomotion; sailing ships and liners, a coach and horses, motor cars, Stephenson's Rocket, an express train and with the statement *100 years cannot improve on the old wish - a Merry Christmas*.

In 1934 he used his yellow correspondence card and on it a sketch at the top of a tram in black and superimposed on it a liner in red. At the bottom, just running off the card is half of *New Ways*. It combines together well and is a bright greeting for the festive season.

In 1935 there is another exceedingly apt caricature, a very good likeness of WJ in typical *rushing* attitude complete with his Homburg hat and his two best friends, his still and cine cameras. This was sketched in black and deep blue by a fine artist friend Ernest Noble, who also did cartoons. WJ is standing on the wing of an aeroplane and apparently waiting to board a liner speedily approaching with the figures 1935 impressed on its bow. There was another in similar colouring with a liner, its

The 1949 Christmas card which illustrates his sense of humour. Visible in the top right hand corner is a special poster done for the Repertory Theatre by local artist Osborne Robinson.

J Bassett-Lowke Collection

funnels touched with yellow, and the message *A Good Crossing 1931-2*. One summer in the 1930s my uncle, aunt and I visited Snowshill Manor in the Cotswolds. It was the home of Mr Charles P Wade, one of uncle's clients for special models. He was interested in farm wagons and the firm was making models of the wagons of the various counties of England. This gentleman had persuaded WJ and aunt Floss to call on him on the island of St Kitts in the West Indies, where he owned sugar plantations. In fact, the cruising vessel they were on had a port of call there, and WJ took a party of friends to view this small island and partake of Mr Wade's hospitality. When we visited Snowshill Manor I was fascinated by the house and garden (he had built a model fishing village in it) and we went upstairs to see the room where the wagons were displayed. Snowshill Manor has been open to the public for many years. The Manor boasted a XVI Century clock that took WJ's fancy as his Christmas Card that year, in white, yellow and black. It featured *time* and a quotation from the clock at Snowshill manor. Entitled on the front *A Christmas Time Greeting* it shows 5 clocks of different types, white on yellow, and a small picture of New Ways inside a large pendulum.

A picture of a somewhat darkened *New Ways* was the subject of the simple card for 1942, with the sombre heading *blacked for the duration* and a quotation from *Sanskrit*. The 1943 offering was also in keeping with wartime feelings. A simple white card with black typescript just relieved by one muted colour, pale blue. Inside there is a quote from Shelley's *Prometheus Unbound* written in

1819/20. WJ sometimes included appropriate quotations such as his 1945 card that quoted words from *Captain Shotover* in George Bernard Shaw's Heartbreak House: *Navigation. Learn it and live; or leave it and be damned.* Showing a picture of a ship called *Mankind* drifting in a stormy sea of *Atomic Power*, WJ gave the clear message: *May our Navigators keep in mind the Christian message when setting our course for the future of civilisation.* This was a small plain card with simply: *Christmas 1945* on the front, and very much reflected WJ's inward thoughts, the mood of the day, and his concern for the future.

Coming to 1947, WJ is in more cheerful vein. His card has an aerial picture of Northampton showing Abington Park and a small inset indicating exactly where New Ways is situated. A band of that favourite daffodil colour is evident, as are the greetings of WJ and his wife for Christmas. Inside is an aerial photograph of Northampton town centre with his *Vision for a City*. 1951 is completely photographic; a postcard filled with miniature holiday pictures and the message: *Some of our Happy Memories of 1951.* There are several views of Switzerland here, for uncle and aunt, without fail always spent a fortnight there. The 1952/53 card shows a birdcage and the dove of peace, with a small leafy branch in its beak and uncle and aunt sitting on its back as it flies from 1952 towards 1953 with *New Ways* down below.

This is just a short résumé of uncle's Christmas cards, which were a feature that his friends on the list looked forward to each season, and which enlivened the December post each year. WJ went to much trouble in deciding on his subject, talking to his artist, and was not satisfied until he was sure that everything was right. 1952-53 was his last offering.

1945

Hector – I do have th
Capt. Shotover an Eng
Hector – And
Capt. Shotover be damn

WHITHER DRIFTING?
MANKIND
ATOMIC POWER

..., in *Heartbreak House*"

May our Navigators keep in mind the Christian message when setting our course for the future of civilisation

With the Season's Greetings from Mr. & Mrs. W.J. Bassett-Lowke
"NEW WAYS" NORTHAMPTON

Time for a change
J Bassett-Lowke Collection
(artist unknown)

Chapter Twelve

'New Ways'

In the meantime, between the various business and personal activities which came his way after the First World War, WJ was taking a long time to find the architect to design his new home as he relates:

> *After the first World War I purchased a piece of land on the outskirts of Northampton. It measured 300ft x 60ft and a garden was already laid out there. Mackintosh was to have designed a house for me to build on this site, but he went away to live in the Pyrenees and I lost touch with him.*
>
> *I tried to find another British architect with modern ideas that suited my taste but was unsuccessful. Then, looking through the German publication 'Werkbund Jahrbuch* in 1913, I saw pictures of work by Dr. Peter Behrens, who designed many large buildings on the Continent. I thought his style of architecture looked simple, straightforward and modern in atmosphere. I obtained Dr Behrens' address from the German Consul and got in touch with him in 1924.*

Whilst WJ was searching for an architect to design his proposed new home, he was able to purchase the Wellingborough Road plot (then 508 Weston Road) from his brother-in-law, Frank Jones, who had moved with his wife (according to Kelly's Directory 1924), to Greenwood House, Harlestone Road, St. James, Dallington. The garden was laid out with a lawn large enough for a tennis court. For many years, members of Aunt Jane's family used to foregather there and enjoy the pleasant days of summer, having perhaps a picnic tea there

Dr. Peter Behrens (later Professor) was born in 1868, the same year as Charles Rennie Mackintosh, and his atelier was at one time the most important in Germany. NEW WAYS was the only building he designed in England. He died in 1940 never having been over to see it.

                    Courtesy Prof. Dr. Ing. Till Behrens

---

* Also referred to as *Deutscher Werkbund* by WJ.

WJ meets Professor Behrens (on the left) in Paris with his builder, Charles Green (in the middle), and Behrens' assistant (right) to discuss the details for the design of his new home, NEW WAYS, *in April 1925.*

J Bassett-Lowke Collection

after tennis on the lawn. At the bottom of the garden there was a delightful lily pond fed by a natural spring, an orchard and vegetable plot, a rose walk on one side of the lawn approaching the house and beds planted out as flower borders. This garden had been maintained in good order by a regular gardener for some time, the whole plot waiting for a house to be built, which would complete the idyllic picture of a happy home.

My uncle at first had Charles Rennie Mackintosh in mind but, by the time he and my aunt had finalised their plans, the Scottish architect was suffering indifferent health. He had left London and was living abroad in France, where he devoted himself to painting watercolours. So there was the task of finding another such rare and gifted an architect as Mackintosh and WJ's early searches did not reveal a British architect with the same views as Mackintosh and himself. It was about 1923/4 when WJ saw the old copy of the 1913 German magazine, referring to the work of Prof. Behrens and he was determined to meet him.

Prof. Behrens strove to make industrial design relevant and modern and his grand idea was to humanise the industrial world. In 1907 he was commissioned as consultant for the design of the A.E.G. Headquarters and the Hoechst building in Frankfurt and his best known building is the Turbinenhalle (Turbine Factory) for A.E.G. *New Ways* was the only building he designed in England. WJ had heard about the house he had planned at Darmstadt, and that he had designed everything in the house and garden. This house and the Villa Obenauer in Saarbrücken are better known, but Behrens himself regarded the English home as a favourite work of his life. His atelier was at one time the most important in Germany and three notable architects worked there for a time in their early days; Walter Gropius, Mies van der Rohe and Le Corbusier. Born in 1868, the same year as Charles Rennie

Mackintosh, Behrens died in 1940 and is known still as a pioneer in industrial building. He was a painter, graphic designer, type-artist and after a short period of experimenting with art nouveau, became architect to the A.E.G. electrical company where he was not only responsible for factory design but also for the design of the products they made, from kettles to street lamps.

My aunt later told me that she and WJ went to an exhibition in Stuttgart where my uncle was particularly taken with a house designed by Behrens. They did not see him then, but WJ went over later and met him in Berlin. WJ eventually travelled to the Continent with his chosen Northampton builder, Charles Green, and in Paris he met Behrens and his secretary. Charles Green was determined to enjoy himself, of course, as it was a rare occasion for a provincial builder to meet up with such an outstanding architect on the Continent. At the same time, he was determined not to be rushed off his feet by any foreign nonsense! Prof. Behrens' assistant was a thin, serious and rather nervous man in a plush hat and clasped a roll of drawings whilst Behrens himself was stout, bow-tied and jovial. WJ was fortunate to find this eminent architect interested in undertaking a commission for an Englishman. Prof. Behrens did not come to England, but swiftly drew up ideas and plans and, in March 1925, the building of this pioneer house began to take shape, being completed in 1926.

Charles Green was not happy with the appearance of this strange looking house and he refused to have his board up outside! He spent much of his time trying to persuade his clients to follow less adventurous ideas, although in vain! *New Ways* stands today much as his clients wanted it to be and as Behrens designed it.

With *New Ways* my uncle and aunt had certain definite intentions. They wished to incorporate into one house every modern aid and comfort possible; a home that would express the spirit of its age. It was, firstly, to be a house of two storeys, all rooms to be contained within the four surrounding walls

The front garden entrance to NEW WAYS *from Wellingborough Road. The pillars, either side of the steps, provide illumination in the dark and illustrate that 'modern' thinking was not just restricted to the house.*

J Bassett-Lowke Collection

Above, the front elevation of NEW WAYS. *The central triangular window illuminates the spacious hall, stairs and landing and, with the canopy, is the dominant feature of this house.*

J Bassett-Lowke Collection

Left, the south facing rear elevation showing the loggia and balcony above, with Mrs. Bassett-Lowke.

J Bassett-Lowke Collection

Opposite, this view from the bottom of the rear garden shows the southerly elevation of the house, and the attraction of the property with its small pool, fed by a spring, and an atmosphere of quietness where there is room for relaxation.

J Bassett-Lowke Collection

with no outbuildings, with the exception of a garage, although he never owned a car. One of our well esteemed architects, Sir Hugh Casson, visited *New Ways* in 1952 when he was around 50 years old and took tea with my uncle and aunt. He afterwards gave a talk on the radio about the house in his series of *places lived in*. Uncle would have been in his seventies and he and aunt had then lived at *New Ways* for a quarter of a century. When commenting on WJ and his new house, Sir Hugh remarked that : *As you peer through the slatted blue garden gate set in the rough stone wall, it is as square and white and uncompromising as a block of stone.*

Both uncle and aunt realised the importance of suitable accommodation for staff. Space was requested for a sitting room downstairs and a bedroom upstairs with washbasin and hot and cold running water for a housekeeper or maid. An essential main room for this house was a spacious warm and attractive lounge, large enough for meetings and parties.

Having entered through the front door there was a modern convenience and washroom on the left, and on the opposite side an ample cloakroom. Proceeding inside, there was the large light and airy hall with a tiled floor in grey and black of an abstract design. According to Sir Hugh Casson, WJ and Mrs B-L themselves laid out the tiles, and the end result was incorrect to the original design. Spreading upwards into space was the wide staircase travelling round 3 walls to the upper floor and guarded by a solid balustrade. This staircase apparently worried Charles Green so much that he actually had another more traditional one made as he thought this more sensible. It was placed in position in a desperate attempt to persuade his clients but, of course, without any success.

The dining room, with space for a table to seat 8 persons in comfort, was planned as a room to be used solely for meals. It looked out over the patio, the large windows giving a view of the garden. On the left-hand side of the house, facing the garden, there was the modern kitchen and larder. Stairs down gave access to the wash house, a wine cellar, boiler room and fuel store in the basement. Convenient for the domestic offices was the housekeeper's room.

On the first floor two fully equipped bedroom suites with sizeable and well appointed bathrooms were planned. A special item my aunt requested was the provision of generous cupboard space and this was placed on the spacious landing. Between the bedroom suites there was room for a pleasant cosy den for Aunt Jane and her hobbies of sewing and embroidery, along with bookshelves for her favourite literature. Prof. Behrens designed the lounge, hall, dining room and exterior of the house whilst the kitchen, bedrooms and bathrooms were by WJ.

The front elevation of the house was planned to give a dramatic effect. A high vertical projecting V shaped window rises from above the front door to the roof, a feature that has been imitated in many houses since. Over the double front doors, painted in glowing ultramarine, was a strikingly designed white concrete canopy. Then, as you looked upwards, there was the flat roof itself broken on the skyline by a frieze of thin battlements along the roof line, very effectively painted black to contrast with the light walls, as did the black painted frames of all the windows.

Close up view of the loggia, with its tiled floor, looking through the French window leading to the lounge and Mrs. Bassett-Lowke perusing the news.
J Bassett-Lowke Collection

The rear elevation had four large windows and, in addition, doors and windows on the first floor giving access to a central verandah. Very much a repeat feature of 78 Derngate and a delightful spot which enjoyed morning sunshine. Access was gained on either side from the bedroom suites, and here guests often joined their hosts for breakfast. Downstairs at a similar central point was a covered loggia, a favourite place for tea on a summer day. A side door off the lounge opened onto this. Some notes survive on *New Ways* in my aunt's clear hand:

> *Commenced March 1925. Ground staked out to Behrens final plan on March 21st. Placed 2 feet forward from original staking. Green's price £2,670 less specified deductions for certain omissions. Paid £25 in gold to settle contract. Cut out 1 ft through centre of house saving approximately £20. Paid visit to Paris with Charles Green (the builder) to see Behrens on April 18th (1925).*

To quote Sir Hugh Casson further in 1952:

> *Although modest in name and size it is in fact a very special house indeed. To architectural students its face is, I suppose, as familiar as that of No. 10 Downing Street or Hampton Court.*

When it was built, *New Ways* was described by its admirers as *a symbol of a new phase of thought* and by its opponents as *the ugliest house in England*. How WJ developed an interest in modern architecture was a question often raised. He became a D.I.A. member and thus absorbed views from the eminent men with whom he came in contact. His motto became *fitness for purpose* and he kept to this maxim all his life. He learned from Charles Rennie Mackintosh and his experience with 78 Derngate, and developed this further in *New Ways*. In the early days, neighbours were a trifle dismayed to be living next door, or near, to this extraordinary house. No doubt WJ was not popular with his neighbours at the time. Visitors to New Ways, who were no doubt curious to see for themselves what the Bassett-Lowke's new home was like, were always given an excellent welcome. In 1932 Sir Clough Williams-Ellis CBE, MC, LLD, stayed the night there. He was a man who had interests much in common with my uncle and whom he met, as we have seen, when he was president of the D.I.A. Sometime in their married life uncle and aunt visited his famous village of Portmerion in North Wales. He commented that *it is now accepted as the first 'modern' house in this country – I found it very pleasantly startling*. One sector, which did not obviously share this view, was some bureaucratic department who wrote to WJ, causing him slight irritation: *regarding your <u>Factory</u> on the Wellingborough Road*!

Uncle and aunt moved from No.78 Derngate to *New Ways* in June 1926. Sad to say that Prof. Behrens never came in person to see this first modern house in England that he had helped to create: either before, during, or after construction. WJ sent him a quantity of photographs to show him the finished house. He replied in broken English from Vienna on the 7th August 1926, the letter being addressed to 76 Derngate (not 78), Northampton; the only letter from him which remains in connection with this impressive commission :

> *Mr. Bassett-Lowke*
>
> *Dear Sir,*
>
> *I herewith beg to accept my best thanks for your favour of the 29th ult. And although for the great number of photos, you have sent. I am very pleased that the impression, I have got out of them is considerable well. You will certainly understand that I have been very curious to see, in which manner our work has been finished, because I have not been able to be on the working-place during the time of building. Selfunderstood it would has been a pleasure for me to help you with regards to the making of the interior. I could see out of the sent photos that you have established the interior with the best of taste, but nevertheless I would like to make some reform-proposals for the case, you will not take it amiss.*

He goes on to say that, whilst he found the hall very beautiful, he thought it was too bare, and would benefit from different stencil decorations the design for which he was forwarding. WJ had also considered the lounge to be a little bare and had obviously asked for advice from Prof. Behrens on the matter. The letter continues:

> *Although re lounge you are quite right that the walls seems to be a little bare. I should like to propose, to place a long picture in the form of a frieze above the side-board, further a fine, but not too large relief above the fire-place. The other free walls could although be animated by pictures or stencils, for which case an ornamentation of the tapestry will not be necessary. But, when you prefer this ornamentation, please do not employ a too animate*

WEST SIDE.

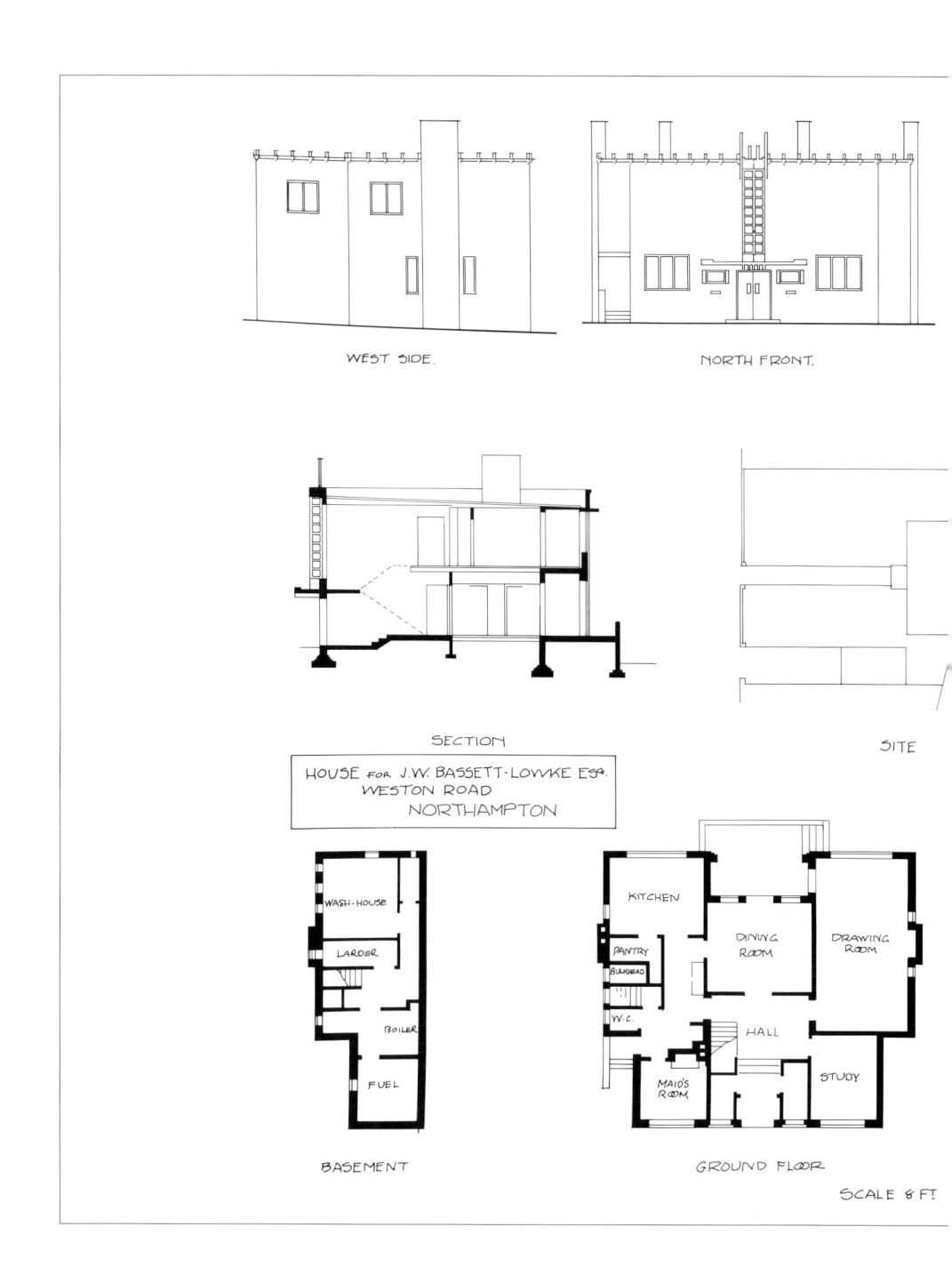

NORTH FRONT.

SECTION

SITE

HOUSE FOR J.W. BASSETT-LOWKE ESQ.
WESTON ROAD
NORTHAMPTON

BASEMENT

GROUND FLOOR

SCALE 8 FT.

'NEW WAYS'

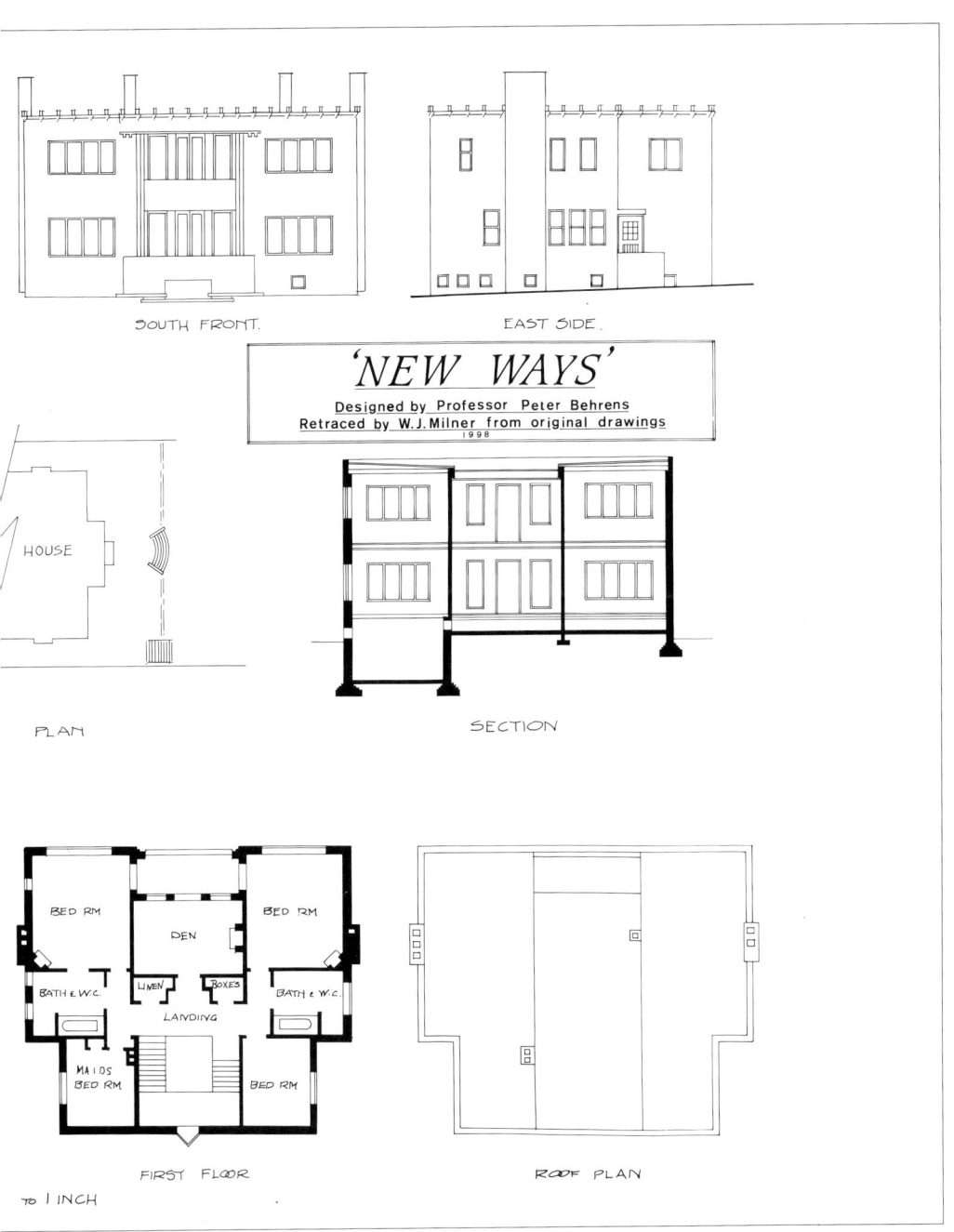

Designed by Professor Peter Behrens
Retraced by W.J. Milner from original drawings
1998

J Bassett-Lowke Collection

The west elevation looking from the front of the house, illustrating its plain design, relieved only by a series of pinnacles around the roofline, the leaded windows, and the attention to the design of the garden gate.
J Bassett-Lowke Collection

Close up of the large and striking window above the concrete canopy over the double front doors. The doors, along with the garden gates, were painted in ultramarine blue.
J Bassett-Lowke Collection

NEW WAYS 179

One of the mirrors in the hall, with an intricate fretwork radiator cover.
J Bassett-Lowke Collection

Above, a view of the triangular window, as seen from the first floor, with the Mackintosh designed standard lamp. The Egyptian style panels on the walls were the first designs to decorate the staircase. The ceiling composition puts the finishing touch to this outstanding interior and, below, the later decorative scheme.

J Bassett-Lowke Collection

The study, which was based on original designs by Mackintosh, including the stencilled pattern in orange, red, blue, grey and yellow on primrose walls. The ceiling light fitting came from the hall at 78 Derngate, as did the radiator cover and furniture.

J Bassett-Lowke Collection

The study in later years with a change of decoration. WJ's set of waterline ship models is on display and a bust of his respected friend, George Bernard Shaw, takes place of honour.
          J Bassett-Lowke Collection

WJ admires his collection of Bassett-Lowke waterline ship models.
          J Bassett-Lowke Collection

A view from the hall towards the dining room which shows the detail of the tiled floor, the flush doors and radiator covers.
          J Bassett-Lowke Collection

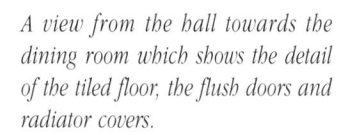

The most attractive room in the house was the lounge, built very much like the first artist's impression. With large windows (behind the camera) it was light and every detail was in harmony, being a restful and charming room to remember. Left, WJ and Mrs. Bassett-Lowke enjoy afternoon tea in the lounge.

J Bassett-Lowke Collection

The colour scheme for the main bedroom, where Mrs. Bassett-Lowke's tastes were predominant, was in cerise and blue with grey painted furniture. The door on the left gave access to the bathroom.

J Bassett-Lowke Collection

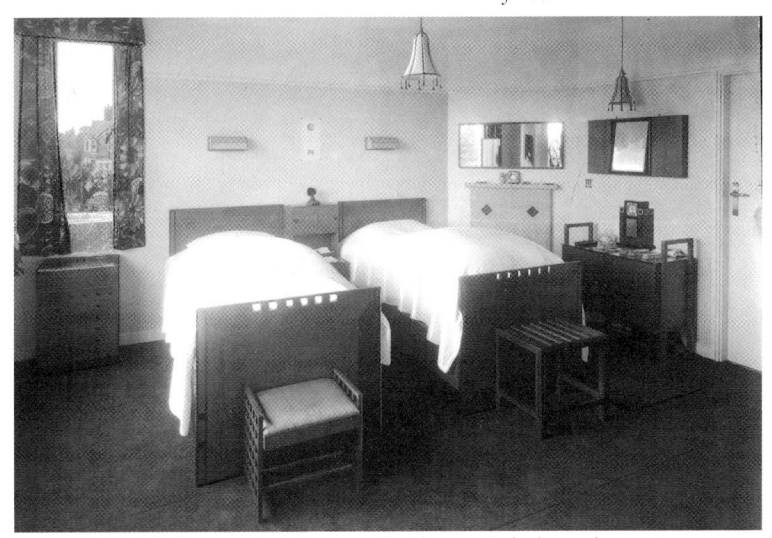

In contrast to the owner's bedroom suite, the guest's bedroom has a vigorous colour scheme. The light oak furniture is placed on a vivid green carpet. This is the Mackintosh suite that was in the 78 Derngate house. On the dressing table is the largest of the Mackintosh clocks, designed with squares of holly and ebony wood and a mother of pearl face with a mirror panel beneath.

J Bassett-Lowke Collection

Opposite page : The dining room at NEW WAYS *was a compact room with attractive lighting. In the right hand corner is the trolley designed by Mackintosh for* CANDIDA COTTAGE.

J Bassett-Lowke Collection

> design, but geometrical designs, in the manner of these, I am forwarding at the same time.
>
> The electric light fitting I have seen on the photo is not according this one, I have proposed. Please be so kind to proof still once the natural detail, I have drawn. To-day I will although forward a proposal re alteration to reform it without difficulty. Another lighting-body would certainly distribute the harmony with the ceiling, because the lighting-body shall be understood as part of the ceiling.

The letter then discusses WJ's plan to publish an article on the house in *The Architectural Review*. Prof. Behrens is obviously concerned that WJ should *finish at first the house without any fault in taste.........that we suppose to carry through the new style to England*. He goes to great lengths to instruct WJ as to what photographic angles are required for the illustrations and ends with:

> I regret very much that I am not able to have a talk with regards to all this with you on the place in England himself, for which reason I beg at the more to let me have further informations.
>
> I would ask you to do so and remain, with regards to Mrs. Bassett-Lowke, dear Sir.
>
> Yours faithfully,
>
> Behrens.

The Professor's grandson, Prof. Dr. Ing. Till Behrens, has followed in his grandfather's footsteps and is an architect, town planner, industrial designer and, until recently, professor at the Wiesbaden Polytechnic who has received national and international awards for his work. Sir Hugh Casson continued his opinion of *New Ways* :

> The really exciting thing about it is not the house itself nor its contents, but the spirit of adventure and experiment which inspired it and which still lives in it today (1952) ....All of it, I think, bears the stamp of that lively and original mind ....some of the architect's detail, particularly, I thought, the living room fireplace, is (like some of Mackintosh's furniture), queer rather than attractive and here and there I saw things which, to be honest, I thought downright ugly. This of course, is to be expected in pioneering design. Often the designer is fighting so hard for a point of view, that in his urgency he overstates his case. Even as late as 1926, remember, modern architecture was generally viewed with suspicion, dislike, and it is easy to forget, now that the battles are largely won, how stern and hardhitting these early struggles were, when every house was a fight for principles and clients were hard to find.
>
> 'New Ways' is a private family house and is not open to the public but, if you are in Northampton, do take a look through the golden gate and see if you can catch, as I did, an echo of the challenge which some 25 years ago

resounded from those whiite and simple walls.

On the 11th June 1976, three years after Auntie's death, *New Ways* was advertised for sale in the *Northampton Chronicle and Echo* and was described as :

> *Unique detached .... the subject of numerous television programmes and articles in 'Ideal Homes' and the 'Independent' .... restored to its original 'Art Nouveau' condition and ready to walk into.*

During both my uncle and aunt's lifetimes, I visited their home on many occasions. I often stayed there for a few days at a time and I remember it as a draught free, easy, bright and spacious house, the embodiment of WJ's maxim throughout life of *fitness for purpose* with a certain quiet beauty about the interiors. The present owner told me that when he first stood in the lounge, looking out over the garden and the park beyond, he decided immediately that this was the house for him. The hall floor tiling, after being laid for over seventy years, is perfect except for an almost invisible crack. The two Mackintosh items in my uncle's study, the hanging light and the coloured patterned glass panes covering the radiator, are still treasured and in place. The materials which builder Charles Green used were of excellent quality and have stood this home in good stead.

Today, New Ways stands as a seemly memorial to the foresight of its first owner, and to the credit of his architect and builder.

Another visitor to New Ways a year or two later was Frank Pick, head of the London Passenger Transport Board, who also knew WJ well through their D.I.A. membership. In 1934 he writes to my aunt *:*

> *I return all the better for my Northampton excursion, which gave me much enjoyment and made me think. I rarely meet Christian people. .... The trains were late so I failed to get to the office until the afternoon .... With many thanks to you and to your household. Frank Pick.*

Mr Pick must have enjoyed his visit as he came again in the March and May of 1941. His signature was noticeable because of the vivid green ink he sometimes used in his fountain pen!

The bathroom attached to the main bedroom, which had both bath and shower and was fully tiled.

J Bassett-Lowke Collection

Uncle and Aunt also had a good friend in the person of the secretary of the Design and Industries Association, Margaret Pheysey. She first stayed at *New Ways* in 1934 and then, after a period of 7 years, she came again and became a regular visitor. The last record of her visiting was over the Christmas period in 1952 - WJ's last Christmas. She was a valued friend, very interested in architecture and the work of Charles Rennie Mackintosh. Family visitors on my aunt's side were often visiting for a night and one was her eldest niece, Doris Cutting, whom she had known very well from the time she was 7 years old when she, and her mother Emily Ann, went to live at the family home in East Park Parade. Doris was in Florence Jane's company years before she married WJ. One disappointment young Doris remembered was when the family party had their supper on a Saturday night, the little girl was not allowed to stay up. WJ, in the early days of his courtship, used to be there often on a Saturday and, as Doris grew up, and aunt Jane and uncle went to live at *New Ways*, Doris and her family used to go frequently to see them.

The guest bathroom.
J Bassett-Lowke Collection

Cyril Derry, Chairman of the firm in the latter part of uncle's life, was another regularly visitor with his wife and sometimes his son, Richard. This was usually at the time of the Bassett-Lowke AGM.

Notables who received *New Ways* hospitality were MP Jim Griffiths in 1945 and in 1946 Professor C E M Joad, who was a member of the *Brain's Trust*, a popular radio programme of the time, which I think was introduced or chaired by Freddie Grisewood. I remember vividly meeting the professor in London in 1942. My fiancée and I were having a day in London on his leave and WJ said *why not have lunch at the Salted Almond? I am going to be there tomorrow with Joad.* We thought we would try this

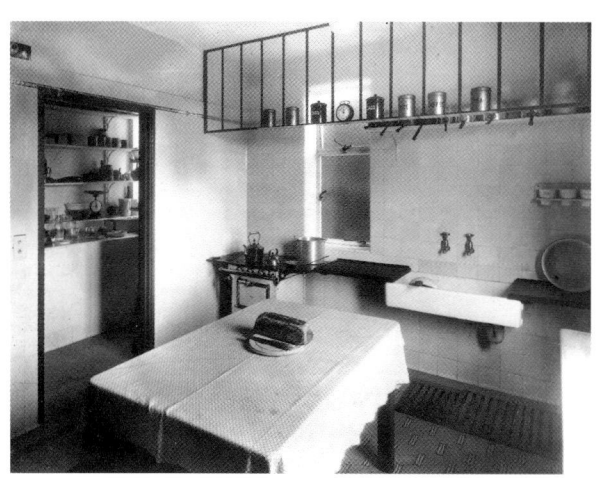

A general view of the kitchen and larder of NEW WAYS. *At a later date the area under the sink was boxed in to form cupboards to store utensils.*
J Bassett-Lowke Collection

NEW WAYS   187

The above illustrates the magnificent open aspect of the rear of NEW WAYS and a view from a neighbour's garden, showing the contrast between old and new.

J Bassett-Lowke Collection

popular place and afterwards went to uncle's table, where the two were in earnest conversation. I am sure the professor could be popular with the ladies, he certainly concentrated on me, which made WJ laugh. When I listened to the Brains Trust after that I tried to think about the serious side of things!

WJ received visits from his German friends in business, Sigfried Kahn and Stefan Bing and their wives. This was before 1939. After the war there was a small cutting from the local paper dated June 29th 1945 which read as follows :

> *During their brief stay in Northampton Mr and Mrs Clement Attlee were the guests of Councillor WJ and Mrs Bassett-Lowke. Yesterday they visited the Public Baths and had the opportunity of seeing elementary and secondary schoolchildren having swimming lessons. They also visited the works of Bassett-Lowke Ltd and they were keenly interested in the special work being carried out for Government departments.*

Then there was Francis Parker of Bewdley, whose family knew WJ well, the acquaintance having begun towards the end of the First World War when Mr Parker's father met WJ, when both were engaged on similar war work. There was also a charming letter from Lord Brabazon of Tara, who gave the address at the Firm's 50th Anniversary Dinner at the Savoy Hotel in November 1949. So there are many memories contained in the Visitors Book.

One intriguing item which was in the hall at *New Ways* and confronted visitors when they arrived, was the tortoise, made of cast iron, which rang a bell when you pressed either the head or tail to announce your arrival. This was in those happy far off days when one could safely leave the front door unlocked - an era when life was much simpler and less stressful. WJ smoked Turkish cigarettes, but only as a social smoker. These were tipped and were a rarity at that time in this country. Auntie Floss never smoked and did not like the smell of tobacco smoke in the house. Ash trays were cleared the moment the visitor concerned had left.

Like all other houses during the War, *New Ways* was fitted with blackouts to the windows. These were made in the Works and Ray Stutley and another workmate were entrusted with the task of fitting them. Being made by Bassett-Lowke, they were top quality blackouts and took a full day to fit!

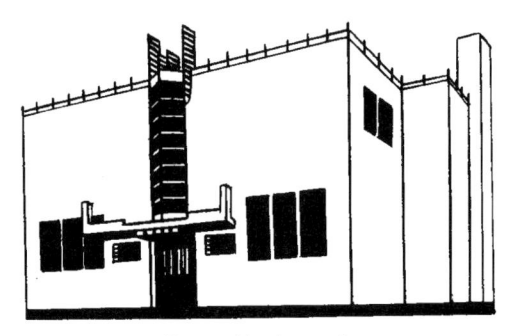

Have nothing in your house which you do not know to be useful or believe to be beautiful.

William Morris

Chapter Thirteen
Life in the 1930s

My sister Vivian was 13 and I was one year older when uncle thought about standing for the Borough Council. On the 1st November 1930, he was elected Councillor for the St. Lawrence Ward, representing the Labour Party. As school children, we were only mildly interested in politics, and about the time he was preparing to defend his seat we were invited up to tea at *New Ways*. We pricked up our ears when we heard the conversation was about swimming and that he was on the Baths Committee. There was some talk of the necessity of a decent new swimming pool for a town the size of Northampton.

As he was canvassing, he told us that he was sending out a special card to all the electors in the ward to reach them on polling day. He looked at us with a smile and said : *How would you both like to deliver some of these for me?*

His ward was in the Kingsley area, which we did know as our grandmother had lived in Kingsley Road. We guessed he might give us a present so we said we would ask our parents! After all, it might be fun, provided we could do some of the streets we knew. Uncle did not mind which ones we did providing that if we met any voters coming from their houses we handed them the card and said our little piece: *We do hope you will vote for our uncle today*. We sorted out the roads with no front gardens or with houses close together and our father popped us up to the district by 4am. We had a busy time, then caught a bus down to the town centre about 8am, in time for school. Uncle got in with a good majority!

Next summer, as mentioned in chapter 1, he surprised the two of us by asking if we would like to go to the Norwegian fjords with Auntie Jane, himself and a party of their friends, on their annual cruise. The time would be towards the end of July when we had broken up from school. He made this invitation to my sister because she had become a Midland District swimming champion and was working her way rapidly upwards in the races for both front and back crawl. I was included in this largesse more for school work than swimming, although I was also a swimming competitor. My goodness, the excitement! Our first holiday without our parents, our first crossing of the North Sea and our first visit to the Norwegian Sea. We rushed to sort out clothes, bathing costumes as; yes, there was a nice little swimming pool on our cruise ship, the *Atlantis*. It was every bit as exciting as we had imagined, the great expanse of sea, the coasts we sailed by to reach our first port of call, Bergen, a wonderfully clean and attractive city. We visited the Sogne, Naero and Hardanger fjords, where there was so much picturesque beauty in calm waters and went inland to view the Brigsdal glacier. Also, we swam round the big ship in the Eidfjord, which was exhilarating and caused a small stir in uncle's party as my sister covered the swim round in record time.

When I joined Bassett-Lowke Ltd, I started right at the bottom of the ladder, mornings only, for the princely sum of 10/6d (52p), or half a sovereign, a week. My first obligation was to be at work half an hour earlier than the general office staff. I was due in the filing room, where there were shelves all round the walls, with big green boxes on them, in alphabetical order. All the previous day's correspondence was in a neat pile and I just had to sort and place them in alphabetical order in the correct boxes. Not too hard on the little grey cells! Then I would climb upstairs to the top floor back room office that was our elderly book-keeper's retreat. There was a desk and typewriter in one corner for me, with a couple of drawers in which to keep necessary possessions. I then began learning about the accounts under Mr Branson's tuition. Actually I knew him quite well from another sphere - he was secretary of the local Royal Life Saving Society. The room smelt faintly of tobacco as the old boy liked his occasional pipe. I was used to my father smoking, so I did not think about saying anything. In those days the evils of smoking had not been realised. WJ's office, large and roomy, was next door and occasionally he would pop his head round our door and ask me to run some errand. On Saturday morning it used to be to fetch the weekly pork pie (home-made of course) he had ordered from the pork butcher's on the Mayorhold, a small square close by. These were splendid and other members of the firm used to buy them also.

I had prepared my cruise essay for him and a few days later carefully typed it out and handed it in. A day or two later he called me in to his private office and said it was quite good. He handed me a newspaper cutting about a postal writing course and suggested I should do this. I had to read the monthly lesson, there were twelve spread over the next year, and produce some kind of writing each month which they would digest and on which make suggestions for improvement. For the second lesson I decided to write on some aspect of swimming; I called it *Learn to swim in your mirror*. My course master made a couple of suggestions and then added: *Try sending this to Titbits*! Uncle, surprisingly enough, concurred. *Titbits* was a weekly national magazine which my parents read occasionally. So, I wrote a neat letter, added a stamped addressed envelope, retyped the article and popped it in the post. In a month's time I opened an envelope with a cheque for 2 guineas inside - my first success. WJ took an interest in these literary efforts each month. I sent my cruise article one month when I was over busy and had not had time to concoct something else. I received quite a pungent criticism saying the English was good, but I must make it topical. At WJ's suggestion I rewrote it and connected it with a new cruise ship. The lessons became more interesting and WJ then gave me a couple of advertisements at which to try my hand. He gave me the current Guard Book to consult. The Guard Books were largish flat scrapbooks, in which press cuttings, photographs and advertisements of the firm were pasted, also articles by WJ. There were several of these books, kept carefully in WJ's office and I was allowed to carry one off next door from time to time to study it. This helped a lot in learning about the firm's progress and various interesting happenings that had occurred before my time. He took me down to Ship Models Ltd to meet the craftsmen there and watch work going through, and I was sent up to Winteringhams, where Mr James Mackenzie showed me round.

Then I went 'over the road', for a few months, which actually meant going out of one front door and in the next, up some steps to the door where Mr William Rowe was in command. He had an office and smart small showroom there on the first floor which led into the stores, with piles and piles of boxes neatly arranged containing Bassett-Lowke goods. Downstairs was the packers department. My small spot was at the top of the entrance stairs, the telephone exchange and reception which led into the showroom. It was the Reception for customers and messengers and at times it could be a busy little spot, particularly when everyone wanted a phone call at the same time!

After a few months, I came back from 'over the road' and WJ installed me as assistant secretary, under the wing of Miss Joan Garrard, his long-time private secretary. Jobs I did included an occasional note for uncle Whynne and pasting up the Guard Book. Also direct from uncle I was sent down to Ship Models to take notes on any special models that were being made. He was always busy on the Publicity side, getting Bassett-Lowke Ltd a good press and it became my job to follow up his ideas and then he would dictate a rough framework for an article leaving me to fill in the details.

One day when I was alone in the office, he came in and said : *Where's Mr Branson?* I told him that he had gone up to the bank. He was going out of the door when a thought struck him and he said: *Would you like to come up to 'New Ways' and have a cup of tea on Sunday. Your aunt has a bicycle she won't be using any more and you can have it.* I went. The cycle was very smart and new looking and royal blue in colour. Just a little small for me as aunt was only 5' 4". But I was able with care not to knock the handlebars as I rode it home. At the time I did not think there was anything behind this gift and enjoyed cycling to work on fine days, putting the bicycle carefully in the stores. But before long my devious uncle suggested I should cycle down to the station on the days when he was travelling to London (at least twice a week) and meet him there at 8.20 am with my pencil and notebook! This meant instructions for the day, taking down any letters he wanted doing and posting them off. He himself was always early on London days and at the office soon after 8 am, opening his post. So, it dovetailed in that I should be at the station as requested. There he would be, on the platform, having walked down quickly from the office. He looked the typical smartly dressed businessman, standing at the door of his 1st class train compartment with open attaché case on the seat and a pile of papers in his hand, and there I was, scribbling away on my pad. Then all at once, signs of action, the train was starting up. Quickly he would shut the door and with a wave at the window would be speeding towards the metropolis. In the winter it was not my favourite job and once or twice I would be late back after lunch, telling myself I'd had to go early, so what. But someone who shall be nameless eventually told on me and uncle was cross and threatened to give me the sack. I did stand up for myself though and told him I did my full day's work if he counted the earlier time I was on duty at the station, and the trouble abated. My father and mother said it never hurt to do that little bit extra, with good grace. I realised they were right and improved my ways!

In 1933 Cyril Derry succeeded G P Keen as Chairman of Bassett-Lowke Ltd and was still in office when WJ died.

The Borough Council

As Councillor, he represented the St. Lawrence Ward for the first 2 years. Then, when the boundaries were changed, he became one of the representatives for the St. George's Ward. It is interesting to look at the leaflet he sent to the electors of his ward for the November 1936 municipal election.

The development for which WJ is best known is the New Swimming Baths. It seems amazing that the Town Council of Northampton had been looking at proposals for a new swimming pool since 1911. Then in 1922 they had the chance to buy a site large enough for a new civic centre when the Government decided to close the Northampton Prison on the Upper Mounts. Until then the swimming amenities

Northampton Municipal Election
November 2nd, 1936

ST. GEORGE'S WARD

X

TO THE ELECTORS OF ST. GEORGE'S WARD

Promises Performed and Pending

Economic and useful expenditure of the Ratepayers' money.

Useful work for the Unemployed.

Slum Clearance and Erection of Modern Inexpensive Flats on suitable sites.

An adequate provision for central Car Parks.

Street Widening and Town Improvements.

New Public Baths worthy of Northampton, the installation of Filtration Plant at the improved Midsummer Meadow Baths, and the all-round improvement of Open Air Bathing Places.

Conversion of the old Grand Stand into an attractive Sports Pavilion and small Public Hall.

Preservation of Trees in St. George's Avenue and Planting of Trees on the main approaches of the town.

Provision of a covered Fish and Meat Market.

A suitable large Public Hall for Northampton.

The laying out of the Abington Square site as a Public Garden of Rest.

GENERALLY TO MAKE OUR TOWN A BRIGHTER & BETTER PLACE TO LIVE IN

NEARLY SIX years ago I was first elected to the Northampton Town Council from the old St. Lawrence Ward and have been one of the representatives of the St. George's Ward since its formation in 1932.

During this time I have endeavoured to serve you conscientiously and have been pleased to give the utmost of my available time to the work, the interests of the electors and the town generally.

I have had the privilege of serving on the Improvements, Housing and Town Planning, Baths, Finance, Highways and Education Committees and have a high attendance record.

The Labour Party has again invited me to stand for St. George's Ward, and if elected, I can assure you of my continued interest in the administration of the Town's affairs and my full and energetic support for any scheme that is beneficial to Northampton, no matter by what party it is proposed.

Three years ago I was honoured by appointment as Chairman of the Baths Committee and advocated the improvement of the open air baths at Midsummer Meadow and the successful scheme for running warmed water. Following the decision of the Council to proceed at last with the Public Baths, I devoted much time to the details of their construction and with the full support of my Committee have endeavoured to see that the ratepayers had value for the amount voted by the Council for this long delayed addition to our town's health amenities.

Previously, in addition to producing a publicity film of Northampton which has made known far and wide the town's industries and amenities, I was also mainly responsible for the formation of an honorary Arts Advisory Committee to safeguard the future Northampton from ugliness and planning errors. I am pleased to say that its first function has been to assist with the layout of the Abington Square site as a Remembrance Colonnade and Garden of Rest.

May I have a renewal of your confidence on November 2nd with further opportunity to serve you and to promote the progress and prosperity of my native town?

Yours faithfully,

W. J. Bassett-Lowke

Sketch by F.E.Courtney of the Public Baths - J Bassett-Lowke Collection

were far behind those in towns of similar size to Northampton. This Upper Mounts site was big enough for other public buildings, so it was decided to organise an architectural competition for the design of the centre and this was advertised nationwide in 1931. In October of that year the results were declared. The first prize (£500) (First Premeditated Design) was won by J C Prestwich and Sons of Leigh in Lancashire, the second (£400) by H J Harding ARIBA of Beauchamp Place, Brompton Rd, London SW3, the third (£300) and fourth (£200) by E B Musman BA, ARIBA of Westminster SW1. The adjudicator was Percy Thomas of St John's Square, Cardiff. This competition certainly generated a great deal of local interest. There were eight other firms highly commended and all the designs were put on exhibition. Mr Thomas, a well known adjudicator, stated :

> *I am satisfied that the Design placed first more nearly than any other fulfils the requirements of the Conditions of the Competition, both in layout, detailed planning and in architectural character.*

The estimated cost of the new Swimming Baths (two pools) Turkish Baths etc. was £103,288 exclusive of fees. This was considered too expensive and was shelved for a less ambitious design which was finally approved in 1933. WJ, as Chairman , together with other members of the Baths Committee, visited many of the latest baths in the country and endeavoured to incorporate their best features. The Turkish baths, Russian and Zotofoam had been previously available no nearer than Leamington Spa. Under the site, foundations of the old town walls were discovered and had to be removed. The baths were actually built on the site of the jail exercise yard! The contract for the work at the revised cost of £52,500 went to Northampton Builders, A Glenn & Sons, in December 1934 and work started a month later.

The baths were opened on October 3rd 1936 when Councillor WJ, as Chairman of the Baths Committee, welcomed the special guests, Lord and Lady Burghley and the Mayor and Mayoress of Hastings, and

The new swimming pool on the Mounts was opened on 3rd October 1936 by Lord Burghley, who praised Northampton for their effort in improving sports facilities in the town . . . .

. . . . and right, the Plunge Bath in the Turkish section.
J Bassett-Lowke Collection

thanked those who had worked on the project. The baths were then declared open by Lord Burghley, the famous British sportsman, who warmly commended Northampton's lead in the nationwide drive to improve facilities for physical recreation.

Mr W V Arnold, Northampton's oldest all-year-round swimmer, made the first plunge into the water. The Chairman's nieces Janet, Vivian and June Bassett-Lowke, gave an exhibition of variety swimming while Freddy Hodges, the well known Highgate Club diver, who represented England at the 1936 Olympic Games in Berlin, gave a splendid diving display. Afterwards, Lord and Lady Burghley and the Baths Committee members made a tour of inspection of the new building. Later, guests were entertained to tea in the Town Hall by the builders and they were a very large crowd, with the Northampton Repertory Theatre orchestra playing in the Great Hall. Not so long ago a diamond jubilee party was held at the Baths for the 60th anniversary celebrations. The pool is still a popular place for those who love the water.

WJ took an active interest in all his Committees. He was a member of the Libraries and Finance Committee, Deputy Chairman of the Planning and Development Committee, and on the Highways and Educational Committees to name but a few. It is interesting to learn from Miss June Swann who worked at the Northampton Museum from January 1950 for 38 years. She mentions that as a new member of staff, the first councillor she began to know was Alderman W J Bassett-Lowke, who was Chairman of the Library and Museums Committee. She was soon aware that the Chairman and Committee had some considerable say in the way the Museums were run. She says :

> *To my youthful eyes, he appeared about the same age as the Curator (Reginald W Brown) who had retired as librarian head of the five libraries to run the two museums and art gallery full time. The staff could see how the relationship between the Chief Officer and Chairman had worked, as Bassett-Lowke dropped in to discuss business before the ten committee*

meetings, then held each year, and often also on the way to Council meetings when important museum business was on the agenda, or just to see how things were going on his way to a Design and Industries meeting. His name of course I had known since childhood, or at least a couple of years after 1935 when my brother was born. The trains we had were Hornby, although I was aware that the alternative was made in Northampton by Bassett-Lowke, but thought to be more expensive and a non-starter in our 1930's household. The friendship between Bassett-Lowke and Reginald Brown was apparent and I took to his friendly manner, as he passed through our office with a kindly enquiry as to how we were. With something of awe I realised there was friendship between his secretary, an attractive smart and very efficient young woman who invariably accompanied him, and the equally smart senior assistant who had worked for the British Council in London, before moving to Northampton. Their pleasant manners, elegance and sophistication left a deep impression and their notable dedication and super efficiency set standards I have never ceased to aim at. An atmosphere of gentleness and gentility seemed to surround all three, revealing a magic world of art and design combined with world-wide reputation in industry, which left an indelible impression, and a pride that my town could produce people of such calibre.

WJ was offered the position of Mayor in 1948 but he declined this honour in kindness to my Aunt who, because of her health, was not really up to facing the social role that she would be expected to perform. In 1952, WJ had been an Alderman for 7 years and he did not seek re-election on the 8th May of that year, retiring from the Council at the age of 75. On one occasion it is said that, as a much respected Alderman, he voiced his

A Northampton postcard which appeared in 1940 when, for wartime charities, well known British champion swimmers gave their services at different galas all over the country, raising a considerable amount of cash for worthwhile causes.

Alan Burman Collection

WJ discussing waterline model ships with George Bernard Shaw at Ayot St. Lawrence in 1934. The photograph was taken by Harold Bassett-Lowke who used to service Bernard Shaw's generating set at the house.

J Bassett-Lowke Collection

opinion that the Guildhall should perhaps be turned into a museum with the Councillors as working exhibits!

Returning to life outside his Council commitments, WJ took part in April 1931 in an early television demonstration called the Baird system. Speaking from studios at Long Acre, London, the pictures of his broadcast were received in Northampton. Also, in the same year, he gave a short talk on cinematography to the Northampton Rotary Club in which he said that the cinema industry was wholly dependent on Berlin, New York and London : Berlin for the brains, New York for the capital and London for the biggest audiences. In the same year, the very fine ship model of *The Empress of Britain* went on display to the general public in the Booking Hall of Charing Cross Underground Station.

Everyone, at some time or another, falls into disfavour with others for one reason or another and WJ was no exception to the rule. The year 1938 witnessed an unpleasant and unnecessary dispute between WJ and his old friend Henry Greenly. At the time that this happened, although I was working for him, I personally never knew anything about the matter and have had to rely on the words of others more closely concerned for this account. Greenly, whilst retained as consultant to Bassett-Lowke, was a free agent and produced a multitude of designs for other manufacturers as well as for his regular articles in the model press and his books, and for sale through his own business. Greenly alleged that F J Camm, an editor and regular contributor to magazines, was using his drawings and was publishing them without his permission. Greenly was extremely hurt by this and wrote to WJ expressing his concern about the pirating of his designs, although the matter had nothing to do with WJ himself. He was probably looking for support from his old friend. For some unknown reason, but more than likely to smooth out the problem, WJ showed the letter to Camm who promptly retained it and refused to return it to him. WJ probably acted at the time, as he thought, in the best interests of Greenly but this action unfortunately backfired. As a result, Camm placed the matter into the hands of his solicitors and action for libel against Greenly followed. Greenly at this time was not in an altogether very good financial position but, even so, he decided to drive the dispute up to the courts confident that he had a good case. Unfortunately, his solicitors considered otherwise and he was advised that his modest

WJ's 60th birthday party celebrated with crackers and paper hats. From left to right, Annie Bassett-Lowke (author's mother), Phyllis Jones, Keightly and Mrs. Cobb, Harold Bassett-Lowke (author's father), W J Bassett-Lowke, Alice Maud Lovejoy (cousin) and Florence Jane Bassett-Lowke.

J Bassett-Lowke Collection

income could not sustain the likely costs if he lost, and his chances of winning were less than 50%. He had to withdraw, lost the case as it was undefended, had to pay Camm damages to the tune of £500 and, as a result, had no option but to declare his bankruptcy. Probably, had WJ not shown this letter to Camm the whole matter would have blown over and been forgotten about by Greenly. It was certainly the finish of him both in financial and health terms. Lilley Greenly never had any contact with WJ after this event.

Greenly did in fact undertake a little bit of double-dealing that annoyed WJ. He very often prepared two sets of drawings; one set supplied to Bassett-Lowke with their name on them and the other set for his own business, and which he technically sold in competition with his client! When Greenly was asked to prepare a set of drawings for a 7¼" gauge *Royal Scot* WJ wrote to him and made it clear that these were to be sold only through Bassett-Lowke. They were in fact never finished, that is until long after his death when his daughter Elenora completed the task.

On a lighter note, Norman Shannon, an Australian visitor to the 1934 Model Engineer Exhibition in London, was pleasantly surprised when Percival Marshall, Editor of the Model Engineer magazine, said he would introduce him to WJ. He was not however prepared for the response : *He unexpectedly turned on me and condemned Australia quite dramatically because of import duties then prevailing and having been imposed during the preceding years because of the depression .... I found most of the other prominent firms all very nice people to deal with.* He never dealt with Bassett-Lowke again!

On the 27th December 1937 the Press reported that :

A youthful looking Councillor Bassett-Lowke celebrated a birthday yesterday said a writer in the local paper. When he mentioned his age I could scarcely believe it. I asked three people who know him well how old the chairman of the Baths Committee was and their replies were 45, 48 and 50. Actually Councillor Bassett-Lowke is now 60. No wonder he is always smiling unless he has just seen some part of Northampton's architecture which he does not like. It is not often a man looks at least 10 years younger than his real age.

Chapter Fourteen
The Model World of Ships

In one of his lectures, WJ related that model ship building was established when the Egyptians built model spirit ships which were placed in the tombs of the dead to carry their disembodied spirits across the waters of the Nile. Waterline model ships were first built by Bassett-Lowke at the turn of the century. They were simple in construction and not to any particular scale. About 1908 the models were sub-contracted out to a small business under the control of Mr Denton and Mr Checker. They, with the assistance of Mr Tranter of 19, Broad Street, Northampton, Miss Tranter, Edward Elkington, Ernie Johnson, L Ashton, and Reg Carroll, were engaged to produce special models for the various shipping lines and collectors.

When WJ's good friend Jack Sears persuaded him in 1908 to open a retail shop in London WJ had not then developed his latent interest in boat and ship models. Edward Walter Hobbs was employed as Manager and he suggested to WJ that there was a market for good quality models in this field. Initially Winteringhams made these but in 1921 Harry Franklin with WJ decided to set up *Ship Models* (later *Ship Models Ltd*) to build ship models exclusively for B-L. George Shaw from Sunderland was engaged to head the metal working team and Percy Claydon, from Glenns the well known Northampton builders and who was a skilled woodworker, was put in charge of this department. Harry Franklin also took over model ship workers from Winteringham Ltd. Franklin and WJ thus had complete control and all work was exclusively for Bassett-Lowke Ltd.

One man who worked for 40 years in the ship modelling side of the business is Ray Stutley. He came to the business in the early 1930s at about the same time as I started in the office section of Bassett-Lowke Ltd. He lives in Northampton and I see him from time to time when we discuss our lives and times at B-L, and remember some of the highlights that occurred while we were there. Like William Rowe, my uncle's first member of staff, Ray was drawn to the fascination of model making and devoted his whole working life to the firm. Gradually over the years, he was transformed from an apprehensive young school leaver into an exceedingly skilled craftsman. In his own words:

> *As the time approached for me to leave school, my thoughts were on my future. I was in the Abington Church Choir, and the Sunday School Superintendent was a Mr Wilcox, a true gentleman. He was a shopwalker at Adnitts haberdashers in The Drapery, a well-known and respected local firm. I had a long chat with him with the idea of joining the staff as a window dresser, and was considering applying. I became interested, but when I told my father of my plans, he flatly refused to listen to me. No, that was not the job for a man, and not at all the situation he had in mind for me. He knew an engineer, Leo Halford, who lived locally and who was the*

> *foreman in the boiler dept of Bassett-Lowke. My father spoke to him and he said 'yes' there was an opening for an apprentice.*

So it all began. He went for the interview and was signed on as an apprentice in the metal department under the foreman, Mr George Shaw, a Northerner with a vast knowledge of real shipping. He attended the local technical college for a year. His early work was making small fittings, stanchions, which were not his favourite, and rigging hooks, which he found rather monotonous. As the 'new lad' there was a certain amount of teasing to take, as usually happens in a group of fellows, but a saviour was found in *Tich* Clark who stood up for him. He was a likeable chap, about five feet tall, but he understood youngsters as he was married with a family of six.

Bob Marriott, the apprentice before Ray, took him under his wing and they worked together very well, but Raymond was impatient to do more intricate work. One of his duties as the youngest there was, twice a day, at 10 am and 4 pm, to walk to the general office, some ten minutes away in another part of Northampton, and take or fetch correspondence or parcels; anything necessary in fact to go from one place to the other. This was pleasant in the summer, but not so in the rain and cold of winter. The months went by and he began to feel it was time that he merited an increase in his wage of eight shillings a week.

> *So, after a year, I climbed the main stairs to Mr Franklin's office at the top of the building and made my request for a rise. The boss was a very careful man about cash. I stood awkwardly in front of his desk, looking at this kindly old gentleman, surrounded by model ships and with papers neatly placed before him, and waited for an answer. I noticed he wore a stiff celluloid collar and smiled to myself to see he had folded a white handkerchief neatly inside it to keep it clean. I thought and concluded that he must be aiming at saving extra washing! The result of my visit was a rise of $^{1}/_{2}p$ an hour, the princely sum of 24 pence a week.*

After eighteen months, George Shaw told Raymond that the apprentice in the wood dept was leaving to join the Army, and that he would like him to take his place. He jumped at the opportunity, knowing that it had been planned for him to work there eventually, but had happened sooner than he had expected. This department was in a large single storey building, spacious and light, with five other employees and the foreman Mr Percy Claydon. As a start he began by making mainly catalogue goods, skylights, hatches and so forth, work which he found more rewarding than metalwork. No more trips however to head office; that job went to *his* junior!

> *As part of my new duties I fetched the food for coffee breaks and tea at 3.30 pm. I would go up to the 'Corner House', a good tea shop in nearby St. Giles Square for rolls and cakes, a pennyworth of butter from Mrs Stevens' Corner Shop and two ounces of Rover Biscuits (perhaps five) and woe betide you if you got any change wrong! Those were happy days, with a grand set of colleagues.*

Ray had only been in this department for 12 months when Mr Claydon approached him and said *I would like to try you out on 'fitting up'*. That was the trade name for assembling all the fittings on

A good example of the craftsmanship which excelled in the ship department, a ¹/₆₄th scale model of 'Red Dragon'.

RailRomances Collection

to the finished model. He was put under the guidance of Harold Kent, who had been an expert on this job for some years and remembers that day with great clarity. The first model on which he worked was a scale *Strathmore* liner ⅛" to the foot, about 7 feet long. The fitting up department was sealed off from the others, to prevent dust coming in and settling on the models, thereby providing ideal working conditions. He enjoyed working with Harold Kent who was known as *Jim*; he had a fantastic sense of humour and a great knowledge of shipping, in particular the rigging of old time ships. He learned a great deal from him and work was now varied and absorbing.

> *One job above all I liked was a ¹/₃₈th scale 'Windsor Castle' made especially for the Union Castle's new showroom in New Bond Street. The starboard side of the hull was cut away to show the interiors. There was even a miniature picture of the Queen Mother (who launched the ship) hanging in the library! We repeated this model years later in 1979 for a private collector.*

The EMPRESS OF GREAT BRITAIN *was launched by HRH the Prince of Wales, at Clydebank, Glasgow, on the 11th June 1930 and became the Flagship of the Canadian Pacific fleet. This 21ft long waterline model was built in record time and took part in the Lord Mayor's show in London, that year, on the Canadian Pacific Railway Company float. The event was filmed by WJ.*

RailRomances Collection

He became more and more engrossed in this original kind of work, which Percy Claydon used to say called for his ***artistic application***. He was also called upon, from time to time, to be photographed with the models and appeared on TV several times, as did other model makers with the firm. I used to meet Ray, when WJ sent me to gather facts about the latest model he was on.

The main array of tools used when working on a scale model ship could possibly be counted on one hand. For the hull, a large handsaw would be used for a big hull like the *Queen Elizabeth* and, for a smaller ship, a bandsaw would be used. Other tools used were a drag (or draw) knife, a 2 inch chisel, inside and outside gouges, an electric drill, a spokeshave, a wheel brace and coarse and fine sandpaper.

When an order was received for a large-scale model, the first preparations were for the materials. While the metal and wire accessories were not a problem as these were kept in stock, timber had to be ordered specially. If the planks were available they would be obtained from a local timber merchant (on the firm's old truck in the early days!). For a large model, Percy Claydon would travel up to Hull to a large timber importer, Mallinson & Son, and inspect planks suitable in length and width. The timber chosen was always Obechi (an African timber also known as White Mahogany). This wood had a very close grain, was fairly light and would clean up to make a very fine surface. The selected planks would then be kiln dried to remove any moisture, so there would be no movement in the hull when it was carved. As soon as they were ready, the kilned planks would be delivered to the works.

The subject of the ship modelling activities of Bassett-Lowke is a subject in its own right and one that

This ¼" to the foot scale model of the Cunard White Star liner QUEEN ELIZABETH *was mooted in July 1938, when the prototype was being fitted out at John Brown's Clydebank yard. Because of the outbreak of war, the project was postponed until just before Christmas 1947, when instructions were received to proceed. It was shipped to the New York offices of the Cunard White Star Line in February 1949. WJ is here seen inspecting the work in progress.*

Ray Stutley Collection

would take more than this book to cover in detail. To give the reader an insight into this aspect of the firm's work, and a feel for the skills required, I give, via the courtesy and expertise of Ray Stutley, some details of the building of a large ship model.

The ship I have chosen is an order from Cunard White Star, who, as early as 1938, were considering a very large scale model (¼" to 1ft) of the famous liner *R.M.S.* (Royal Mail Ship) *Queen Elizabeth*, then under construction at John Brown's Clydesbank yard. Because of the advent of war in 1939, this project did not become a firm order until 1947.

The timber for the hull came from Bassett-Lowke's usual importers, who selected a log weighing 6 tons, 25 feet long, with a diameter of 5 feet at the base. As a matter of interest, this log cost £80. Of necessity it had to be sawn into planks of suitable thickness, from which the best pieces would be chosen. There are always, despite the quality of any log, certain parts where the wood is of lower grade and these would not be used. In the case of this giant ship the process of seasoning or *kilning* the wood took 8 weeks and in that space of time it was said to have lost 110 gallons of water. The boards were ready by June 1948. During this time also, much activity in other areas took place.

MODELLING R.M.S

Scale: $1/4$ inch to the foo

1. 2 inch thick planks of Obechi (white mahogany) are sawn by hand to form the laminates for building up the hull.

2. The sawn out laminates are glued and screwed together with some 2000 screws.

3. The outside of the hull was then planed by hand to the correct profile.

4. The stern of the hull, illustrating true craftsmanship in carving out the propeller shaft housings from solid.

Ray Stutley Collection

THE WORLD OF MODEL SHIPS 205

QUEEN ELIZABETH
1/8th actual size

5. The hull, all finely sanded, ready for the detail work and superstructure.

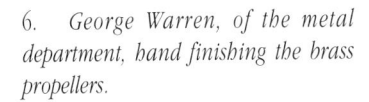

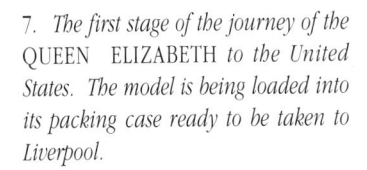

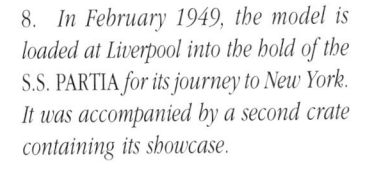

6. George Warren, of the metal department, hand finishing the brass propellers.

7. The first stage of the journey of the QUEEN ELIZABETH to the United States. The model is being loaded into its packing case ready to be taken to Liverpool.

8. In February 1949, the model is loaded at Liverpool into the hold of the S.S. PARTIA for its journey to New York. It was accompanied by a second crate containing its showcase.

Left, Percy Claydon at work on the ceiling panel for one of five 1 inch to the foot models of the room interiors of R.M.S. QUEEN ELIZABETH, built for display at the New York World's Fair and, opposite, a catalogue page showing more of these realistic models.

J Bassett-Lowke Collection

Bassett-Lowke was supplied with the necessary original builders' drawings. These were very carefully examined and from the hull drawings, the templates were prepared to enable the model hull shape to be carved. Details were also collated for the decks and superstructure and the bridge. The timber was delivered to Northampton in June 1948 and the workmen started immediately on the hull. Each 2" plank was marked out and cut to the rough shape externally with a large handsaw. Some were also cut internally so that the finished hull would not be too weighty. In addition to this, each of the planks was carefully finished so that it would unite together smoothly when glued. Altogether, to make sure the joints were permanent, over 2,000 screws were used on this particular model to secure the laminations. The electric drill would have certainly been busy and there were no electric screwdrivers in those days!

The first tool to continue the hull shaping was the drag or draw knife. This is a tool of ancient origin, said to have been in use at the time of primitive man. It removes most of the rough surplus timber. Then the gouges, inside and outside, came into action, taking out other surplus wood gradually, carefully to fit the template. The propeller bosses were carved in one piece with the hull. After this operation, the desired smooth finish was achieved by using a spokeshave with, finally, a rubbing down with coarse and then fine sandpaper. All handwork without the benefit of modern power tools.

This was a very long 'hard work' job, taking in this case 1,100 man-hours and at this point the hull weighed 1 ton. As the fashioning of the hull was proceeding, the decks and super-structure were being prepared.

We now come to the metal work, to reproduce all the elaborate structures above decks. In this model all visible detail was reproduced. The total number of individual pieces turned in brass was over 3,000. These were such items as life boats with boat lowering davits, masts, derricks, cargo winches, bollards, fair leads, window frames, portholes, handrail stanchions, hand rails, propellers, rudder, ladders, rigging, flagstaffs, brass lettering for the ship's name at bow and stern, navigating instruments on the bridge, accommodation ladders, ventilating fans and some items too small to specify.

A special effort from the metal workers was the set of 4 propellers. These were fashioned by hand, an exceptional example of fine workmanship. But the pièce de résistance was the radar scanner, housed

UNSURPASSED REALISM IN MODEL WORK

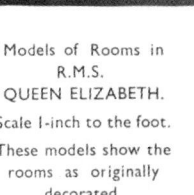

Models of Rooms in
R.M.S.
QUEEN ELIZABETH.

Scale 1-inch to the foot.

These models show the rooms as originally decorated.

The above three models formed part of a special display by the Cunard White Star Line in the British Shipping Pavilion at the New York World's Fair. The display was entitled "A Century of British Trans-Atlantic Shipping".
In a central position was a model of R.M.S. "Queen Elizabeth" and underneath were five models of different rooms on the ship, of which the above three are examples. The rooms were the tourist swimming pool, first-class lounge and first-class dining-room, tourist lounge and a suite de luxe. By pressing a button on the indicator rail, the particular room the onlooker desired to view was illuminated and lights shone through the sidelights of the ship above indicating exactly where the room was situated in the hull. Built to a scale of 1 inch to the foot, one-twelfth actual size (whereas the model mounted above was one thirty-sixth) they show a tremendous amount of detail. In fact it is practically impossible to say whether the untouched photographs on this page are of the actual rooms on the ship or "merely models."

Much work and ingenuity were expended on their building—the swimming pool called for a careful selection of materials to produce the right effect, and the modelling of the actual art work of the lounge and dining hall required more than "model" skill.

BASSETT-LOWKE LTD. LONDON AND NORTHAMPTON

in its glazed casing and visible in a prominent position aft of the bridge. This small detail served, at that time, to express the modernity of this marine masterpiece. 2,000 stanchions were needed, each being turned from brass wire (Ray Stutley was exceedingly glad he had long passed this job to less experienced model workers!). These were no thicker than large needles and less than an inch in height and the varnished wood handrails no bigger or wider than a book match was.

The hull superstructure and deck details had to be assembled and checked over to ensure complete accuracy. Then they were dismantled for painting, plating and finishing.

To achieve the highly polished surface of the finished hull, there was no speedy method. The first coat, the 'priming coat', had to be brushed well into the grain of the wood. This first paintwork on the hull was vital to achieving the flawless finish, the foundation of final success.

At least 20 coats were applied and after each coat the 'rubbing down' or 'smoothing' was as necessary as the application of the first paint had been. This slow and steady means ensured that the perfect mirror-like surface was eventually obtained.

The straight white riband along the water line, the Plimsoll lines and the loading marks were examples of very fine painters' skill. Also the entire superstructure, fittings and ships' boats were made ready all hand-painted in their correct colours. One of the most exacting tasks was marking out the decks. It was estimated that there were 5,000 ft of careful lining in Indian ink with a draughtsman's pen and straight edge to be ruled, a delicate and monotonous task for a skilled and patient worker.

After 4° months the entire component parts were finished ready for assembly and the final stage of fitting up was reached. For this last 12 weeks, the *Queen Elizabeth's* hull, and the whole paraphernalia for fitting up needed to be moved. The works did not have a room that would contain the 22ft giant plus the 5 men working on the 'final stages'. Suitable space in a nearly hall in a quiet neighbourhood eventually solved the problem.

So many small jobs had to be delicately accomplished. There were 1,700 sidelights (portholes) to be marked out and fitted into the sides of the hull with scrupulous care. These were in three sizes. Then the anchors were fixed into their recesses, specially hollowed out each side of the hull and the propellers had to be put in place.

Many metal fittings of a standard type were not suitable, so certain individual pieces had to be fabricated by hand in brass as a correct replica of the original. So the time came when the work had progressed far enough for an inspection by the marine architect of the Cunard Line, and all the workers, and particularly the Works Director, were happy and proud when complete satisfaction was expressed with their work. The job was done! It had taken 6,900 man-hours to build, contained no less than 4,600 individual metal parts, was 21ft 7ins long by 2ft 7ins wide, and weighed 1 ton 7 cwt.

The showcase for this model was made by a local firm, A Glenn & Sons, and was constructed of Honduras mahogany for the base and 350 square feet of half inch plate glass contained by a bronzed frame. Early in February 1949, two great packing cases, one containing the model and the other the showcase, were hoisted onto a low slung lorry and set off for Liverpool docks. There they were loaded onto the *S.S. Parthia* at Liverpool, en route for the main office of the Cunard Company in New York, bearing the words painted on the outside of the crates *The Biggest Model of the World's Largest Liner 'R.M.S. Queen Elizabeth', 83,672 tons.*

Ray Stutley often tries to recall the many models that passed through his hands, bound for so many different parts of the world. He wishes sometimes that he had made a note of each interesting item.

> *Often when a model came to be fitted up, and before I laid the decks I would sign the bottom plank and maybe some others, who had worked on it, would also put down the date, maybe a local newspaper and some coins. Who knows? Say in 50 years' time, a model might need restoration, and a model maker of the future might run across this small collection of items. He would have a fellow feeling with us, maybe.*

As an example of the amount of work involved in building a ship model, the *Majestic*, made for the White Star Line in 1923 to a scale of $1/96th$, consisted of 12,000 parts, took 10,000 man-hours to construct, and cost £600. On labour alone this equates to 1s 2d (6p) per hour not taking into account material, overheads and profit.

WJ was based at the offices of Bassett-Lowke Ltd, and was particularly interested in anything to do with ships, whether full size or models. He used to go down to the ship department in Kingswell Street several times a week to see the orders he had obtained in progress. Ray further relates that :

> *Even when I was a beginner apprentice and had to ask afterwards who he was, he had a smile for me and for other workers. As I was moved onto more skilled work he would stop and chat. When, during one conversation he found I lived quite near 'New Ways', he had a word with Percy Claydon to ask if sometimes it could be arranged for me to take messages to Mrs Bassett-Lowke on my way home. When I arrived at 'New Ways' Mrs Lowke would call me in and give me a bunch of flowers for my Mother.*

Waterline ship models of the Blue Riband holders (left to right) the MAURENTANIA, CONTE DE SAVOLA, BREMEN, NORMANDIE, *and* QUEEN MARY. *In the foreground, by way of comparison, is the* SANTA MARIA. *Scale 50ft to 1 inch.*

RailRomances Collection

W J Bassett-Lowke and Ray Stutley with the ⅛ inch to the foot scale model of H.M.S. ANSON *built for Messrs. Swan Hunter and Wigham Richardson in 1946/47 and below, this photograph of the 3/16 inch to the foot scale model of* HMS HOOD *was taken by WJ's brother Harold and was placed on the honours list of the Royal Photographic Society of Great Britain (c 1939), being reproduced in 'The Year's Photography'. Also selected was Harold's photograph of his daughter Vivian diving, entitled 'The Spirit of Holiday', and both were exhibited at the Society's Galleries in Princes Gate, London.*

Ray Stutley Collection

I grew to realise Mr Whynne was the entrepreneur salesman of the firm who knew the 'powers that be' connected with the big shipping firms and he was the man who obtained the orders.

Some of Ray's workmates talked amongst themselves about his regular visits to take messages from WJ to Mrs. B-L at *New Ways* and the upshot was : *Why can't WJ ring home direct himself?* Ray was proud of the team with whom he worked. They were the men whose quality of work ensured that the firm continued to get asked to make the models!

There were many types of men who came to work in the firm. The father of one was a retired bank manager, the father of another the chief huntsman to the Pytchley hunt, and yet another had a father who was cartoonist for the local paper. One man employed by Bassett-Lowke Ltd was particularly popular when any goods had to be sent by rail; his father was stationmaster at Castle Station! One thing the ship modellers had in common was a pride in the work that they produced and a desire to make whatever they did to the best of their ability. Every year in the summer, one day was set aside for a free day out in the country by 'char-a-banc', with free meals at some suitable pub. Every Good Friday, the staff were treated to a hot cross bun, paid for by Harry Franklin, from the baker next door to the workshops in Kingswell Street. It is summed up in Ray Stutley's own words:

Personally, I know that I count myself fortunate to have had such an interesting and fulfilling occupation, meeting so many interesting people, which I am sure would not have been the case had I become a window dresser!

The *Queen Elizabeth* is perhaps the finest and most famous example of all the model ships built, but it is only one of the very large number of models of various scales built over the years. One can pick out at random a host of historic names such as the *Olympic* and *Britannic* for the White Star Line, the *Aquitania*, *Mauretania* and *Queen Mary* for Cunard, working steam models of *HMS Hood*, one for Lord Howard de Walden and the other for the Maharaja of Patiala, and *HMS Ark Royal* for Cammell Laird. Strangely, a model of the ill-fated *Titanic* was not built until 1977. The Compagnie Générale Atlantique, owners of the giant *Normandie*, decided on a large waterline model, to a scale of 1:100 with the added attraction of internal illumination. The hull was specially hollowed out and white light shone out through transparent windows in the upper structure and from the 1,500 sidelights, glazed and fitted in the hull. The modelled bow wave gave an amazing resemblance of life and movement to the whole scene. The list of these superb ships is endless.

Among the great ship builders for whom Bassett-Lowke made scale models was John Brown of Clydebank. In 1947 Bassett-Lowke built for them a model of *HMS Vanguard* to a scale of $1/48th$. Dr. John Brown, now 97 and head of the firm in his day, relates that :

'HMS Vanguard' was built on Clydebank towards the end of World War II but was not finished in time to take part in it. The Admiralty had a model of it and the then Chairman of the John Brown Group thought that we should have a similar model although, as builders, we seldom had models made to our own account. The one made [by B-L] *I consider to be the finest ever example of ship modelling.*

It is interesting to note that when HRH Princess Elizabeth, then in her 21st year, went with the Royal Family to South Africa the ship chosen to take them was the brand new *HMS Vanguard* and the local press recorded that :

> *It is more than likely that the Princess, her interest sharpened by her maritime environment, will dip into 'Ships and Men', the new book by Northampton Alderman W.J.Bassett-Lowke and Mr. George Holland, for Alderman Lowke despatched a copy to her prior to her departure.*

Following the cessation of shipbuilding, the John Brown Group was split and the Clydebank operation is now part of Kvaerner Energy Limited. Throughout these changes, the model of *HMS Vanguard* has retained its proud place in the foyer of the main Clydebank building.

Apart from the manufacture of model ships, the firm produced a vast range of products to satisfy the then extensive market of model ship builders. Everything conceivable was available from modestly priced yachts, clockwork and electric motor boats and super detail marine models, kits for sailing ships, scale fittings covering everything you would need to build a model ship, silk flags, blue prints and of course the well known range of waterline models.

When Harry Franklin retired in 1938, Ship Models Ltd continued as a separate entity, although now more directly supervised by Bassett-Lowke, whose new director, Captain Lockhart took a special position there for a short while until recalled to the Navy in the same year, and directed to submarine duty in Scotland despite having a heart ailment. Captain Lockhart was eventually invalided out of the service and died a fortnight afterwards. Ship Models Ltd became a wholly owned subsidiary company of B-L and eventually the name was changed to Bassett-Lowke (SM) Ltd.

The extent of the skills of the modelmakers at Bassett-Lowke are well illustrated in this close up photograph of the $1/64th$ scale model of H.M.S. VANGUARD, built in 1947 for John Brown & Co. Ltd., Glasgow. Dr. John Brown, now 97 years old, considers that in his opinion it is 'the finest example ever of ship modelling'.

Courtesy Kvaerner Energy Ltd

Chapter Fifteen
Later Years and The War

As the 1930s advanced, our lives were changing and WJ was showing increased interest in both of his elder nieces. In me, because he saw me practically every day, and in Vivian because of her continued swimming prowess. My sister left school when she was 15 in order to concentrate on her swimming. She trained as often as possible and my father, in conjunction with her London coach, oversaw progress and acted as trainer. He took her to pools all over the Midlands before the new *Mounts Baths* were built in Northampton. They often went to Kettering, Bedford or Rugby, if and when the pools could grant her training times. In the summer she used the pool at Franklin's Gardens and the one by the river at Midsummer Meadow. In the winter, twice a week would be as often as she could train. At home she learnt other useful skills like photography and, although too young to drive, knew more than most girls about what went on under the bonnet of a car.

When the New Baths were opened there was much more activity in the sport in the town. Our swimming club was granted one evening a week as club night for activities like swimming practice, water polo and teaching beginners. I helped with teaching youngsters, an activity of which WJ approved and once a week for one hour, 5 pm to 6 pm, I was allowed out early from work to take a class of YSL's (Young Sea Lions) - boys and girls in their first stages of learning to swim. At one period I had 30 or more youngsters turning up and teaching was hectic. As soon as these juniors became adequate swimmers many of them transferred to the swimming club on Club Night proper and some grew to be valued members of the club.

In the summer of 1936 uncle invited me and my best friend to go on a cruise to the Canary Isles, calling at Madeira and the Spanish port of Corunna. We were lucky to experience a holiday like this in carefree surroundings before the war. We were young and unattached but had uncle and aunt to keep watchful eyes on us and we had a wonderful time.

The author as a schoolgirl in a silk racing costume. At the age of 15, she achieved the Gold medal of the Royal Life Saving Society.

J Bassett-Lowke Collection

By the late 1930s Vivian had become one of the foremost women backstroke swimmers in the couIn the summer of 1936 uncle invited me and my best friend to go on a cruise to the Canary Isles, calling at Madeira and the Spanish port of Corunna. We were lucky to experience a holiday like this in carefree surroundings before the war. We were young and unattached but had uncle and aunt to keep watchful eyes on us and we had a wonderful time. ntry. At the National Championships in 1938, she recorded the fastest time overall in the heats for the 150 yards backstroke championship of Great Britain, but in the final she missed winning by a touch. She was disappointed that she was not chosen that year to represent England, her greatest aim, so she made the decision to go for the long distance championship of the country. This was about 3½ miles in the Thames, over the Boat race course and was being held later that year.

Vivian and my younger sister decided to go camping on the island of Guernsey, to train there for this championship swimming in the sea across the various bays and testing out the best stroke to use. They were away a full fortnight and came back looking fit and bronzed. Vivian had elected to use the back crawl for most of the distance and had worked out a way of keeping a straight course by lining up 2 points. Each competitor was provided with a boat and I and a swimming friend, Rory Robinson, who had had previous experience of this particular race, followed her within safe distance. It was an exciting afternoon on the Thames, by the waterside the watching crowd, and in the river itself there was a tide and various obstructions like floating bits of wood and other items along the way, but she won by a wide margin. She brought home a large silver trophy, which certainly made friends open their eyes! She was honoured by being received by the Mayor and Mayoress, Councillor and Mrs W Howes Percival, the Town Clerk, Mr W R Kew, and other worthies including the Chairman of the Baths Committee, her uncle WJ, and the Baths Manager, Mr George Richards. Champagne was ladled out of the trophy to celebrate.

The following year, in July 1939, she became backstroke champion of England at the Nationals held in Minehead and was on the list of swimmers to be selected to represent Britain in the 1940 Olympic Games, scheduled to take place in Helsinki. She had achieved her goal, but directly war was declared on September 3rd 1939, the Games were cancelled. She went to Erfurt in Germany representing her country and the British team only returned home 10 days before war was declared.

Disappointing to a keen young swimmer, but she and other champion swimmers decided to use their talents in aid of war charities during hostilities, giving swimming displays all over the country. She married in December 1940 and a few months later her husband, who was an observer in the R.A.F. on Wellington Bombers, was shot down and was missing. She did not hear for some time where he was and it was a relief when the news eventually came through that he was alive. She took the test to become an Inspector for the Aircraft Inspection Directorate and continued with this work of national importance from then on throughout the war period. Her husband spent the war in a Nazi prisoner-of-war camp.

Working for Bassett-Lowke's I was in a reserved occupation. The firm was working overtime, with our craftsmen making literally thousands of small waterline models for the Navy and Army for reconnaissance purposes. After 5.30 pm each evening, our female staff went into the workplace where the models were waiting. We all sat round a big table packing the so delicate small scale models. Our simple task was to label each model and tie it safely into the special box prepared for its reception. Some of us were entrusted, under guidance, with preliminary work on the models, not

In 1938, Vivian Bassett-Lowke won the Womens Long Distance Championship of England in the River Thames. This Christmas card, which she compiled herself, shows the start of the race, the contestant in the water doing the back crawl, which she did for most of the way, and the victor clinging to the boat that accompanied her with the author and Rory Robinson, a well known coach. At the bottom Vivian is welcomed at the Town Hall, Northampton, with (left to right) W R Kew (Town Clerk), the Mayoress, Mrs. W Howes Percival, Vivian Bassett-Lowke, the Mayor, Councillor Howes Percival, and W J Bassett-Lowke, Chairman of the Baths Committee.
J Bassett-Lowke Collection

difficult tasks but each had to be performed with the utmost care. WJ, as usual, came round to see our progress and to discuss matters with Percy Claydon. At 7.30 pm work stopped, benches were tidied, we straightened our backs, put on our coats, collected our gas masks, which went everywhere with us, and made our way home in the blackout.

My boyfriend had been called up and was in the Army. We got engaged and in the summer of 1942 were married. Shortly afterwards he went to an Officer Cadets Training School and emerged as a 2nd Lieutenant. In early December he came on embarkation leave and departed these shores early in January 1943. I continued working for my uncle. I was having a baby and stayed working until the last month before my child arrived. After a few months, with both grandmas lending a hand, I was able to return to work part-time, to help with various kinds of literature for WJ.

WJ was writing a full length book with a colleague, Mr George Holland, to be called *Ships and Men*, which was planned to give an account of the development of ships from their prehistoric origin to the present time, along with the achievements and conditions of the men who built and worked upon them. This, WJ said, would take years! He was as busy as ever with his Council Committees and those to do with the Design and Industries Association.

One particular D.I.A. friend, Mr Noel Carrington, had introduced him to Mr Allen Lane of Penguin Books Ltd. Mr Carrington was editor of the new Puffin series of coloured picture books for children and in April 1941 WJ was asked to link up with an artist to write *A Book of Trains*. Mr Frederick E Courtney, Principal of the Northampton School of Art, undertook to do the pictures. I had already helped with the text. This was the start of a series and the correspondence between WJ and with Mr (later Sir) Allen Lane and with Noel Carrington is preserved in the archives of the library of Bristol University. In 1971, Noel Carrington, then about 76 years old, requested my help as he was writing about the D.I.A. pioneers with whom he worked in the 1930s, including WJ. My aunt was by then in her eighties and in a nursing home, and I went to see her to go through his questions. One was: *was he interested in trains before he became so keen on ships?* My aunt's reply was: *yes, but eventually his love of ships became stronger than anything else that the firm modelled.* He duly replied and the last sentence of his letter was: *I have the liveliest recollection of your blooming youth - a contrast to most of my authors and artists. yours ever.* A thrilling and unexpected compliment and still remembered!

In connection with his first book, *A Book of Trains*, WJ shows his ever present keenness for, as soon as it was published, he wrote: *Yes I would prefer to send off the review copies myself, because then I can send a different note to each of my friends.* He personally handed over a copy to Bernard Holloway, Editor of the *Northampton Independent* and sent his local review to the publishers. In November he sent copies to most of the railway magazines including the *LMS Staff Magazine* and signed the letter *Trusting the Book will be a success.* It ran into a second edition in its first year and was, of course, on sale at the London Branch and whenever he gave one of his popular talks. In July 1942 he writes to Penguin's:

> *Am I right in believing that 37,500 copies were printed as a first edition and 37,500 as a second, making a total of 75,000 copies. .... I also understand that the price has now been increased to 9d. which affects the amount of the royalty due.*

Amongst the correspondence there is a letter from Noel Carrington to one of WJ's artists when he admits:

> *I have known Bassett-Lowke long enough to take his enthusiasm with a grain of salt. One cannot always do things the way Bassett-Lowke would like. On the other hand, without his energy behind things, how little would get done*

How I agree - this was the secret of so many successful projects; he was the mainspring behind them. In a letter to Allen Lane in February 1943 he alludes to war conditions, saying:

> *As regards Model Railways, we ceased making these at least two years ago and only have a few left in our stores, which are under the limitation of supplies regulations, or what we call 'frozen'. Our London shop is hardly worth visiting these days but we are sending up in the course of a few days some of our sample models to make the showcases look a little more attractive. Here is our gauge 'O' catalogue of railways we <u>used</u> to be able to supply.*

By spring 1943 the Puffin book of *Wonderful Models* was being discussed and the artist Paul B Mann, was in London on leave and lunched with WJ and Noel Carrington. It was decided to change the title to *Marvellous Models,* which flowed more smoothly. In the final paragraph of a letter about this he writes: *I find a difficulty in getting the Penguin Books I specially want. Can you oblige me with the enclosed? Four books in all.* And the books? *An Anthology of Wartime Poetry; European*

Architecture and *What about Business?* by John Gloag (2 copies). The cost 3s. 3d. (16p) - marvellous value!

Paul Mann used to live in nearby Kettering and trained as a graphic artist and illustrator. During the War he served in the Royal Engineers in Jamaica and started painting seriously in oils and watercolours. After leaving the Army in 1946 (except for two short periods away in 1947 and 1950) he became a full time professional painter. After experimenting in the development of cellulose colours, he returned to his favourite medium of watercolour and held a one-man show in his native Northamptonshire, also exhibiting in many parts of the world.

In July 1943, WJ paid a rare visit to Fairbourne on the Mid Wales coast, and the location of one of his miniature railway ventures, the Fairbourne Miniature Railway. The purpose of his visit was to see his old friend John Wills who was losing his eyesight. This was the last time they met as John Wills died in the October of that year.

Late John Harrison

In February 1944, *Marvellous Models* was at the 'dummy' stage and WJ wrote to the printer, R Geoffrey Smith, about one of the figures drawn. He sent a photograph of the actual person and indicated : *he hasn't a funny nose like the artist has shown*. The date moves on to March 1944 and the publication of *Canals and Waterways* book, with Laurence Dunn as artist. It is evident that I typed one letter, for the postscript at the end reads : *My niece today showed me the rough dummy she has prepared for the Swimming Book and I hope that now you have found an artist this book will go forward. I am sure she will make a good job of it and I shall of course be pleased to help in any way I can*. This book, entitled *The Book of Swimming*, was published with illustrations by Lunt Roberts.

In these war years, when he could not travel abroad, WJ used to go up to the English Lake District for a holiday, and was there in May 1944. In a letter to Carrington he adds : *where I met no aircraft, no tanks, and only one soldier and I think he belonged to the Home Guard*.

Uncle decided to take aunt Jane for a second time that year in September and said to me : *Can you get a Grandma to look after your baby? Then you could come up with us and have a little holiday? Bring a friend*. My mother-in-law was only too pleased to oblige so I was able to go with Uncle and Aunt with a light heart. She was an expert on such a task, having had six children, and already several grandchildren. It was my first holiday for two years and an old school friend joined in the party, which added to the pleasure of the trip.

Whilst my husband was abroad during the War, I enjoyed working part-time with uncle and I also visited him and Aunt Jane often at *New Ways*. In fact, most Sundays WJ and I formed the habit of going to church together. I used to catch a bus to Abington Park and he would walk down from nearby *New Ways* and we would continue along The Avenue to Abington Avenue Congregational; the church where he and Aunt were married.

He was still working away at *Ships and Men* and this book of over 300 pages with over 150 illustrations was published by George G Harrap & Co Ltd of London towards the end of 1946. He sent a copy to my parents for Christmas that year.

On May 8th 1946 there is a letter I wrote to Carrington referring to *Marvellous Models*, WJ being away in his favourite Lake District at the time : *All the text for the new pages has been supplied 1) Opening pages - ancient model, 2) Coal Mining in Miniature 3) Farm wagons in Miniature 4) The Bailey Bridge as a Model and also Mann's Farm Wagons sketch.* The typescript had already gone - the Durban model and all the drawings with the exception of the Egyptian carpenter's shop which was coming direct from the artist Paul Mann. He concluded : *Please let me know if there is anything further I can do.*

WJ's letter of June 10th speaks of his holiday in Switzerland and return by Swissair in 2 hours 56 minutes, *a lovely journey above the clouds.* These days it is just a hop of scarcely half the time. Later on in the month he receives the drawing and mentions trying to get a map of the South African city of Durban. By August the second printing of *Marvellous Models* is taking place and in September WJ's letter lists the Puffin books he is connected with and asks about their progress. These included *Marvellous Models*; *A Book of Swimming* by me, which was having a hardback and French edition printed; *Book of Locomotives*, a new book in progress; a revision of *A Book of Trains*; *Waterways of the World*, where his artist is Lawrence Dunn, and lastly *The Inside of Things*. The price then of these attractively coloured books was only ninepence (c.4p). In 1947 *Marvellous Models* was, I believe, the book selected in the top 100 out of 5,000 titles published.

In January 1947 WJ is still battling with his books. *A Book of Trains* was noted as being the most popular of Puffin books and was to be reprinted in the stiff cover series. WJ notes that he is going through the long mentioned *How it works* and *The Inside of Things*. Lane had been to America looking at matters from a business point of view in his unceasing drive for better publications and Bassett-Lowke Ltd are only just getting back into production, the first products being earmarked for overseas. In September 1947, WJ wrote to Carrington after seeing the first finished publication with Paul B Mann as artist and wrote : *I think this is a very good edition of 'Locomotives', a bright and colourful book and feel it will be a better seller than the Book of Trains, although it has a more limited scope.* In September, Lawrence Dunn is seen to be re-drawing all illustrations for *Waterways of the World*, and Courtney is redrawing his pictures for the *Book of Trains*, under WJ's persuasion. WJ seemed pleased with life and very enthusiastic about the new Puffin book *Locomotives*, then just out, with the new *Marvellous Models* also ready and he was anxiously awaiting the arrival of a batch of each book to supply a long waiting list of orders. *How it Works* and *The Inside of Things* were presenting problems! *A Book of Trains* is noted for being one of the most popular books of the series, and had a second edition as did *Marvellous Models*. WJ's last letter is dated August 1951 in which he admits to Carrington : *I was pleased to hear this morning from Penguin Books that they are repeating 'The Book of Trains' for delivery in October. This pleases me as it is a very good seller.*

Returning to 1946 and the business, the opening of the extension to Messrs Bassett-Lowke's premises at 112 High Holborn, London took place in December of that year, within 16 days of WJ's 69th birthday. Cyril Derry, Chairman of the Company, welcomed the assembled company of friends from the model railway world and Percival Marshall, the man my uncle had first met at the very beginning of his business dream spoke of this :

> *I am sure we would all like to empty our glasses and to echo Mr Derry's charming words, and to wish the greatest possible success, not only to the firm of Bassett-Lowke Ltd. but also to their staff and to this very fine extension to their London premises. It may not be a large gathering, but if one looks round the room it represents the world of those interested in the Model Railway and Engineering. We know that Montgomery is Chief of the General Imperial Staff, but I regard our friends here today as the actual 'General Staff' of the Model Engineering World, and I am very honoured to take part in the proceedings today.*
>
> *It is good to know that we are all very good friends and all interested in the one hobby which we have at heart, and that is the development of the model engineering and model railways in all possible directions. In particular, if I may mention names, I would like to mention Mr H W Franklin who is the son of one of the founders of Bassett-Lowke Ltd. We all have the greatest respect for Mr Franklin senior, and are very glad to know that this family is represented by his son.*
>
> *Just a word about Mr Cecil J Allen our friend from the Railway Magazine, which does much to keep alive the interest in model railways. Myself, I do not feel that railways are going to die out. Some people may imagine that air and other forms of transport are going to dispose of railways altogether, but I do not think that this is so. The interest in railways is going to last for many generations to come and it is of the greatest interest and a pleasure to us to have with us Mr Cecil J Allen who is doing so much with the Railway Magazine to preserve the interest in this side of the hobby*
>
> *I have been very interested to come to see this new showroom, and I regard it as the nearest rival to the Model Engineer Exhibition. One thing, you have to pay for admission to the Model Engineer Exhibition, but you can come out without paying; however, the public who come to this 'exhibition' will be able to come in free of charge, but I am quite sure that with all the delightful examples of model making on view they will not be able to go out again without putting their hands in their pockets!*
>
> *One thing about the firm of Bassett-Lowke Ltd - they are always up to date -*

sometimes a little bit ahead. I have heard that the Chief Mechanical Engineers of the various Railways are going to send their representatives round to Bassett-Lowke's showrooms to see what is happening, or about to happen in the model locomotive world, so that they can get some new ideas before they put fresh designs on the drawing board.

Now I want to be a little personal about a few old friends. I have known Mr Bassett-Lowke for 48 years - that is a long time. I knew him when he was just emerging from the chrysalis stage when he was an apprentice at his father's works - and he had some ideas then. He looked ahead and he could see that there was going to be a great interest in the model trade in all its branches and he started right away to supply the growing demand for materials and finished parts for craftsmen and for those interested in model railways and their working.

I have watched him many hundreds of times since those days and have seen him trying to 'grow up' but he has never grown up.

Today he wears that youthful expression, that youthful smile which has always marked his appearance, and he is just as much a boy as ever and I am sure we all hope he will still preserve that delightful outlook on life. It is a very pleasant thing to know that whenever you meet Mr Bassett-Lowke he greets you with a smile. People say you should say it with flowers, but I believe there is an alternative - I think you should say it with a smile. This has always been characteristic of the staff of Bassett-Lowke Ltd. Mr Bassett-Lowke started this, and I think it has gone right through the staff. I remember Mr Gooday who used to be the General Manager of the Great Eastern Railway and how his personality extended from his own office right through the staff of the G E Railway down to the humblest porter on the smallest station, and just in the same way I think our friend W J Bassett-Lowke has extended his personality right through the staff of the great Company from the top 'noises' down to the friends and colleagues at London Shop. On the many occasions I have had contact with Bassett-Lowke Ltd I have always been met with a smile.

At this stage Mr F J Camm arrived and Mr Marshall broke off to say : *We are very delighted to see Mr Camm here today and we hope you will carry away a very good impression of the new showroom which has just been declared open.*

We all know how busy Mr Bassett-Lowke has been developing the various extensions to his business, but he has not been too busy, as he has found time to write a new book entitled 'Ships and Men' .... I have not had the opportunity of reading it yet, but I have seen some of it in manuscript form and I am sure it is an admirable book and one of the greatest interest to those interested in maritime supremacy - if I can tear it to pieces in the Model Engineer I shall do so! It is a tribute to his unending energy that he has been able to do this as well as settling the many problems and developing and organising a business.

One thing I should like to congratulate the firm on - one thing which many publications and many publishers look upon with a little bit of envy and that is the production of their many interesting catalogues. They are some of the most interesting 'textbooks' in the schools of Great Britain, and I tremble to think of the number of boys who have been found studying a Bassett-Lowke catalogue when they should have been absorbing algebra or history and the like!

Mr Derry says that he could have gone on talking for a long time - so could I - the firm of Bassett-Lowke Ltd has had a most remarkable history, and I feel that this is coupled with Mr Bassett-Lowke himself. His personal enthusiasm, his smile, his 'looking ahead' has been communicated to his staff, and this is well known by all the friends of the firm. This applies also to Mr Franklin Senior, Mr McKenzie, and Commander Lockhart, who are not now with us, to Mr Bindon Blood - after two minutes discussion with him one finds oneself involved in a discussion on gauges etc. - he is a real technical enthusiast. Then of course we have our old friends Mr Sell and Mr Foreman, who have done so much for the firm in London.

I would like to express a welcome to Mr Cyril Derry on his Chairmanship of the Company because I am sure he will be a great inspiration to the firm.

Thanking Cyril Derry and Percival Marshall, WJ responded :

I must say that I have loved model railways and model ships from my childhood and shall do so all my life. I hope to reach the age of 70 next year and to still be useful at that age. To be youthful at 70 is, I think, better than being old at 40. I will conclude by saying that I hope the extension of our premises will be a success and thank you for all your good wishes for the future.

At this gathering, besides Cyril Derry and Percival Marshall, editor of the Model Engineer, were J N Maskelyne, Editor of the *Model Railway News* and H Coleman of *Modelcrafts*. Cecil J Allen of the *Railway Magazine*, D A Russell, an editor of several model publications, and F J Camm, editor of *Practical Mechanics* and two gentlemen from Germany, Franz Bing and Siegfried Kahn of Trix Ltd. Members of the firm present were H M Sell, Manager and H C Foreman, senior member of the London shop, Harry Franklin, Director and William Rowe, the senior member of the Northampton staff.

Two fine examples of Bassett-Lowke 'O' gauge production, illustrating the ultimate of W J Bassett-Lowke's objective, back in 1900, to produce more realistic models than had hitherto been produced. Above is the DUCHESS OF MONTROSE *(1938) and below the* FLYING SCOTSMAN *(1947).*

Bob Burgess Collection

Chapter Sixteen

The End of an Era

At Head Office in Northampton, Mr. Whynne, as WJ was known by the staff, was now over retirement age. There was an evident need for an extra person on the office staff there, to take some of the workload from him. Roland Fuller was asked if he would transfer to Northampton. For a while he commuted from London each day and, with his new position being a proven success he was made General Manager in 1945 and in 1947 moved with his family to Northampton. As WJ aged, Roland gradually took over the running of the office on both the retail and manufacturing sides. At that time, Percy Claydon was in charge of the industrial side of the business. If WJ had a meeting to attend or a talk to give, Roland was by his side and if necessary made the speeches as well as presenting some of WJ's talks whilst he sat by.

Roland Harrington Fuller started work at the London shop, 112 High Holborn, in 1917 where he was engaged as a shop boy, under the instruction of Bert Sell. Mr. H C Foreman was at that time Manager. Gradually he learned about the model trade and in 1920 became a salesman. Derek Brough was at

At home
Wenman Joseph and Florence Jane Bassett-Lowke
J Bassett-Lowke Collection

the shop over their busy period in 1937 to early 1938, and his job was to demonstrate the new *Trix Twin* '00' gauge railway layout that Roland Fuller had built in the basement. He said that it was an excellent layout and whilst he was there this particular product range sold well.

The London staff had to learn everything to do with the products they sold, and all were proficient and able to deal with small repairs. From the early days, there was a small workshop behind the scenes. At the beginning of World War II there were goods to sell, but a quiet period inevitably followed when it was mainly war production at the works in Northampton. Roland was asked to create a workshop in the basement of 112 High Holborn, to engage two young men and train them to make waterline models. More especially they were constructing recognition models of all the new equipment, particularly supplied by the USA under lease to the UK, and the unique elements designed for the Allied Invasion of Europe. This proved to be a very sensible plan and helped towards an increase in output. When it came to 1943, the outlook for model work seemed more hopeful and it appeared probable that models would come back into their own before too long.

During the 20 or more years while I have been searching and trying to contact people still alive who knew Uncle, I have been fortunate to trace a select few who have given me their thoughts and views about WJ. One such man is Derek Brough who worked for a time as a youngster at the London Branch.

He first met WJ in 1937 when he was temporarily employed at the London shop in High Holborn. He did not see WJ again until after the war, when they met on several occasions and it was at Brough's instigation that WJ was made a Vice-President of the Historical Model Railway Society, shortly after the Society was formed in 1950.

Derek said he had the chance of a long quiet talk with my uncle one evening during a dinner in Cambridge in 1947. Between courses WJ took from his pocket a tiny model he wished to show him and he could not wait for the meal to finish. *That, I thought,* said Derek, *was typical of him, for he certainly knew how to use that most valuable commodity - time - for he never wasted a second. On this same occasion he surprised me when he said that he liked ships best, then locomotives and then stationary engines. Until then I had always thought that locomotives were his first love.*

At that time Derek was living in Cambridge and had become a member of the Cambridge University Railway Club. The President of the Club, Viscount Garnock, who later became the Earl of Lindsay, asked him if he knew someone who might be willing to give a talk to the club and Brough immediately suggested WJ. So it was arranged for him to go over one evening by car with Roland Fuller, who actually gave WJ's talk. He was at that time nearly 70 and felt he was getting too old to do it himself.

Derek related that when at the London shop in 1937: *I did serve a member of the Royal Family, although I did not realise this until the Manager, Mr H C Foreman, asked me if I knew who he was.* It seems that this customer was the Hon. Gerald Lascelles, the younger son of the Earl of Harewood and the then Princess Royal. Another customer particularly remembered was Sir Thomas Salt, a most charming man, who built a passenger carrying railway around his estate at Shillingstone, Dorset. *I was quite excited too when Jack and Claude Hulbert came in,* he said, *but I could not get to speak to them - my great heroes!.*

WJ, dressed for the tropics, on one of his many cruises. Date unknown but probably on the way to the West Indies.
J Bassett-Lowke Collection

During the early part of the war (1940/1) Derek was in the Royal Engineers and on the Headquarters staff of the Longmoor Military Railway in Hampshire, where there was a Bassett-Lowke model railway in the Signal School used for training the Sappers.

Returning to my Uncle's activities, David St. John Thomas, Chairman of David & Charles the publishers, related that in 1940 WJ, whilst on a visit, was strolling over his lawn at Teignmouth, just after the air raid siren had gone off, and made the somewhat pessimistic remark : *we are bound to lose the War!*

As a member of the Town and Country Planning Association, WJ was on their 1947 tour to Sweden and made a cine film of this event in colour. He was elected a Fellow of the Royal Society of Arts in 1946 and in 1948 he gave one of the Society's Juvenile Lectures with the help of Roland Fuller on the subject of *Model Railways*. After all, model railways should rightly be regarded as a form of art! Also, on the 13th April 1951, a paper was read to the Junior Institute of Engineers entitled *The use of Models in Industry, Education, Invention and Recreation* by Roland Fuller with the introduction being given by WJ. It was reprinted from the Junior Institute Journal in 1952 and produced as a booklet.

WJ continued to be immersed in his book writing and in the last few years of his life he had a very good secretary, Mollie Harvey, who guided him everywhere; to his various Council meetings, outside visits, and who even went on holiday to Switzerland with him and Aunt Jane. He loved Switzerland

50 Years of Model Making
1899 – 1949
BASSETT-LOWKE
Northampton, 6 PM, 8 NOV 1949

Bassett-Lowke Ltd.
50th Anniversary Dinner
Savoy Hotel, London, 15th November, 1949.

…

We are delighted that you have accepted our invitation and look forward to the pleasure of your company on this occasion.

Guests are requested to enter the Savoy Hotel by the Embankment Entrance.

Reception 6.30 p.m.
Dinner . 7. 0 p.m.

Dress Optional
(Business Dress or Dinner Jacket)

The Savoy Adelphi Garage entrance is in Savoy Place.

GUESTS

1. Lord Brabazon
2. F J Camm - *Practical Mechanics*
3. George Dow – British Railways
4. R Bindon Blood – Precision Models
5. J D Ki,ey, M.P.
6. C E Rowe – Town Clerk of Northampton
7. C Courtice – Passport Office
8. S Kahn – Trix Ltd
9. W H Rowe – First employee of Bassett-Lowke Ltd
10. Victor Harrison – Harrison Stamp Printers
11. J C Cribbin – Model Engineer
12. J E Timmins – David Harcourt Ltd
13. E H Clifton – Twining Models
14. Chairman of Model Engineers Trade Association
15. H M Sell – London Shop Manager for B-L
16. E W Stogdon – *Model Engineer Exhibition* Manager
17. H C Foreman – London Manager 1919-45
18. G L Lake – Model Engineering Trade Association
19. P Oppenheim – Trix Ltd
20. R J Hingley – Holders Ltd
21. J H Saillil – ICI Ltd
22. *The Daily Telegraph* representative
23. R A Rautin – French Lines
24. J Aggett – Blue Star Line
25. D Caird – Royal Mail Lines
26. F Bing – Trix Ltd
27. H Glenn – Northampton builder
28. R Saunderson – Stuart Turner Ltd
29. F E Courtney – Principal Northampton Tech. College
30. R H Fuller – Bassett-Lowke Ltd
31. A J White – Harrap & Co. Ltd.
32. J R Cox – Editor *Boys Own*
33. G Lewis – Bassett-Lowke shareholder
34. A Robson – Union Castle Co.
35. P F Claydon – Bassett-Lowke Ship Models Ltd.
36. A H Ridrup – Cunard White Star Lines
37. G Archer – Jarrolds, printers
38. Unknown
39. B W C Cooke – Editor *Locomotive Magazine*
40. A B Storrar – Chairman, *Society of Model Engineers*
41. Ernest Steel – Henry Greenly's son-in-law
42. H W Franklin – son of joint founder of B-L
43. J N Maskelyne – *Model Railway News*
44. Editor of *English Mechanics*

W J Bassett-Lowke is out of the photograph to the left of Lord Brabazon with a few more unknown guests

THE END OF AN ERA

THE

FIFTIETH ANNIVERSARY

OF THE FOUNDING OF

BASSETT-LOWKE

CELEBRATION DINNER

HELD AT THE SAVOY HOTEL, LONDON

Tuesday, 15th November, 1949

Guest of Honour

THE RT. HON. LORD BRABAZON OF TARA P.C., M.P.

TOAST LIST

His Majesty The King

*

Mr. Bassett-Lowke and the Company

Proposed by ... ... LORD BRABAZON OF TARA, P.C., M.P.
Response by ... ... MR. W. J. BASSETT-LOWKE, M.I.Loco.E.

*

The Craft of Model Making

Proposed by ... ... MR. GEORGE HOLLAND

*

The Visitors

Proposed by ... ... MR. H. M. SELL
Response by ... ... MR. GEORGE DOW

*

The Gentlemen of the Press

Proposed by ... ... MR. R. H. FULLER
Response by ... ... MR. F. J. CAMM

*

Chairman ... ... MR. CYRIL DERRY

Lord Brabazon of Tara with WJ at 'New ways' on one of his social visits.
J Bassett-Lowke Collection

and went each year, 1952 being the last time. He produced an album of holiday photographs on each trip, some of the photographs being of railway subjects. In September 1949, they went by Swissair and visited Zurich, Vitznau, Rigi, Engelberg, Lucerne, Olten and Lake Lucerne. Engelberg, it will be remembered, was the scene of his winning a championship in a bobsleigh team in 1912 with Jack Sears, his first Chairman. In 1950 their points of call were Basle, and the Swiss Industries Fair, Coire, Zurich, Bad Ragaz, Lucerne and back to Basle. In 1951 it was back to Basle and this time they visited Loetschberg and took the Simplon Tunnel route to Locarno and Lugano, then by road to Cadenabbia and via the St. Gotthard route to Lucerne. The last trip was just to Lucerne and small places such as St. Niklausen, Tribschen, Brunnen, Schwyz, Vitznau, and Rigi Kaltbad, finishing off in Berne and Zurich. Truly a traveller to the last! The 1950 – 1952 trips all took place in April. WJ learned to enjoy flying in those last days.

As children we three girls had little to do with WJ. It seems on consideration as if he spoke a different language. My sister June, who was his goddaughter, remembers as a youngster his arguments with our father – brief and sharp. Naturally he understood boys best. He did make an effort to entertain the assembled company with Mickey Mouse or personal films and delighted in running them backwards. He never learned to drive; he loved travelling by train or bus and would happily cadge a lift. Auntie Jane once said *he spends pounds while I save pennies*.

One item my sister does recall was one lunchtime when I remarked that Uncle had been to the doctor's that morning. A most unusual occurrence and the only time I remember him doing so. I added that he had been ordered to rest and had gone home at 11.00 am Returning to school at 1.30 pm she had spotted him running to catch the bus! *A pity*, says my sister June, *that my memories are not more flattering because this jack-in-a-box man left a legacy of inventiveness which still fascinates generations.* My sister considered that a more accurate picture of both Uncle and Aunt might be obtained from the Jones side (Mrs B-L) of the family. Doris Cutting was able to provide this.

Somewhere between 1950 and 1952, just before WJ's death, an enquiry was received from British Columbia for a model locomotive and the purchaser wished to pay in gold! The locomotive is illustrated with its pile of gold as payment. I suppose the same purchaser today would wish to pay in drugs!

Bob Burgess Collection

WJ's 75th birthday party in 1952 at 'New Ways' with, from left to right, Miss. Pheysey, Mrs. Joan Derry, WJ, Harold Bassett-Lowke, Mrs. WJ, Annie Mary Bassett-Lowke and Cyril Derry.
J Bassett-Lowke Collection

Doris, who was my aunt's eldest niece, saw quite a lot of WJ in his courting days and was obviously very fond of both aunt and uncle. She considered they were an ideal pair, except for the fact they did not have a family. She had wondered a lot about this but, according to what she told me, auntie Jane had said quite sadly to her that children *just didn't happen*. This coincides with my mother's remark to me that they did want children but in those days there was no IVF treatment to aid young couples, if they did not strike lucky. It was evident that they did seek medical help. It would be typical of WJ to accept that if things were not going to happen they wouldn't and it was no good fretting. One could not have everything one wanted in this world so one must get on with life. They became a very well liked couple, enjoying entertaining their friends, going to parties and out to shows, and they cultivated a wealth of interests. Auntie was a superb cook, and was noted for being able to tell each year to the nearest penny what she spent on housekeeping. She was an excellent seamstress and embroiderer and took a great interest in the garden. There was always a meal on time awaiting her hungry husband coming home from work, which he, having an excellent appetite, did appreciate, but he had to be home on time!

Aunt Jane had sisters and brothers who were married, and accepted her nieces and nephews with pleasure. She had a favourite younger sister who never married and they were often together when WJ was out on business or at one of his many meetings. His life appeared one rush after another; he was the dashing, pushing businessman on his way up in the world. He was a ladies' man, popular without appearing to make any effort to attract the opposite sex. If any of his friends made a rueful remark about this, he brushed the joking taunt away with a smile and continued on his winning way.

My aunt was not a jealous woman and he once said to me *there's no one I want but your auntie*, a considerable compliment to one who was troubled with arthritis but who always had a smile for the world. As much as her condition would allow, she would join wholeheartedly in his various activities. When he took a crowd of their friends on a cruise to the Mediterranean, the West Indies or the fjords of Norway, there she was, smart and good looking, seated to watch the games or on deck with friends enjoying the sun. A smile goes a long way and that was her good nature carrying her through life. I think he was a lucky man and, busy as he nearly always was, he discussed matters with her and on every occasion he kowtowed to her selection of the clothes he wore. Shirt and tie, socks and shoes, all must be in harmony. This discussion came naturally because he was colour blind!

It was several years after WJ's death before I began to be interested in Charles Rennie Mackintosh and his connection with WJ. Maybe this was because, during the Second World War, I married and in the 10 years following my husband and I produced a family of girls and boys, the youngest of whom was born in May 1953. At that time I was very pleased to take Christopher Joseph to see WJ and my aunt. Though uncle was getting quite noticeably older, he showed great pleasure in that we had named our second son after him.

Not long after, the family was taken up with a tragedy when my champion swimmer sister Vivian died suddenly at the end of June 1953 leaving a family of four young boys including a 2-month old baby. In life we all meet some happening which remains the greatest sorrow, and for me this was it. Today, I do find consolation in the knowledge that she would have been proud of all her sons.

1953 was that year of years when I grew swiftly out of my youth. In the July and August of that year WJ had become fragile and was losing his lively memory. On the last day of August my aunt wrote to their old friend Francis Parker :

My Dear Francis,

How very kind of you to send us such a lovely tin of honey. It was a lovely surprise – thank you very much indeed. I told my husband all about it, where it had come from, but he did not seem to remember you. However he thought he would like to send you one of his latest catalogues, so if you get one and a letter from his secretary you will understand about it. It seems such a long time since we saw any of you – if you are ever this way do let me know so that I can be in and give you a meal. I was sorry to miss you last time you called.

Whynne gets gradually worse and I shall soon be faced with getting a permanent nurse attendant. It seems so very sad because he had such a quick alert brain. The doctors say it is all a matter of the circulation and there is no treatment at all for it. It is very difficult to deal with and so very tiring – some days he does not even know who I am. Again many many thanks for your kindness. With regards to you and all the family when you see them.

Yours sincerely,

J. Bassett-Lowke.

Sadly my aunt was right. At first it appeared to be just a troublesome memory problem but things did not improve. He depended on the continued support of his staff and had a wonderful helper in his secretary and companion Mollie Harvey, but overstrain began to be seriously apparent. He was persuaded to go for treatment in a private hospital. For the first time in his life he had to take real relaxation and rest, but unfortunately it was too late to restore him. In the few weeks he was in hospital, my father visited his brother and each time came home saddened.

On Wednesday the 21st October 1953, the anniversary of the Battle of Trafalgar, WJ passed peacefully away at the age of 76. The funeral service took place on the Saturday at 11.30 am at Abington Avenue Congregational Church, Northampton.

As recently as the beginning of that month, his firm of Bassett-Lowke Ltd was moving from the St Andrews Street premises to their original starting point in Kingswell Street. Returning home again to occupy the extensive new building that had been erected over the past year with a fine showroom and works, a building which presented a modern look to the old street. The special room made ready, complete with a specially painted triptych portrait of their Managing Director, was waiting, never to see the founder of the business again.

All who knew WJ found it hard to believe that such an active man was gone and many hundreds of letters poured through the letterbox of his firm with their messages of sorrow and sympathy. Amongst the hundreds of tributes which arrived at the offices of Bassett-Lowke was one from Mr S K R Rutherford of Newbury, a customer of the firm who never met WJ, but who sat down to write a 600 word appreciation on receiving news of his death. Writing to Harry Franklin he declared :

> *I can think of nothing which has given me more pleasure than the outcome of his work. The passing of Mr Bassett-Lowke has affected me, in a way quite like that of a close friend. Upstairs in my railway room, all the models will stand quiet today - a simple tribute such as we can offer.*

The *Northampton Independent*, on the 23rd October 1953, wrote that :

> *All who knew Mr W J Bassett-Lowke well will find it hard to realise that he has passed for he was a man of such amazing activity and vitality throughout his seemingly tireless career. Although he was 76 years of age, his life appeared to be one of continual hurry up to a few months ago when signs of overstrain began to be seriously apparent. By his death, Northampton has lost one of its most remarkable men. His inventive ingenuity as a model maker won him a world-wide fame and incidentally enhanced the reputation of the town for craftsmanship. He also brought Northampton into prominence through his architectural ideas some of which were strikingly embodied in his home at 'New Ways', Weston Road, Northampton.*

Herbert M Prentice, The Beehive, Chipping Campden, Glos. sent a letter to the *Northampton Independent* :

> *Sir. I have just read of the death of Mr W J Bassett-Lowke, and whilst respecting the wish that there should be no letters, I should like to pay tribute to his memory and my association with him when I was at Northampton and to the work he did for the theatre during its early struggles.*

> *I have always been proud of my association with the Northampton Repertory Theatre and was very happy in my friendship with Mr Bassett-Lowke, whose enthusiasm and dynamic qualities contributed so much in those early days. There could be no finer tribute to his memory than the realisation of his aspirations and those of the whole Board, especially those who have worked for it since its inception and continue to do so.*

Before the start of business of Northampton Town Council tributes were paid to the memory of WJ. The Mayor, Alderman W A Pickering, said he was a genial personality who was well known, not only in Northampton but also throughout the country. The Mayor recalled his hard fight to secure the borough's public baths, saying he had rendered the town very good service for many years.

The monthly luncheon of Northampton Chamber of Trade was chaired by the President, W T C Smeathers, and Mr G Foster paid tribute to WJ, describing him as *a man socially a delight to know* and referring to his skill, craftsmanship and business acumen. Those present stood in silence. Following the luncheon, the speaker was Roland Fuller, whose subject was *models in war and industry*. The Design and Industries Association, paying tribute to WJ in their magazine, remarked that:

> *He will always be remembered for his great interest in improvement of design, which extended into the field of town and country planning. He was one of the founder members of the Design and Industries Association. He was with the T.C.P.A. Swedish Tour in 1947 and took an excellent colour film of it.*

The *Daily Mail* proclaimed:

> *The land of make-believe loses 'king'.*

> *The King of Lilliput is dead. And in the Land of Make-Believe there is mourning today for 74 [76] year old Wenman Joseph Bassett-Lowke - the model maker whose tiny trains, ships and planes were known all over the world. His customers ranged from small boys to Oriental princes, from millionaires to kings.*

> *Some of Wenman's models were only inches long. Others, like the ones he built for funfairs at Blackpool and Rhyl, were big enough and strong enough to haul passengers.*

> *Whatever the model however, there was always the same advice to salesmen in his shops in Manchester and London; 'Concentrate on the father. He's the one who wants the train set'.*

In his Will, WJ left £22,992 8s. 1d. (£22,992.40) gross, £22,840 17s. 9d. (£22,840.88) net. He left his set of cut-out models of locomotives, including the case they were in, to his friend Harry Franklin. His set of model waterline ships, showing the progress of transport by water, to be fitted out at the expense of his estate by Bassett-Lowke Ltd, in a flat wall case, to the County Borough of Northampton, to form part of the collection at Northampton Museum. The sum of £20 was bequeathed to the Design and Industries Association; £20 to the Friends Relief Committee Service; and £50 to Abington Avenue Congregational Church. Five hundred £1 Ordinary Shares in Bassett-Lowke Ltd were held upon trust

Throughout his life, WJ was always smartly dressed and wore distictive shirts. He always had two holes specially pierced in the collars to allow his favourite tie pin to keep his tie in order.

J Bassett-Lowke Collection

for his brother Harold for life. £500, the effects not otherwise bequeathed, the freehold property in Kingswell Street and the residue of the estate, was left to his wife upon trust for her life, and thereafter between his nieces.

Correspondence between WJ and Ernest Steel, Henry Greenly's son-in-law, in 1952 indicates that he was seriously in the process of preliminary work on his autobiography. In one letter he enquires about a booklet and photographs which Greenly had produced after one of their early visits to Messrs Carette in Germany. We are today the worse off for his failure to complete this task.

Tributes came from far and wide including, as one would expect, from the *Model Engineer* magazine:

> *We had the privilege of knowing him closely for many years and during the whole time he remained the same loveable personality; prosperity never changed him or dimmed his characteristic energy and drive. His interest and enthusiasm were infectious and inspired everyone associated with him.*
>
> *But it is as one who took so many first steps which enabled our hobby to attain its present state of perfection that he deserved and received the respect of model railway enthusiasts in every walk of life, and we feel that many of our readers will wish to join us in this affectionate salute to his memory.*

There is one final letter written by Sir Allen Lane of Penguin Books addressed to the Directors of Bassett-Lowke Ltd.

> *Dear Sirs*
>
> *It is with great regret that I received your yesterday's letter informing me of the death of your founder. As you may know, he and I had known each other for a large number of years and it was always a considerable pleasure to meet him and to share his enthusiasms.*
>
> *Having known the house of Bassett-Lowke since my early school days I had imagined before meeting Mr Bassett-Lowke himself that he must have been a very old man and it was a great surprise to me to sense his youth which remained with him up to the time of our last meeting.*

I would like to end this memoir with the obituary that first made me decide to write this book.

> *Occasionally the founders of colleges, schools and businesses become legends in their lifetimes. W J Bassett-Lowke certainly became a legend to me. As a boy I waited more impatiently for his catalogue of model locomotives than for almost anything else the postman brought. His standard of accuracy was so high that I remember being impelled to measure a railway bridge with exemplary care and making a model of it in which even rivets were not forgotten, in order to live up to his scale permanent way! But when, just after the 1914-18 War, I came to know him as one of the founder members of the Design and Industries Association I realized that his interests were far wider than railway engineering, on which his knowledge was encyclopaedic.*

He was passionately keen on improving standards of design in everyday things. In order to encourage architects who were thinking along new lines he built a house which appeared revolutionary to his neighbours in the 1920s, but has since come into its own. He used to boast that there was nothing in it older than himself! On the other hand he took a great interest in the Museum and Art Gallery at Northampton, which, like many other good causes in the city, owes much to his help and encouragement, always practical and quietly given. He retained his zest for new ideas into old age, and his death will sadden many of all ages and conditions in many walks of life.

Sir Gordon Russell

This narrative ends on the 21st October 1953; the close of a busy and rewarding life, a dear uncle and friend to many, not least his niece Janet.

THE END OF AN ERA

AND

MY SMALL TRIBUTE TO

BASSETT-LOWKE LTD.
MODEL ENGINEERS

NORTHAMPTON   **LONDON**   **MANCHESTER**

DIRECTORS OF BASSETT-LOWKE LTD. AND BASSETT-LOWKE (S.M.) LTD. (Subsidiary Company)

CYRIL DERRY, M.S.E. (Chairman)	H. F. R. FRANKLIN
R. H. FULLER } (Joint Managing Directors)	H. W. FRANKLIN
P. F. CLAYDON }	R. BINDON BLOOD
B. C. TIPPLESTON	

THE REPORT OF THE DIRECTORS

To be presented to the Shareholders at the FORTY-FIFTH ANNUAL GENERAL MEETING of the Company, to be held at the Registered Office, 18-25, Kingswell Street, Northampton, on Friday, 25th June, 1954

YOUR Directors beg to submit the Company's Balance Sheet and Profit and Loss Account for the year ending 31st March, 1954. They also submit, in accordance with the provisions of the Companies Act, 1948, the Consolidated Balance Sheet and Profit and Loss Account of the Company and its Subsidiary, Bassett-Lowke (S.M.) Ltd.

	£	£
Your Directors report that the result of the trading for the year under review is a Net Profit of		2,731
Provision for Taxation amounts to		1,536
Leaving a Balance to carry to the Appropriation Account of		1,195
The Balance brought forward from the previous year was		12,063
		13,258
It is proposed, with the approval of the Shareholders to pay the Dividend of 5% on the Cumulative Preference Shares .. .. Net	27	
and the Directors recommend that a Dividend of 10% for the year be declared and paid on the Ordinary Shares .. .. .. Net	986	
		1,013
		£12,245

The death of Mr. W. J. Bassett-Lowke—founder and first Managing Director—at the age of 78 was deeply regretted, not only by those near to him, but also by many thousands throughout the world who had known him personally or by repute.

Messages of sympathy received from so many countries are an appreciation of the man and his achievement and a reminder to us that his personality had created a universally accepted connection between good craftsmanship in models and the name " Bassett-Lowke." No greater respect can be paid to departed merit than that the standard of the Company should be maintained at the highest level.

During the year reviewed by these accounts, the Northampton Building Scheme was completed and the premises finally occupied on the 5th October, 1953. Although full occupation commenced only recently, it is clear that the new premises will provide for more economical working. These economies are not reflected in these accounts, but the benefits will accrue in a full year's experience.

Trade generally throughout the year provided a satisfactory turnover at £129,000 of which £66,000 was for special products by the subsidiary company and the balance of £63,000 by retail sales through the branches and by mail order. The retail trade of model railways by mail order and through our London and Manchester shops continues to be subject to a fluctuating market, but your Directors have confidence that the forward position is satisfactory.

Despite the considerable cost and disturbance of removal to new premises, the nett profit remains at the same level as last year. It is hoped that this will be considered satisfactory since the Company may now be regarded as settled in circumstances which will enable it to accomplish increased production with savings in cost.

The Consolidated Balance Sheet and Accounts disclose that there is an aggregate credit carried forward on Profit and Loss Account at 31st March, 1954, of £15,056 after making provision for the Dividends recommended above.

In succession to Mr. W. J. Bassett-Lowke, Mr. R. H. Fuller and Mr. P. F. Claydon were appointed Joint Managing Directors on the 22nd January, 1954.

In accordance with the Articles of Association, Mr. Bernard Tippleston, elected Director on the 22nd January, 1954, in place of the late Mr. W. J. Bassett-Lowke ; and Mr. Cyril Derry, Mr. R. Bindon Blood and Mr. H. W. Franklin, elected Directors at the last Annual Meeting, retire from the Board, but being eligible, offer themselves for re-appointment.

The Auditors, Messrs. A. C. Palmer and Co., offer themselves for re-appointment.

Dated this 1st day of June, 1954,

By order of the Board,

CYRIL DERRY,

Chairman

Postscript

by John Milner

As related in Chapter 9, Precision Models who were Bassett-Lowke's main source of supply and who were under the control of Trix Ltd, folded. This left the company without any input into the rapidly developing '00' market, which WJ had started, and no future supplies for the '0' gauge market, which was in decline anyway. After WJ's death, Roland Fuller and Percy Claydon became joint Managing Directors of the firm. In 1964, Claydon died and Roland was left as Managing Director on his own with Arch. Cox becoming General Manager.

In 1958, the manager of the London shop retired and his place was taken by a new one. He failed to produce what was required if the business was to survive. A last ditch attempt was made in 1962 by way of a marketing campaign which proved a failure and, in 1964, the retail side of Bassett-Lowke was sold to Beatties who already had toy shops in London. In the same year, Cyril Derry (Chairman of Bassett-Lowke) died and Percy Claydon (Joint Managing Director) retired. Bassett-Lowke had lost a lot of its expertise, other than in the field of specialist model making. The management over the years had failed to recognise the rapid change in the market and the opportunities which were there, and the company had eaten up its reserves and was now under-capitalised. A retired Bank Manager, H Talbot Butler, who was a close friend of Mrs. Bassett-Lowke and advised her after WJ's death, became Chairman but, sadly, he was ill experienced for the job.

The Bassett-Lowke and Franklin families sold all their shares in 1966/67 to Richard Derry (son of Cyril Derry) and Barrie Riley, who ran mail order and cleaning firms respectively. Bassett-Lowke ceased all of its traditional model railway production, although there was a small exception. It still had a stock of parts for the '0' gauge *Mogul* locomotive and these were later assembled, producing what was the last of its own railway products from Northampton. The company, although in a smaller way, continued with its specialised architectural, industrial and ship modelling, but this also was starting to decline, and continued to do so.

In 1968, Bassett-Lowke (SM) Ltd were approached by Steam Age of Cadogan Street, London, in order to see whether or not an arrangement, for selling the Bassett-Lowke ³/₄ inch scale *Burrell* traction engine on an exclusive basis, was possible. Ivan Rutherford Scott, the proprietor of Steam Age, discussed the matter with Allen Levy (who was the inspiration behind the London Toy Museum) who suggested that it would make more sense to take on the whole range of Bassett-Lowke model trains. In return for being given the sole right to market Bassett-Lowke model railway products, Bassett-Lowke (Railways) Ltd. would offer the Northampton factory all the restoration work from Steam Age, and also give them first option to manufacture new products. Thus, the two companies entered into an arrangement. Steam Age was basically a retail outlet, dealing in new and secondhand model and miniature railway equipment, and what one would call today, collectables in the model and toy field. As a result of the arrangement, the '0' gauge live steam *Mogul* was re-introduced on to the market. After several years, Allen Levy resigned from the Company and his intterest was acquired by Marcel Darphin, the founder of the Swiss model railway producer Darstead. Several years later, Ivan Scott died and his widow inherited the business. After several years of trading at new premises in Kensington, the name Bassett-Lowke (Railways) Ltd was transferred back to the main Company.

In 1970, the firm took on a new lease of life when it was acquired by Ann Ritchie (ex. Wife of Richard Derry née Wates of the Wates building firm) acquired the firm and became Chair of Bassett-Lowke Holdings Ltd. Three major appointments were made. In November 1970, Mike Fielding, C.Eng., M.I.Mech E., M.I.E.D. joined as Director, who in turn appointed John Ashby as Works Manager. In 1972, Arthur Tobbitt joined as Group Managing Director. The models, which the company built at this time, were very different from those during WJ's era. Now there were models of spacecraft, communication satellites, a training railway for Egyptian Railways, another such railway for Malaysian Railways, a model of the Hong Kong transit system and even channel tunnel boring machines. The tradition of Bassett-Lowke was carried on with many private commissions for ships and locomotive models.

In 1984 moved into 4000 sq. ft. purpose built building in Harvey Reeves Road, Northampton, abandoning the original Kingswell Street premises. The order book remained good and included models of the *Mary Rose*, two one fifth scale Rover Metro cars, along with work for numerous regular customers. It was perhaps fitting that one of the last models built, before the company changed hands, was a $2\frac{1}{2}$" gauge model of a rebuilt Bullied Pacific, constructed to the finest detail.

Due to the pressure of her other business interests, Ann Ritchie sold the business in 1989 to Nigel Turner, a successful Northampton businessman well known for his Turner's Musical Merry-go-Round Ltd tourist attraction in the town. He enlisted the help of Design Consultant Marcel van Cleemput who, for 30 years, had been the Chief designer for Mettoy, manufacturers of Corgi toys. Throughout these changes Mike Fielding kept the threads of the business together, but was to leave the company in 1990.

Despite their attempts to develop and diversify, Nigel Turner decided to sell the business in 1991/92 to Ken Robinson (Acorn Models), a Wellingborough businessman and, under the leadership of his son Andrew along with Paul Martin, the business concentrated on limited edition die-cast models.

Corgi Classics Limited, of Leicester, acquired certain assets and the intellectual property relating to the Bassett-Lowke business from Channel Asset Management Limited in August 1996, and the company is now a wholly owned subsidiary of Corgi Classics Limited, thus ending 97 years of association with Northampton. Hopefully, this latest change will usher in a total new lease of life for Bassett-Lowke, and carry its name forward into the next century. Despite all the changes since 1953, of which WJ would perhaps have not approved, at least on the 100th anniversary of his company the name of Bassett-Lowke is still with us and about to perhaps take on a new lease of life into the next century.

Lowko is now a registered Trade mark of Corgi Classics Ltd

Acknowledgements

I have many people to thank, from near and far, for their help with these memoirs of my uncle. I apologise to anyone I may have missed. First of all the Bassett-Lowke and Jones families; my Aunt Jane (Mrs. B-L), her niece Doris Cutting, great niece Jane Preston, my mother and father, my youngest sister June and my daughter Marilyn, who has spent many hours deciphering and typing the early drafts of the book; she has been a pillar of support over the years. I have been fortunate to have invaluable assistance from Raymond Stutley, who worked at Bassett-Lowke at the same time as myself and altogether gave 40 years service to the firm.

Here I must mention the aid of three local people, who are no longer with us, being the late Victor Hatley, Northampton librarian who, with his enthusiasm for the whole project, convinced me that I was the only person left in the family who could make it become reality, and the late Councillors (and Mayor) Alwyn Hargrave and Roger Alder who took much interest in 78 Derngate and local work which my uncle had done for the town.

I much appreciated the asssistance from Roland Fuller's daughters, Jane and Susan, who allowed me access to the family records at what was a difficult time for them. I thank Sir Hugh Casson for his permission to quote from his 1952 broadcast and Dr. Ing Till Behrens for information and use of the photograph of his eminent grandfather.

My introduction to WJ's connection with Charles Rennie Mackintosh sparked my interest. In this connection, I am indebted to Roger Billcliffe, Keeper of the Mackintosh archive at the Hunterian Museum (1970s); the Hunterian Museum's Senior Curator, Pamela Robertson; and Patricia Douglas MBE (ex. Director of the the Mackintosh Society) who have given me valuable assistance on Mackintosh matters.

Thanks go wholeheartedly to Mr. Roger Morris (Chief Executive and Town Clerk, Northampton Borough Council) who undertook to edit the entire manuscript; a task which he admirably performed; Councillor Les Patterson, recently Mayor of Northampton and now secretary of the 78 Derngate Trust; Sheila Stone, Curator, Angela Edgar, Collections Manager, Judith Hodgkinson, Keeper of Social History, of the Central Museum, Northampton; and Rachel Watson, Northamptonshire County Archivist.

On behalf of John Milner and myself I thank all those who have assisted, too numerous to mention in detail here, but in particular R. Avery; Bob Burgess and Peter Parks of the Bassett-Lowke Society; Corgi Classics Ltd.; Rachel Boom, Royal Collection Enterprises Ltd., Windsor Castle; Dr. John Brown (ex. John Brown of Clydebank); Alan Burman; the staff of Bristol University; Mike Fielding, Chris Fincken; John Hall-Craggs; S. Tarig Ibrahim; Mr. Christopher Packard, Doreen Curran and Joanne Sherwin of Kvaerner Energy Ltd; Allen Levy; Les Patterson, 78 Derngate Trust; Andrea Peach; John Roan Photography, Northampton; Simon Townsend; Nigel Turner; Peter Trowles, Glasgow School of Art; Winnie Tyrrell, The Burrell Collection, Glasgow; Sydney Wainright; Katrina Milner for anicillary typing; Alistair Kerr for specialist photography; the staff of Lazertype, Wrexham, for their devoted attention and the staff of Jazz Design, Chester. Special thanks go to Robin Butterell who kindly made available his early and more recent research work on Bassett-Lowke.

Finally, my grateful thanks for the generous financial assistance given by Northampton Borough Council, the 78 Derngate Trust and anonymous donors, which enables us to include colour illustrations in the book.

Lastly and most important of all, I must thank the greatest assistant one could wish to have, my editor and publisher John Milner, for the tremendous amount of energy and time he has spent in bringing this book into being for me. He deserves success in this enterprise.

Bibliography

The Bassett-Lowke Story : Roland Fuller	1984
Bassett-Lowke Waterline Ship Models : Derek Head	1996
Charles Rennie Mackintosh: Art is the Flower : Pamela Robertson	1995
Charles Rennie Mackintosh and The Modern Movement : Thomas Howarth	1977
Charles Rennie Mackintosh - Complete Furniture, Drawings and Interiors : Roger Billcliffe	1979
C.R.Mackintosh - The Chelsea Years : Alan Crawford and incorporating *A Memoir of W.J. Bassett-Lowke* by Janet Bassett-Lowke	1994
Charles Rennie Mackintosh : Edited by Wendy Kaplan	1996
History of Scouting in Northamptonshire : Brian Brayshaw	1984
Craftsman and Quaker, The Story of James T. Baily 1876-1957 : Leslie Baily	1959
The Maharajahs : John Lord	1972
Freedom at Midnight : Larrie Collins and Dominique Lapierne	1989
Adventure in Repertory : Aubrey Dyas	1948
Rails Through The Sand : W J Milner	1996
50 Years of Model Making : Bassett-Lowke Ltd	1949
The Miniature World of Henry Greenly : E A Steel and E H Steel	1973
Liliputbahnen : Jng. Dr. Walter Strauss, Germany	1938

Northamptonshire County Records Office (Wootton Park) - Deposited Plans Register.

    A E Anderson - Work for Lowke and Bassett-Lowke families:
    Warehouse in Kingswell Street for J T Lowke J163
    Warehouse 10/11/1903 - *Model Steel* 12/2/13 A230
    78 Derngate for W J Bassett-Lowke 1/6/1916 F250
    Additions to Albion Place House for H A Bassett-Lowke 16/1/1922 N208
    New Ways, exors of Henry Green and owners of the site - 10/2/1025 V217
    Francis Parker Collection

Bassett-Lowke family records (private collection)

Mackintosh Collection - Hunterian Museum, University of Glasgow.

RailRomances archive collections (private collection)

The Royal Institute of British Architects collection - Professor Dr. Peter Behrens and *New Ways*.

The Model Engineer magazine 1898 forward.

Catalogues and publications of Bassett-Lowke - Basset-Lowke Society archive collection.

78 DERNGATE

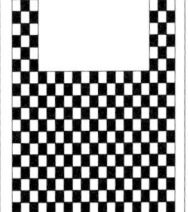

The 78 Derngate Northampton Trust is a registered charity and was formed in February 1998 its purpose is:

To restore and make available to the public 78 Derngate and to thereby deepen understanding and broaden awareness of the work and contribution of both Charles Rennie Mackintosh and W. J. Bassett-Lowke to its creation

If you would like to find out more about the work of the Trust please contact:
The Secretary,
The 78 Derngate Northampton Trust,
c/o 4, Clock Tower Court,
Thorplands,
Northampton. NN3 8YP.

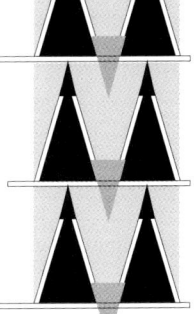

The 78 Derngate Northampton trust is a Charity Company Limited by guarantee. Charity No. 1068270
Registered office, The Guildhall, St. Giles Square, Northampton NN1 1DA.
Trustees: Mr. K. Barwell; Mrs. M. Barwell; Dr. M. Gaskell ; Mrs. P. Douglas MBE; Mr. L. Patterson

78 DERNGATE

Appendix 1

PROFESSOR Dr. PETER BEHRENS, WIEN, VII, KARL SCHWEIGHOFERGASSE 3/III, TEL. 30-4-95

                                        Vienna, 7th August 1926.

Mr.

B A S S E T T - L O W K E

                              N o r t h a m p t o n
                              76 , D e r n g a t e
                              E n g l a n d .

Dear Sir.

    I herewith beg to accept my best thanks for your favour of the 29th ult. and although for the great number of photos, you have sent. I am very pleased that the impression, I have got out of them is considerable well. You will certainly understand that I have been very curious to see, in which manner our work has been finished, because I have nOt been enabled to be on the working - place during the time of building. Selfunderstood it would has been a pleasure for me to help you with regards to the making of the interior. I could see out of the sent photos that you have stablished the interior with the best tast, but nevertheless I would like to make some reform - proposals for the case, you will not take it amiss.

    I found the hall not only roomy, but although very beautiful, nevertheless I think, just so than you that the hall is too bare and that different stencil - decorations would be of advantage. I suppose, it is of importance in which manner such pictures are placed, for which reason I have made a sketch, showing the placing of these stencils, as I am thinking.

    Although re lounge you are quite right that the walls seems to be a little bare. I should like to propose, to place a long picture in the form of a frieze above the side-board, further a fine, but not too large relief above the fire - place. The other free ~~plans~~ walls could although be animated by pictures or stencils, for which case an ornamentation of the tapestry will not be nessecary. But, when you prefer this ornamentation, please do not employ a too animate design, but geometrical designs, in the manner as these, I am forwarding at the same time.

The electric light fitting I have seen on the photo is not according this one, I have proposed. Please be so kind to proof still once the natural detail, I have drawn. To - day I will although forward a proposal re alteration to reform it without difficulty. Another lighting - body would certainly distribute the harmony with the ceiling, because the lighting - body shall be understood as a part of the ceiling.

I am seeing with much interst, you are proposing a publication of the house in the periodical " The Architectural Review ", at which I have been co - worker some time ago. I think, we shall try to finish at first the house without any fault in tast, not only in consideration of the periodical but although with regards, that your house is a novelty for England and that we suppose to carry through the new style in England; then we must try to get beautiful photos, being of course well reproductions. Certainly there are some photos, very well to need, but I think, that they will nevertheless not be satisfying. I would like to publish a discourse about your house in a german periodical, but then I must have effectively well photos.

PROFESSOR DR. PETER BEHRENS, WIEN, VII., KARL SCHWEIGHOFERGASSE 3/III, TEL. 30-4-95

2.

I would remark re photo of the entrance, being certainly a very well picture, that the small trees are deranging, although the lamp, placed inside must be removed, when taking the photo.

Aspects of the facade are omitted; an aspect of the northern front would be of great importance, further a photo of the staircase with the ~~pump~~ basin on the southern side.

The small photo of the lounge without table is roomy much better than the large one.

Photo of the hall must ba taken, when the stencils are placed-. The rails of the fire - body are very hard in effect. They can be coloured dark in the shade of the mirror - frame or, there can be placed a fine rail of light metal behind the wood.

I have proposed to make a small basis for the lighting - pillars by a listel. In my plan I did not suppose to place the pillars on the wall; there will mow certainly be nessecary abasis.

Further I would recommend to make the photo of the hall against the entrance from a place in larger distance, therefore from the dining-room.

In consideration of all, the places from which the photos have been made, seems not to be the best. It would be of advantage to make a considerable number of small photos, of which you will get certainly the best directions, how to make the large photos.

I regret very much that I am not enabled to have a talk with regard to all this with you on the place in England himself, for which reason I beg at the more to let me have further informations.

I would ask you to do so and remain, with kind regards to Mrs. Bassett - Lowke, dear Sir

Your faithfully
Behrens

Appendix 2

Chronological Events 1859 - 1953

1859

The engineering business of Absalom Bassett established in Northampton.

1877

W J Bassett-Lowke was born.

1899

Bassett-Lowke & Co. established in Kingswell Street, Northampton. First catalogue published and advertising inserted in the new journal, *The Model Engineer*.

1900

New types of low pressure slide valve steam engines introduced to this country from the Continent. First high pressure Gauge 1 steam locomotive, a Lancashire and Yorkshire inside cylinder locomotive, placed on the market. Paris Exhibition - beginning of Continental influence.

1901

Low pressure steam model of the famous L.N.W.R. *Black Prince* locomotive in 2½" Gauge introduced. First quantity produced scale model to be placed on the English market. Mr Henry Greenly appointed consulting engineer and designer to the Company.

1902

Small scale model permanent way devised by Mr George Winteringham offered for the first time both as separate parts and ready-laid track. A new Works was erected for the manufacture of scale model railway components under the direction for Mr George Winteringham.

1903

A ¾ inch to the foot model signalling instruction table constructed to the order of the Great Western Railway.

1904

Formation of subsidiary company, *Miniature Railways of Great Britain Ltd*, for the operation of passenger carrying railways up to 15in. gauge. First complete Gauge 1 model railway set advertised in the national press. A new 3¾" gauge model of the Midland 4-4-0 locomotive and tender constructed entirely of castings. Range of model locomotives offered totalled 40 in number.

Sultan of Turkey ordered complete model railway for his palace in Constantinople. Special model of the latest Great Northern Railway locomotive was ordered by the Duke of Zaragoza, Spain.

1905

New Bassett-Lowke products included first mass produced stationery steam engine, Gauge 2 model great Northern *Atlantic* locomotive, high pressure locomotives in Gauges 2 and 2½" and a new model locomotive injector displayed on the first Bassett-Lowke public exhibition stand at the first Model Engineer Exhibition held in London. First edition of the *Model Railway Handbook* published and the new catalogue divided into three sections.

1906

First scale model electric locomotive, a Gauge 2 G.N.R. single driver introduced.

A silver model table railway constructed for the Maharajah of Gwalior.

1907

On the Company's stand at the Model Engineer Exhibition was demonstrated for the first time a complete electric model railway using centre rail conductor.

Two demonstration model railways made to the order of the L.N.W.R. Co. for the Trades Exhibition at Bingley Hall, Birmingham, and the Irish International Exhibition at Dublin. Also introduced of special locomotive motor for models in all gauges up to 3½in. advertised under the new trade name *LOWKO*.

1908

First retail branch opened in London at 257 High Holborn, with Mr E W Hobbs as Manager.

A large Gauge 2 electricity operated model railway built for the L.N.W.R. exhibit at the Franco-British Exhibition at White City, London.

Formation of subsidiary company, Messrs. Winteringham Ltd. with greatly enlarged manufacturing facilities for Bassett-Lowke products.

1909

Formation of Bassett-Lowke Ltd., a limited liability company, with Jack Sears as first Chairman. The Northampton business moved to entirely new premises.

Gauge 1 working model railway built for the Imperial Services Exhibition.

15" gauge steam locomotive *Green Dragon* awarded Gold

Medal at the *Model Engineer Exhibition*, London, and *Entente Cordiale* a gold medal at *International Exhibition*, Nancy. 7¼" gauge Great Central Railway locomotive built for Mr Coates of Paisley. 15" gauge 4-4-4 petrol driven locomotive made to the order of Mr C W Bartholomew at Blakesley Hall, Northamptonshire.

Fleet of waterline models of three ships to a scale of ¹/₁₀th inch to the foot supplied to the order of the Navy League.

New Racing Hydroplane model introduced.

1910

The London Showroom and Retail Shop moved to larger premises at 112 High Holbourn. Bassett-Lowke Ltd., awarded the *Diploma of Honour* at the Brussels Exhibition for working model railway designed and built for the East Coast Joint Stock Railways.

The Caledonian Railway Co. placed orders for 30,000 clockwork models of the 4-6-0 tender locomotive *Cardean* to a scale of ¼ inch to the foot.

The Prince of Wales purchased a model electric lighting plant, Special model Mono-Rail built for Governor of Kostroma, Russia.

New range of scale model ships fittings introduced.

Signalling instruction model to a scale of ¾ inch to the foot for the L.N.W.R. Co.

1911

Miniature Railways of Great Britain Ltd liquidated and superseded by Marrow gauge Railways Ltd. Locomotives and rolling stock supplied for the 15in. Gauge railway at Rhyl, North Wales and Llewellyn Miniature Railway, Southport.

Two special models of locomotives built for the Crown Agents for the Colonies for the presentation to the Emir of Katsena, Nigeria.

Complete model railway supplied to the Kwong Tung Yueh-Han Railway.

Models of the airships flown by Ms. Paulhan and Mr Graham White made and exhibited in Northampton.

For the *Glasgow Exhibition* a complete Gauge 2 electrically operated model railway built for the Great Northern, North Eastern and North British Railway Companies combined exhibit.

1912

Architectural model of Blackpool to a scale of 40ft. to the inch built to the order of the Blackpool Corporation.

A 15in. Gauge complete model railway built and despatched to the King of Siam at Bangkok.

A similar 15in. Gauge model also supplied to Sir Robert Walker of Sand Hutton. A complete 15in. Gauge passenger-carrying railway constructed for Luna Park, Geneva.

First Continental retail agency established in Paris.

1913

Architectural models made of Port Sunlight for Messrs. Lever Bros., and Immingham Docks for the Great Central Railway Company.

Fleet of working model battleships ranging from 12 to 20 feet long built for the Imperial Services Exhibition, Earls Court.

Imperial Services Exhibition, Earles Court. First introduction of miniature, scale, waterline ship models for public demonstration.

A model of the site of the Aisgill Railway disaster built to the order of the Court of Enquiry.

1914

Special model of the site and foundation stone for Port Sunlight Garden City used when H.M. King George V performed ceremony of laying the foundation stone.

Children's Welfare Exhibition at Olympia- 9½" gauge model railway installed – Winston Churchill as passenger.

Model of Dye Works built to the order of Messrs. Pullars of Perth.

Model motor car chassis built for the Rover Company of Coventry. Model of Rotterdam Dock works to the order of the Wilton Engineering and Shipway Co.

1914-1918

W J Bassett-Lowke purchased *Candida Cottage* in Roade – 1914

J T Lowke purchased *78 Derngate* for W J Bassett-Lowke - 1916

During the entire period of World War I the Company's facilities were used entirely for the production of screw gauges for the Ministry of Munitions. During 1915 the 15" gauge *Ravenglass and Eskdale Railway* and the *Fairbourne Miniature Railway* were built.

1919

Works enlarged and mass production plant installed for manufacture of popular small gauge models hitherto made on the Continent.

During this period Bassett-Lowke Ltd. were engaged to some extent in making various models of wartime equipment for record purposes and for museums.

1920

A large number of models of warships, aeroplanes, tanks, road vehicles were constructed.

1921

¹/₁₂th inch to the foot scale model S.S. *Olympic* built to the

order of the White Star Line.

Special department organised for the production of exhibition models of ships, etc.

1922

First quality production '00' Gauge model railway placed on the market.

New retail Branch opened in Edinburgh.

Working models of Post Office Mail Vans operating with ground gear for Gauge '0' and Gauge '1' model railways.

Half inch scale model of a Burma Railway 4-6-0 Tender locomotive build to the order of the Locomotive Superintendent's Department.

First American Agency established in New York City. $^1/_8$ inch to the foot model *Massilia* built to the order of the Companie Sud Atlantique.

1923

Extension of Works for the exhibition and ship models. $^1/_8$ inch to the foot scale model *Majestic* for White Star Line.

1924

New Ways house, designed by Prof. Dr. Peter Behrens, built for W J Bassett-Lowke.

Smallest model railway in the world made for the Queen's Dolls House.

Models included Cunard Line *Aquitania*, *Mauretania*, *Berengaria*, built for the *Wembley Exhibition*.

2$^1/_2$ inch Gauge model of Canadian Pacific Railway system. Challenger locomotive trials at the *Model Engineer Exhibition*.

1925

Harwich-Zeebrugge train ferry model for L.N.E.R.

Wembley Exhibition, second year. Treasure Island Railway. H.M. King George V and Queen Mary visited the Exhibition and rode on the railway.

1 inch scale 2-8-2 locomotive for Nigerian Railways.

New *King Arthur* class locomotive for S.R.

1in. scale model railway for Sir Berkeley Sheffield.

$^1/_{10}$th inch to the foot model of *Cutty Sark*.

1926

2 inch scale garden railway for Maharajah of Jodhpur.

$^1/_8$th scale *Asturias* model for R.M.S.P.

$^1/_2$ inch scale Compound locomotive for L.M.S. 10ft. to 1in. scale model *Shrimp* for Lord Louis Mountbatten.

1927

Manchester Branch opened. 30,000 Gauge '0' locomotives distributed under B.D.V. gift coupon scheme.

1928

2 inch Scale garden railway for Sir Edward Nicholl, of Littleton Park.

$^3/_4$ inch scale *Royal Scot* locomotive for L.M.S.

1$^1/_2$ inch scale garden railway installed on roof of Messrs. Pontings, London.

2 inch scale garden railway supplied to the Maharajah of Patiala.

1929

$^1/_{10}$th scale model *H.M.S. Hood* for Lord Howard de Walden.

Three models of *Carnarvon Castle* for Union Castle Co.

Full-size replica of the front of the L.M.S. *Royal Scot* used for Model Engineer Exhibition Stand.

First mass produced scale model of *Royal Scot* introduced.

1930

Model railway supplied to racing motorist Sir Henry Seagrave.

$^3/_4$ inch scale model of *King George V* locomotive for Great Western Railway Company.

Express of Britain model, 21ft. long, for the Canadian Pacific Exhibit in the Lord Mayor's Show.

Langibby Castle models for Union Castle Mail Steamship Co.

Antwerp Exhibition, British Section. Working scale model $^1/_{16}$ inch to the foot made of Harwich-Zeebrugge train ferry and the dock at Harwich end of journey. Electrically driven.

1931

Miniature Railway ticket sorting device supplied to the Irish Sweepstake, Dublin.

M.V. Bermuda, scale $^1/_4$ inch to the foot for Shaw, Savill and Albion. Twenty-nine models *L'Atlantique* for the Charguers Reunis, Paris.

Series of sectional models of *Empress of Britain* for the Canadian Pacific Railway Co.

1932

Waterline models of *Champlain* for the French Lines.

2 inch scale railway installed at Southsea.

$^1/_4$ inch scale *Marnix van Aldegaande* for Nederlands Royal Mail.

Strathmore 1/12th scale, for P. & O. Company.

$^1/_4$ inch scale *Arandora Star* for Blue Star Line.

$^1/_8$ inch scale model *Georgie* for Cunard-White Star Co.

1inch scale Pullman car *Hazel* for the Southern Railway.

1933

$^1/_8$th scale model of the *Britannic* for Cunard-White Star.

¼ inch scale model presented to the driver of the *Royal Scot* during official visit to Northampton.

Cabin models of the Heysham-Ulster route vessels for the L.M.S.

Publicity aircraft models made for Imperial Airways.

1934

Models of pylons for the new electric grid system. Scale milk pasteur)sing plant for United Dairies Co.

¼ inch scale model of the underground system for the London Passenger Transport Board.

⅛th scale models of the *Champlain* and *Colombie* for the French Lines.

¼ inch scale working model Canal for the Grand Union Canal Co.

1½ inch scale model *Locomotion No. 1* for Robert Stephenson & Co., makers of the original.

¾ inch scale model of de luxe tourist car for Great Indian Peninsular Railway, modelled in section.

⅜ inch scale Travelling Post Office model for G.P.O. Exhibit at Radiolympia.

1935

⅛th scale *Normandie* waterline model, internally-lit, 10ft. 4in. long, for French Lines.

¼ inch scale model of the *Queen Mary* for the Cunard-White Star Co.

Model of Graf Zeppelin for the Science Museum.

Trix Twin Trains first introduced.

1936

7¼" gauge *Royal Scot* locomotive for C. N. Rinek of Easton, Pennsylvania.

9½" gauge garden railway for Capt. Ward Jones.

Gauge '0' model railway installed in the Children's Playroom of the R.M.S. *Queen Mary*.

1937

⅛th scale *Awetea* for the Union Steamship Co.

⅛th inch scale model of the yacht *Endeavour* for Mr T. O. M. Sopwith.

1 inch scale model dual purpose fire engine for Messrs. Dennis Bros.

1½ inch scale model *Rocket* for the Royal Scottish Museum.

Panorama Model of British Merchant Navy for the Paris Exhibition.

1938

Exhibition model railway for the four British Groups for the *British Empire Exhibition*, Glasgow.

1inch scale model *Hampton Ferry* train ferry model for S.R. ¼ inch scale model motor yacht *Philante* for Mr T.O.M. Sopwith.

Centenary model of Euston Station and train of the period 1838 for L.M.S. Railway Company.

Three ⅛th inch scale models *Dominion Monarch* for the Shaw, Savill and Albion Co.

¼ inch scale model of coal mine and surface workings for British Mining Association, for *British Empire Exhibition*, Glasgow.

1939

10¼" gauge, *Royal Scot* locomotive supplied to Marquis of Downshire.

Six models of *Strathaird* and *Strathmore* for the P. & O. Steamship Co.

3/16 inch scale model new *Mauretania* for Messrs. Cammell-Laird & Co.

3/16 inch scale model *H.M.S. Hood* for Messrs. John Brown, Clydebank.

Introduction of new set of parts for constructing Gauge '0' Mogul Locomotive.

1940-1945

In contrast to World War I, the entire capacity of the Bassett-Lowke factory was concentrated on model making throughout the Second World War. Many thousands of model were supplied to the Services for rapid training of personnel. A considerable proportion of the work was of a highly confidential nature, but amongst the more famous war-time developments first modelled in Northampton were the Ingles Bridge, the Bailey Bridge, the Mulberry Harbour, every type of landing and assault craft, new types of vehicles and armaments, etc.

In the closing stages of the war, permission was given for part of productive capacity to be employed in the supply of models for post-war developments in Town Planning and re-housing schemes. Also, in support of the anticipated Export Drive, many models of new designs of motor cars were made for the Rootes Group.

1946-1949

British Industry now faced the stern problem of re-establishment to peace-time conditions. The *Britain Can Make It Exhibition* held to show the high quality of British products included a display of new Bassett-Lowke models.

1/48th scale model of *H.M.S. Vanguard* built for John Brown Shipyard – 1947

¼ inch to the foot model of *R.M.S. Queen Elizabeth* built for Cunard.

APPENDIX 2

New models and many accessories added to the standard range of Basset-Lowke products. Industrial re-building and re-equipment of factories, town planning and re-building schemes, new products for home sale and export required a medium for publicity - the post war period saw a flood of special models being commissioned and supplied to :

The Anglesey County Council
Messrs. D. Badcock (Marine) Ltd.
Messrs. Beyer Peacock & Co.
The Blue Star Line,
The Borough of Tynemouth
Th British Electrical Development Association.
The British Gas Association.
The British India Steam Navigation Co.
British Railways.
The British Thomson-Houston Co.
Messrs. Henry Browne & Son Ltd.
Messrs. John Brown Clydebank.
The Burntisland Shipping Co.
Messrs. Cammell Laird & Co.
Messrs. Camper & Nicholson Ltd.
The Canadian Commercial Corporation.
The Canadian Pacific Steamship Co.
The Central Office of Information.
Messrs. Clarke Chapman & Co.,
Messrs. Cohen & Wilks Ltd.
The Colombo Port Commission.
The Commonwealth of Australia.
The Consett Iron Co. Ltd.
Messrs. Richard Costaine Ltd.
The Coventry City Council.
Messrs. Crossley Motors.
The Crown Agents for the Colonies.
The Cunard-White Star Co.
Messrs. Cussons & Sons Ltd.
Messrs. William Denny & Bros Ltd.
The Department of Scientific and Industrial Research.
The Design Research Unit.
Messrs. Dorin & Leach.
The English Electric Co. Ltd.
Messrs, Evans Medical Supplies Ltd.
Messrs F. T. Everard & Co.
The French Line.
The General Electric Company.
Messrs. Gilfillan & Co.
The Gloucester Corporation.
Messrs. Harland & Wolff.
Messrs. C. R. Harper & Co. (Agencies) Ltd.
Messrs. Wm. Harvie & Co.
Messrs. Raymond Hawkins (Lotus Shoes).

Messrs. Hawthorn Leslie & Co.
Messrs. Charles Hill & Co., Bristol.
Messrs. Kilpatrick & Son Ltd.
The Kingston-upon-Hull Corporation.
Messrs. Lewis Berger & Sons Ltd.
Messrs. Lobnitz & Co.
The Measham Motors Sales Organisation.
Messrs. Mechans Ltd.
The Metropolitan Cammell Carriage & Wagon Co.
The Miners Welfare Commission.
The Ministry of Works.
The Motherwell Bridge Engineering Co. Ltd.
The New Zealand Shipping Co.
Nottingham University.
Messrs. Odhams Press Ltd.
The Oxford Stadium Ltd.
Messrs. E. O'Sullivan Ltd.
The Palliser Works.
The Peninsular & Oriental Steamship Co.
Messrs. Wm. Pickersgill & Sons Ltd.
Plymouth Breweries.
The Port of London Authority.
Messrs. Robert Pringle & Sons.
Messrs. Richard Johnson & Nephew.
Messrs. Rootes Securities Ltd.
The Royal Mail Lines.
Messrs. Rushton Bucyrus Ltd.
The Scotch Whisky Association.
Messrs. Shaw, Savill & Albion Co. Ltd.
Messrs. Shelvoke & Drewry.
Messrs. Thomas Smith & Sons (Rodley) Ltd.
The South American Saint Line Ltd.
Messrs. James Stott Ltd., Oldham.
Messrs. Clifford Strange & Associates.
The Superheater Co.
Messrs. Swan Hunter & Wigham Richardson.
The Union Castle Line.
The Van Leer Equipment Co.
Messrs. Vauxhall Motors Ltd.
Messrs. Vickers Armstrong Ltd.
Messrs. Walker Bros. (Wigan) Ltd.
The Wallsend Slipway & Engineering Co. Ltd.
The Wandsworth & District Gas Co.
Messrs. Wests Gas Improvement Co.

1953
Wednesday 21st October 1953, W J Bassett-Lowke died at the age of 76.

Index

A

Abington Avenue Congregational Church 232
Adnitts Haberdashers 199
Advertising labels 108
Alexander Thomson Studentship 96
Allen, Cecil J 119, 219
Allied Invasion of Europe 224
Anderson, Alexander Ellis 31, 43, 96, 103
Anderson, William J 96
Anniversary, 50th 36, 188
Arthingworth Manor 32
Ashby, John 238
Ashton, L 199
Attlee, Clement 188

B

Bailey Bridge 155
Baily, James T 106
Barber, William 39
Bartholomew, C W 42
Bashir, S M 140
Bassett, Absalom 15
Bassett and Sons 15
Bassett, Frederick George 22
Bassett, Harry White Birdsall 19
Bassett, Tom Absalom 19
Bassett-Lowke & Co. 32
Bassett-Lowke (Railways) Ltd 237
Bassett-Lowke (SM) Ltd 212
Bassett-Lowke, Harold Austin 20
Bassett-Lowke Ltd 58
Bassett-Lowke, Vivian 189, 213, 230
Baths Committee 189
Battle, Charles Henry 43, 100, 161
Beattie, H Musk 161
Beckonscot Model Village 70
Behrens, Professor Dr. Peter 77, 169, 184
Bernard Shaw, George 165
Beyer Peacock & Co. Ltd 146
Bing Bros. 37, 113
Bing, Franz 118, 221
Bing, Stefan 37, 188
Blackpool Model 137

Blakesley Hall 42
Blook, Bindon 221
Boer War 25
Bonaventure Press 163
Bond, A W 113
Book of Locomotives 218
Book of Swimming 217
Book of Trains 215
Boots Pure Drug Company 141
Boy Scouts 77
Branson, Mr 190, 191
Brewer, Carl 75
British Charities Association 139
British Empire Exhibition 139, 142
British Industries Fair, 1936 142
Brough, Derek 224
Brown, General Sir John 163
Brown, Reginald W 77, 195
Butler, H Talbot 237

C

Cadbury, Mr. 50
Cagney 42
Caledonian Railway Co. 65
Cambridge University Railway Club 224
Camm, F J 220
Campbell, Sir Malcolm 61
Canadian Pacific Railway Co. 141
Canals and Waterways 217
Candida Cottage 103
Carette et Cie 113, 234
Carette, Georges 37, 113
Carrington, Noel 76, 215
Carroll, Reg 199
Carter, Stabler & Adams 75
Casson, Sir Hugh 173, 184
Channel Asset Management Limited 238
Character Assessment 72
Checker, Mr 199
Children's Welfare Exhibition 50
Chloride Electrical Company 141

Christmas Cards 165
Churchill, Winston 50, 152, 154, 158
City of Coventry Model 158
City of Durban Model 69
Claret, John 34, 38
Clark, Tich 200
Claydon, Percy 111, 144, 199, 223, 237

Cleemput, Marcel van 238
Clements, John 61
Clyde Model Dockyard 34
Coal Mine Model 142
Cobb, Thomas Keightly 31, 43, 96
Coleman, H 221
Colour Supplement 121
Compagnie Générale Atlantique 211
Corgi Classics Limited 238
Cornish, R 65
Courtney, Frederick E 76, 215
Cox, Arch. 237
Cox, Cecil B 62
Cranston, Miss Catherine 83
Cranston Tea Rooms 83
Crockett & Jones 11, 55
Crockett, Sir James 55, 163
Crompton Parkinson 29, 36
Cross, W P 161
Cullen, Kenneth S 119
Cutting, Doris 186

D

D-Day 159
Daimler Motor Company 31
Damage Control School 154
Darphin, Marcel 237
Dell, Ethel M 59
Dennis and Faulkners 66
Denton, Mr 199
Derngate, 78 12
Derry, Cyril 186, 191, 219, 221, 237
Derry, Richard 237
Design & Industries Association 11, 74, 215
Disney, Walt 61
Doddridge Chapel 100
Doddridge Church 19
Doddridge Young Men's Class 43
Domino clock 108
Duckett, Lewis 76, 77, 163
Duke of Clarence 22
Duke of Westminster 61
Dunn, Lawrence 76, 217

E

Earl of Harewood 61, 224
Earl of Lindsay 224
Earl of Moray 61
Eaton Hall 42
Edinburgh Branch 61

Eisenmann & Co 116
Elkington, Edward 199
Erinoid, translucent green 92
Exposition Universelle et Internationale 44

F

Fabian News 74
Fabian Society 74
Fairbourne 49
Fielding, Mike 238
Fifty Years of Model Making 119
Films 70
Finniston, Sir Montague 75
Fire Brigade 19, 20, 42
Fitness for Purpose 100
Fletcher, B J 75
Flinton-Harris JP 18
Flooks, George 44
Foreman, H C 61, 221, 223
Foster, G 232
Franco-British Exhibition 44, 59
Franklin, Harry 32, 111, 211, 212, 221
Franklin's Gardens 213
Fresh Air Fund 18
Friends Relief Committee Service 232
Fuller, Roland 119, 223, 225, 231
Fullerton, M B 161

G

Galsworthy, John 59
Gardam, Dacre 63
Garnock, Viscount 224
Garrard, Miss Joan 191
Garside, Bertrand 34
Gas Street 15
General Post Office 142
General Strike 33
George, D Lloyd 158
German prisoners of war 106
Glasgow School of Art 83
Glenn & Sons, A 194, 208
Glenn, Herbert 111
Gloag, John 77
Godfrey Phillips & Co. 114
Godwin, E W 31
Goodman, Eliza 17
Goodman, John 17
Gramophone Company 141
Grand Union Canal 142

Graves, Francis 163
Great Central Railway 65
Green, Charles 171, 173, 185
Greenly, Elenora 198
Greenly, Henry 35, 42, 44, 50, 66, 74, 142, 197
Greenly, Lilley 198
Griffiths, MP Jim 186
Gropius, Walter 170
Grose, Joseph 32, 36
Guard Books 190
Guinness, Alec 61

H

Halford, Leo 111, 199
Harding, H J 194
Harrap & Co Ltd, George G 218
Harris JP, J Flinton 37, 100
Harrison & Sons Ltd 70
Harrison, Victor B 70
Harvey, Mollie 225, 231
Heal, Ambrose 75
Hearn, Richard 61
Heywood, Sir Arthur 42
Hichens, Dr P S 161
Highways and Educational Committee 195
Hills, Sir Graham 75
Historical Model Railway Society 224
Hobbs, Edward Walter 58, 111, 138, 199
Holborn, 112 High 58
Holder, Sir John 70
Holding, Edward de Wilde 31
Holding, Mathew 31
Holland, George 36, 114, 212, 215
Holloway, Bernard 216
Honeyman and Keppie 83
Hornby 118
Hornby, Sir John 75
Hornimans Tea Plantation 141
Horseshoe Street 15
Horstman, Sidney 103
Howes Percival, Mrs W 214
Howey, Captain 49
HRH Princess Elizabeth 212
Hughes, Doris 55
Hulbert, Claude 61, 224
Hunslet Goods Yard 36
Hunterian Art Gallery 83

Hutchison, John 81

I

Ideal Home Exhibition, 1925 139
Ideal Home Magazine 85
Immingham Docks Model 137
Imperial Services Exhibition 137
Inside of Things 218
Iolanthe 33

J

James, Arthur 111
Joad, Professor C E M 186
John Brown's Clydesbank 203
Johnson, Ernie 199
Jones, Annie Marshall 55
Jones, Charles 11, 55
Jones, Florence Jane 11
Jones, Francis Marshall 55
Jones, Frank 108, 169
Josephthal, Paul 113
Junior Institute of Engineers 225

K

Kahn, Siegfried 118, 188, 221
Keen, G P 191
Kensitas Cigarette Company 114
Kent, Harold 200
Kew, W R 214
King George V 50, 78, 138
King of Lilliput 232
King of Siam 44
King Peter of Yugoslavia 61
Kingsthorpe Tennis Club 31
Kingswell Street 65, 234
Kingswell Street College 32
Knockaloe 106
Kvaerner Energy Limited 212

L

Labour Party 189
Lane, Sir Allen 76, 215, 234
Larkman, Rev. C S 100
Lascelles, Hon. Gerald 224
Le Corbusier 170
League of Work Exhibition 49
Levy, Allen 237
Lewis, Edward 113
Lewis, Major J C 161
Libraries and Finance Committee 195

Library and Museums Committee 195
Lifu steam car 36
Liquid Fuel Engineering Company 36
Lockhart, Captain 142, 212, 221
Locomotives
  Black Prince 38
  Black Watch 142
  Colossus 49
  Count Louis 50
  Diamond Jubilee 38
  Duke of York 114
  Entente Cordiale 50
  George the Fifth 140
  Green Dragon 50
  Immingham 140
  John Anthony 49
  Kovek 44
  Little Giant 44
  Mogul 114, 237
  Nipper 44
  Peter Pan 50
  Princess Elizabeth 114
  Royal Scot 114, 142, 198
  Sir Alexander 65
London & North Western Railway 38
London Underground Model 142
Lord Aberconway 75
Lord and Lady Burghley 194
Lord Brabazon of Tara 188
Lord Cowdray 61
Lord Downshire 61
Lord Glenconner 61
Lord Howard de Walden 61, 211
Lord Jellicoe 61
Lowke & Sons, J T 22, 42
Lowke, J T 81
Lowke, J T & Son 65
Lowke, John 15
Lowke, Joseph 15
Lowke, Joseph Tom 20, 43
Lowke, Tryphena 15
Lowko 113
Lutyens, Sir Edwin 138

M

Macdonald, Margaret 83
Mackenzie, James 190
Mackintosh, Charles Rennie 11, 81, 103, 106, 165, 170

Mackintosh House, The 83
Mackintosh Screen 12
Maerklin 40
Maharajah of Gwalior 145
Maharajah of Jodhpur 140
Maharajah of Patiala 140, 211
Malaret, M E P 61
Mallinson & Son 202
Mann, Paul B 76, 216
Marquis of Anglesey 61
Marriott, Bob 200
Marshall, Percival 35, 40, 66, 198, 221
Marvellous Models 216
Mary Rose 238
Maskelyne, J N 221
Matt, Charles 106
Mayor and Mayoress of Hastings 194
McIntosh, Margaret Rennie 81
Michael Rennie 61
Mill Lane 17
Miniature Railways of Great Britain Ltd 43, 49, 63
Model Club Railway Club, The 58
Model Engineer & Amateur Electrician 35
Model Engineer Exhibition 198
Model Engineering Exhibition 66
Model Engineering Trades Association 113
Model Railway Club 114
Model Railway Handbook 50, 118
Money, Sir Leo Chiozza 18
Moss, Stirling 61
Mountbatten, Lord Louis 61
Mounts, Upper 191
Mulberry Harbour 154
Mulliners Coach Works 32
Musman, E B 194

N

Nancy 44
Narrow Gauge Railways Ltd 63
National Union of Manual Training Teachers 106
New Ways 108, 111
Newbery, Francis 83
Northampton Borough Council 191
Northampton Chamber of Trade 232
Northampton Chronicle and Echo 184

Northampton General Hospital 43, 100
Northampton Independent 216, 231
Northampton Machinery Co. 31
Northampton Repertory Theatre 77, 163, 195, 232
Northampton Rotary Club 161, 197
Northampton School of Art 163
Northampton Town Council 232
Northamptonshire Natural History and Field Club 67, 71
Norwegian Exhibition 49

O

Olympic Games, 1940 214
Opera House 77, 162
Oppenheimer & Erlanger 117
Oracle Wireless Receiver 113
Oriental Steam Navigation Company 75

P

P Phipps & Co. 113
Palmer, A C and Co. 32
Paradis des Enfants 61
Paris Fair 38
Parker, Francis 73, 188, 230
Parker MP, John 74
Parker, Sir Peter 75
Peach, Harry 75
Peacock Hotel 55
Penguin Books 215, 234
Perfection in Miniature 100
Pheysey, Ethel M 76
Phipps, C W 161
Photography 68
Pick, Frank 75, 77, 185
Pickering, Alderman W A 232
Planning and Development Committee 195
Plummer, Raymond 74
Port Sunlight 137
Porteous, John and Alice 55
Precision Models 237
Prentice, Herbert M 77, 231
Prestwich and Sons, J C 194
Prince Bira 61
Prince Chula of Thailand 61
Prince of Wales 145
Princess Marie Louise 138

INDEX 253

Princess Mary, the Princess Royal 61
Puffin Books 215

Q

Queen Mary 50, 78, 138
Queen's Dolls House 138

R

Radiolympia 142
Radwell 33
Railway Bridging School 156
Railways
 Abington Park 43
 Blackpool 44
 Blakesley Hall 42
 Breslau, Germany 44
 Bricket Wood 44
 Broome 70
 Brussels 44
 Budapest 44
 Children's Welfare Exhibition 50
 Eaton Railway 44
 Empire Exhibition 50
 Fairbourne Miniature Railway 49, 50, 61
 Franco-British Exhibition 44
 Halifax Zoo 44
 Luna Parc, Geneva 44
 League of Work Exhibition 49
 Llewellyn Miniature Railway 49
 Longmoor Military Railway 225
 Nancy 44
 Ravenglass & Eskdale Rly. 49, 50, 61
 Rhyl 44, 50
 Roubaix 44
 Staughton Manor 49
 Sutton Coldfield 44
 The Norwegian Exhibition 49
 Treasure Island Railway 50
Ravenswood 55
Recognition Models 155
Rees & Co. Ltd., L 116
Rees, Frank 117
Rees, Leon 116
Registered Trade Mark 66
Reid's Public School 81
Richards, George 214

Riley, Barrie 237
Riley, J D, MP 113
Ritchie, Ann 238
Roberts, Lunt 217
Robinson, Ken 238
Robinson, Tom Osborne 163
Rohe, Mies van der 170
Rokeby, Captain H L 32
Rowe, William 42, 190, 199, 221
Royal Society of Arts 225
Royal Theatre 163
Royal Train 29
Russell, D A 221
Russell, Sir Gordon 11, 75, 77
Rutherford, S K R 231

S

Saloman & Sons 32
Salomans, Sir David 36
Salt, Sir Thomas 224
School, All Saints' Church 24
School, Northampton Grammar 24
Scott, Ivan Rutherford 237
Sears, Jack 58, 62, 113, 199, 228
Sears, William Thomas 63
Segrave, Sir Henry 61
Sell, H M 59
Sell, H M 221
Shannon, Norman 198
Shapland, H P 77
Shaw, George 111, 200
Shaw, George Bernard 59, 74, 100, 103
Ship Models Ltd 33, 111, 190, 199, 212
Ships
 Almanzora 141
 Aquitania 211
 Arandora Star 111
 Asturias 111
 Britannic 211
 Cerannic 141
 Doric 111
 H.M.S. Hood 140
 HMS Ark Royal 211
 HMS Hood 211
 HMS Vanguard 211
 Majestic 141, 209
 Mauretania 111, 211
 Normandie 211
 Ohio 141
 Olympic 141, 211

 Oraca 141
 Ordana 141
 Queen Elizabeth 70, 202
 Queen Mary 211
 S.S. Parthia 208
 Strathmore 201
 Streamlinias 111
 The Empress of Britain 159, 197
 Titanic 211
 Windsor Castle 201
Ships and Men 215
Sideshow Railways Ltd. 44
Silver Train 145
Sir Gordon Russell 235
Smeathers, W T C 232
Smith & Co., D J 31
Smith, David 32
Smith, R Geoffrey 217
Smith, Raalf 161
Society of Model Engineers 35, 63
St. Augustine Street 17
St. George's Ward 191
Stabler, Harold 75
Stanley MA, Rev. R M 100
Staughton Manor 49
Steam Age 237
Steel, Ernest 234
Steel Sheet to Royal Scot 114
Stevens' Corner Shop 200
Steven's Model Dockyard 34
Sturrock, Mrs Newbery 84
Stutley, Ray 76, 188, 199
Swimming Baths 194

T

Table Top Railways 116
Tangye Gas Engines 31
Thomas, David St. John 225
Thomas Hyler-White 31
Thomas, Percy 194
Tobbitt, Arthur 238
Town and Country Planning Association 225
Tranter, Mr 199
Travelling Post Office 142
Trenery, Ernest Arthur 43
Trix Ltd 118, 237
Trix-Twin 117
True Form Boot Co. 58, 63
Trust, 78 Derngate 102
Turner, Nigel 238

Turner, Sidney Marmaduke Stuart 40
Twining, E W 33, 61, 66, 119, 137
Twining Models 113, 138

U

Uncle's Toys 78

V

Vincent Astor 61

W

Wade, Charles P 166

Walker & Holtzaphell 113
Wallace, Edgar 59
Wallas, Graham 74
Waterline ship models 70
Waterways of the World 218
Webb, Beatrice and Sidney 74
Wedding of W J Bassett-Lowke 100
Wells, H G 75
Werkbund Exhibition 75
White Rabbit 152
White steam car 33
White, Thomas 15
Why We Use Photography 68
Will - W J Bassett-Lowke 232
Williams-Ellis, Sir Clough 75, 175

Wills, John 44, 61, 63
Wills, Margaret Anne 63
Winteringham, George 65
Winteringham Ltd 65, 113, 199
Wonderful Models 216

Y

Young, Mr. 61

Z

Zborowski, Count Louis 50

For the benefit of readers, in addition to the 78 Derngate Trust, local and national museums, the following organisations support the preservation of Bassett-Lowke history.

Charles Rennie Mackintosh Society,
Queen's Cross,
870 Garscube Road,
Glasgow
G20 7EL
Tel. : 0141 946 6600

The Bassett-Lowke Society,
George Lane,
Stanton
Nr. Bury St. Edmunds
Suffolk
IP31 2UB

The Friends of 78 Derngate,
32 Ryland Road,
Moulton
Northamptonshire
NN3 7RE

Hunterian Museum and Art gallery,
University of Glasgow,
82 Hillhead Street,
Glasgow
G12 8QQ

The life of Time is motion: his glory perfection
Time attendeth None, Yet is servant to All
Swifter than the winde, Yet still as stone
The Time Man's Peace and Thief's perdition
The Lawyer's Gain the Merchant's hope
He openeth the eye of day and spreadeth the cloak of night
Agent of the living Register of the dead.

Quotation on the 1930's Christmas Card from the XVI century clock at Snowshill Manor in the Cotswolds.